Literacy Learning in Australia: Practical Ideas for Early Childhood Educators

Literacy Learning in Australia: Practical Ideas for Early Childhood Educators

Caroline Barratt-Pugh, Judith Rivalland, Judy Hamer & Paul Adams

THOMSON

DUNMORE PRESS

Australia · Canada · Mexico · Singapore · Spain · United Kingdom · United States

THOMSON
™
DUNMORE PRESS

Level 7, 80 Dorcas Street
South Melbourne, Victoria
Australia 3205

Email: highereducation@thomsonlearning.com.au
Website: www.thomsonlearning.com.au

This first edition adapted from Judy Hamer and Paul Adams *The New Zealand Early Childhood Literacy Handbook*
first published by Dunmore Press in 2003.
First published in 2006
10 9 8 7 6 5 4 3 2 1
10 09 08 07 06
Copyright © 2006 Caroline Barratt-Pugh, Judith Rivalland, Judy Hamer and Paul Adams.

National Library of Australia
Cataloguing-in-Publication data

Literacy learning in Australia: practical ideas for early
childhood educators.

Bibliography.
Includes index.
ISBN 0 17 012801 6.

1. Early childhood education. 2. Children – Language. 3.
Literacy. I. Barratt-Pugh, Caroline.

372.6

Editor: Anne Mulvaney
Project editor: Chris Wyness
Publishing editor: Elizabeth Vella
Publishing manager: Michael Tully
Indexer: Julie King
Cover designer: Olga Lavecchia
Original cover concept: Patrick Jennings
Typeset in New Aster, Gill Sans, Futura and Times Ten by Chris Ryan
Production controller: Jodie Van Teylingen
Printed in Australia by Ligare Book Printers

This title is published under the imprint of Thomson/Dunmore Press.
Nelson Australia Pty Limited ACN 058 280 149 (incorporated in Victoria)
trading as Thomson Learning Australia.

The URLs contained in this publication were checked for currency during the production process.
Note, however, that the publisher cannot vouch for the ongoing currency of URLs.

LAW-DAVIS

Contents

Foreword

This book has an important and ambitious remit. Children's early literacy development is an area rich with debate and full of contention about the optimum ways for early educators to play their part in this arena. That the contributing authors have taken a clear stand about adults having a role in children's literacy development *from birth* is important and reassuring. This orientation, and a focus on practical ideas, invites all those engaged with young children – parents, family members, carers, teachers and educators – to dip into these pages for understandings, insights, ideas and practical ways to play a positive role in young children's literacy development.

The book works across the levels of theory, policy and practice. Australia has followed a strong pathway in matters of Early Years curriculum and pedagogy, a pathway that reflects national commitment to early literacy development. Throughout Australia, policy statements that include reference to children's language and literacy pertain both to care- and education-focused services. In this country, therefore, the care, education and upbringing of children is imbued with the importance of 'making it' in the literacy stakes. However, it is important to remember that understandings of the child influence the shape of curricula and pedagogy. Different understandings of the child, and the varied contexts and localities of children's learning, can result in substantial difference in the *processes* and *outcomes* of literacy events. Adults engaging with young children may view a child as: a unique personality in the present; a citizen with individual rights and agency to choose his/her participation in events and activities; an individual of the future who must be prepared for pre-determined challenges ahead; or, because of age, a person who is incapable or incompetent and needing direction. As readers think about and implement the ideas presented in this book, it is important to reflect also on the ways that children and childhood are considered in local settings, in different contexts, by different adults and importantly, by the reader.

Not all children have access to registered early childhood services of high quality in the years from birth to age five. Indeed, Australian investment in early childhood services for children under four or five years is relatively low when compared with other OECD countries. In particular, children in the period from birth to thirty-six months are poorly served by ECEC programs designed to enhance literacy capacity through early childhood education, care *and* upbringing – few *comprehensive* programs are in place for this age group. This is particularly so for children of diversity groups – those with organic disabilities, Indigenous children, children from culturally and linguistically diverse backgrounds, children who live in low-income households and/or with sole parents, and children in the care of statutory authorities as a result of abuse or neglect. The limited availability of well-researched programs for infants and toddlers, combined with limited professional training for staff in many centre-based and informal care settings, makes this book an important resource for the early childhood field.

In Australia's multi-cultural society, social cohesion is a time-honoured and on-going developmental process. For the children of the twenty-first century who grow, learn and engage in contemporary society, literacy involves not only English proficiency in multi-text environments, but also cross-cultural sensitivity and understandings and the capacity to communicate through multi-symbol systems (verbal, written, dramatic, artistic …). The experiences encountered through early childhood programs influence children's developing capacity as communicators in contemporary society and affect children's attitudes towards diversity, difference and the commonalities of human activity. The authors of this text have paid special attention to cultural and linguistic diversity in the developing literacies of young children, a critical orientation in Australia in the twenty-first century.

Building on home languages and practices is an aspiration that is fundamental to the socio-cultural orientation portrayed and advocated in this book. Yet parents in Australia do not hold uniform commitment to such an aspiration. Some want their children to focus only on Standard English. Some are perplexed as to why educators want to engage with home languages that are different from Standard English. Some are concerned that educators are poorly equipped to develop literate behaviours in non-standard English and other languages. Some consider that time spent flourishing home languages and culture limits the opportunity for full proficiency in Standard English. As educators seek and discover the varied views of families on this matter, rich opportunities emerge for dialogue about children's learning in contemporary times. Children's progress in literacy and their views of themselves as capable persons functioning in different settings, increase through coordinated action by early educators and families. Educators who listen to, and learn from families, and work to support literacy development in family and community contexts, are more likely to ensure successful outcomes.

This book is not about contesting current Australian policies in early literacy but about assisting readers to take a socio-cultural orientation while enhancing early childhood learning and development. The authors translate the literacy policies evident within Australia in the new century, giving ideas and practices that may assist educators to create literacy rich environments for learning. It is timely to note also, that, in Australian policies, the dominance of attention to prevailing education themes – literacy development, learning and teaching standards, cognitive outcomes, and mastery of specific skills – is not the central interest of ECEC programs in many European countries. The themes evident in contemporary Australia are more clearly apparent in countries with dominant English language contexts. In these contexts, the outcomes of children's literacy learning depend on the ways in which educators engage young children, respect their home languages and culture, and build new, common experiences in and beyond the centres in which educators work.

Working in ways that are sensitive to contexts (local, regional, national and global) is a key plank that holds together ideas put forward by the authors of this text. Sensitivity to context inoculates against the use and transmission of pre-determined, 'format-programs' for young children – those prepared for a 'typical' child, or for children of a specific chronological age, or popular programs taken from a different location and context. Such programs, applied without sensitivity to context, are of poor quality because they are transferred without consideration of local children and contexts. Context sensitivity enables educators to recognise and employ diverse ways of learning, seeing, creating and representing ideas with children.

I commend this book to you, the reader. May you find its pages are a vehicle for professional thinking, argument and enjoyment of the wealth of ideas that are available to you at this time. Contemporary Australia is an exciting and diverse place for human learning, development and ingenuity. The young children and families engaging with educators as they continue to grow in literacy capacity would be well served if the ideas herein are taken up with sensitivity, enthusiasm and commitment.

Dr Collette Tayler
Professor in the School of Early Childhood Education at
Queensland University of Technology, Brisbane

Acknowledgements

The authors would like to acknowledge all the individuals, colleagues and early childhood centres, both in Australia and New Zealand, who generously provided the time, materials, work samples and photographs used throughout this book. Their enthusiasm and generosity has made a significant contribution to the book.

We would like to acknowledge Edith Cowan University, the Open Polytechnic of New Zealand, and Massey University for the opportunity to research and write this book; Judy Hamer and Paul Adams for persuading us to collaboratively research and write an Australian version of the *New Zealand Early Childhood Literacy Handbook* (Palmerston North, NZ: Dunmore Press, 2003); Dunmore Press for permission to use material from Adams P. & Ryan H. (Eds), *Learning to Read in Aotearoa New Zealand: A Collaboration Between Early Childhood Educators, Families, and Schools* (Palmerston North, NZ: Dunmore Press, 2002); and Routledge publishers and Gunther Kress for their permission to reproduce the diagram on page 67 of Kress G., Before Writing (London: Routledge, 1997).

We also acknowledge all the people at Thomson Learning for their ongoing support and advice; and the early childhood students, early childhood educators and other professionals who have been so interested in early childhood literacy and freely provided ideas and feedback for this book.

About the Authors

Caroline Barratt-Pugh is a Senior Lecturer in Early Childhood Education at Edith Cowan University in Western Australia. She worked as a child care officer in long day care centres and nursery schools in the United Kingdom before training to be a teacher in early childhood education. Her research and teaching focuses on language and literacy in the early years with a special interest in bilingualism, multiliteracies and family and community literacy. Her PhD explored the development of English as an additional language in early childhood. She teaches language and literacy studies on undergraduate and postgraduate courses and has been involved in a number of national literacy research projects. Caroline has completed the first Australian evaluation of a library-initiated family intervention literacy program, *Better Beginnings: an evaluation from two communities* (Barratt-Pugh, Rohl, Oakley & Elderfield, 2005) and she is co-editor of *Literacy Learning in the Early Years* (2000). She has written a number of journal articles and book chapters on early literacy and has recently completed a second chapter for the *Birth to Three Matters* series edited by Abbott, and published by the Open University Press.

Judith Rivalland is Professor of Language and Literacy at Edith Cowan University where she is the Associate Dean of Teaching and Learning in the Faculty of Community Services, Education and Social Sciences. She is also Director of the Fogarty Learning Centre: Centre for the teaching and research of language and literacy, numeracy, science and curriculum studies. She is an experienced classroom teacher having spent six years teaching in Western Australian schools and eight years in the Northern Territory as a primary teacher and language consultant working with primary students needing special help with literacy. Judith was seconded to the Education Department of Western Australia to help write the K-7 English Syllabus in 1986 and was instrumental in the conceptualisation of the continua for the First Steps Spelling and Writing Developmental Continua. Her special interests are in literacy development, the effective teaching of early and primary literacy and literacy difficulties. Over the last nine years Judith has worked on six Department of Education Science and Training National Literacy Research Projects. These projects include two major studies of early years literacy reported in *100 Children Go to School, A Hundred Children Turn 10* and *In Teachers Hands: Effective Literacy Teaching Practices in the Early Years of Schooling*. Judith has published extensively on the topics of literacy development, and the effective teaching of literacy in the early and primary years of schooling.

Judy Hamer is a Senior Lecturer in the Centre for Education Studies at the Open Polytechnic of New Zealand and teaches in the Diploma of Teaching (Early Childhood Education). Judy worked for a number of years in early childhood education as well as in early childhood teacher education for Te Tari Puna Ora o Aotearoa/New Zealand Childcare Association. She is co-author (with Paul Adams) of *The New Zealand Early Childhood Literacy Handbook* (2003), and co-editor (with Roger Openshaw and Paul Adams) of *Education and Society in Aotearoa New Zealand* (2nd edn) (2005). Her research interests lie in early childhood education and include curriculum studies (including literacy) and social and policy issues.

Paul Adams is a Senior Lecturer in the Department of Social and Policy Studies in Education at Massey University, New Zealand. His research interests lie in policy studies, and he teaches professional studies papers in pre-service teacher education and in the BA, BEd and MEd programs. He is the co-editor (with Heather Ryan) of *Learning to Read in Aotearoa New Zealand: A Collaboration between Early Childhood Educators, Families and Schools* (2002); co-author (with Judy Hamer) of *The New Zealand Early Childhood Literacy Handbook* (2003); co-editor (with Kathleen Vossler and Cushla Scrivens) of *Teachers' Work in Aotearoa New Zealand* (2005), and co-editor (with Roger Openshaw and Judy Hamer) of *Education and Society in Aotearoa New Zealand* (2nd edn) (2005). Paul is also joint editor (with Dr John O'Neill) of the *New Zealand Journal of Teachers' Work*. His qualifications are in the areas of sociology, special education, educational psychology and music.

Collette Tayler, author of this book's Foreword, is Professor in the School of Early Childhood at the Queensland University of Technology, Brisbane. Her research and teaching is focused on policy development, design, implementation and tracking of effective early childhood education and care (ECEC). This includes ECEC policy origins, directions, and effects on both services and communities. The studies address access; quality; monitoring and accountability; community engagement; children's learning and development; diversity; curriculum and pedagogy; leadership and staff professionalism. Collette was a principal researcher in the Queensland Preparatory Year Trial evaluation (2003–04). She established and leads an Australian Research Council funded study of the impact of Queensland Childcare and Family Support Hubs in local communities (2003–06). In 2004–05, with Dr John Bennett, OECD Paris, Collette is completing a 20-country analysis of ECEC policy and provision that will culminate in the publication by the OECD of *Starting Strong 2005*. Collette is reviewing the Australian child care standards for long day care, family day care, outside school hours care and in-home care services in 2005.

Introduction

How do young children learn to read and write? What is the role of the adult in the process of becoming literate? At what age do children start to notice and use print? These are some of the questions that have been puzzling parents, early years professionals and researchers for many years. Over the last two decades our understanding of early literacy learning has changed. There has been a growing body of evidence that suggests literacy begins at birth and that early literacy learning forms the basis of later educational achievement. As babies, toddlers and young children strive to make sense of their world through everyday interactions, they gradually become familiar with the ways in which literacy is used in their family and wider community. Adults play a central role in this process as they help the child to explore different ways of making meaning, from sharing books and print in the environment to making marks on paper. In this book we explore ways in which adults working with babies, toddlers and young children can support their early literacy learning through policy, planning and practice in a range of different early childhood contexts.

The importance of literacy learning in early childhood is reflected in federal, state and local community policy documents about language and literacy in the range of settings that young children attend prior to school. At the federal level, the National Agenda for Early Childhood has identified early childhood literacy as an area of concern (2004). In seeking to make a difference to outcomes for young children, the National Agenda has targeted the development of higher levels of literacy. As part of the National Agenda, a number of early childhood literacy research and development projects are currently being undertaken across Australia, funded through the Stronger Families and Communities Strategy (2004). For example, this includes an Early Learning and Literacy Intervention (ELLI) Program developed in New South Wales. ELLI brings together the existing research and knowledge on the influence of preschool experience and family interaction on the language and literacy of children from low socio-economic groups (http://www.ku.com.au retrieved 3.11.2005).

In addition, the Commonwealth Government has set national goals and priorities through the national literacy plan: Literacy for All: the Challenge for Australian Schools (DEETYA, 1998). In March 1997 Commonwealth, State and Territory Education Ministers agreed to a national literacy and numeracy goal:

> That every child leaving primary school should be numerate, and be able to read, write and spell at an appropriate level. (p.8)

The National Literacy plan highlights the importance of developing strong foundation literacy skills in the early years through appropriate educational experiences. It is argued that, by the end of primary school, for children who have not achieved appropriate literacy skills, closing the gap through the rest of their schooling will be extremely difficult. Thus, emphasising the need to build on and extend children's literacy skills from an early age. In addition, in 1998, the Ministerial Committee on Education, Employment, Training and Youth Affairs resolved that all states would conduct full status testing of literacy in years 3, 5 and 7 and that these would be reported to the Commonwealth against national benchmarks. Literacy attainment in Year 3, will depend to some extent on the literacy knowledge, skills and understanding that children have developed prior to school. The National Literacy plan has been supported by a research agenda that had funded a number of national children's literacy projects. Key projects that specifically focus on the early years of schooling are as follows:

❖ *Literacy in its place. Literacy practices in urban and rural communities* (Breen, Louden, Barratt-Pugh, Rivalland, Rohl & Rhydwen, 1994)

❖ *Developing partnerships: The home, school and community interface* (Cairney, Ruge, Buchanan, Lowe & Munsie, 1995)

❖ *Community literacy practices and schooling: Towards effective support for students* (Cairney & Ruge, 1998)

❖ *100 children go to school: Connections and disconnections in literacy development in the year prior to school and the first year of school* (Hill, Comber, Louden, Rivalland & Reid, 1998)

❖ *Preschool Profile* (Raban, Griffin & Coates 2000, DETYA Indigenous Education Branch)

❖ *A hundred children turn 10: A longitudinal study of literacy development from the year prior to school to the first four years of school* (Hill, Comber, Louden, Rivalland & Reid, 2002)

❖ *In teachers' hands* (Louden, Rohl, Barratt-Pugh, Brown, Cairney, Elderfield, House, Meiers, Rivalland & Rowe, 2005).

These reports reinforce the importance of early childhood educators understanding early literacy development and the value of literacy-related activities in the early years to assist in children's learning and future school achievement.

In line with the National Agenda for Early Childhood, the need to build on and extend children's literacy skills has been recognised in the Quality Assurance systems for long day care centres and family day care centres. In the Quality Improvement and Accreditation System Handbook (2005), Quality Area 4: Children's Experiences and Learning, principle 4.3 requires staff to promote children's language and literacy abilities. In the Family Day Care Quality Assurance System Under Standard 3: Program Procedures, carers are asked to plan for the language potential of all children in ways that are appropriate to each child's level of development, which includes the importance of sharing stories, songs and rhymes (National Standards for Family Day Care, 2005). This is a significant development because these are the first quality assurance programs in which funding is linked to the Child Care Benefit approval for centre based long day care (National Childcare Accreditation Council, 2001).

At a state level the fundamental importance of literacy has been incorporated into a range of early childhood initiatives. These include, the Early Years Strategy in Western Australia, Families First in New South Wales, the Putting Families First Policy in Queensland, Early Chance for Every Child in South Australia, Our Kids Action Plan in Tasmania, A Vision for Territory Children and Children's Policy Framework in the Northern Territory and the Best Start Strategy in Victoria. There are a number of programs which target early literacy development. These include support for literacy from birth, such as the Better Beginnings Program in Western Australia in which a literacy resource pack is given to every new baby, to community based projects such the Aboriginal Best Start Projects in Victoria.

The Early Childhood Australia Association (ECAA) also recognises the importance of early literacy learning. The ECAA, which represents professionals involved directly and indirectly in the provision of early childhood services for children between birth and 8 years of age, has developed a detailed policy on language and literacy. The policy states that literacy is critical to a child's success in life and that literacy development for every child is a shared responsibility of families, communities and early childhood programs (ACAA, 1999).

Literacies and cultural and linguistic diversity

Literacy learning is seen as crucially important in relation to improved educational outcomes for Indigenous children and children from diverse cultural and linguistic communities. The Australian Bureau of Statistics (ABS) reported that approximately 20% of Australians speak a language other than English at home (ABS, 2001), and altogether 240 languages including 48 Indigenous languages were identified. In addition there are variants of English that include 'Aboriginal English, forms of immigrant English and the non-standard dialect (sociolect) sometimes called "broad Australian"' (Martello, 2002, p.40). In order to support children's home languages and achieve better literacy outcomes for Indigenous children, the Commonwealth provides supplementary funding to the Department of Education, Science and Training (DEST) through the Indigenous Education Agreement (IEA). This is targeted at improving the literacy skills of Indigenous children, through the:

❖ National Indigenous English Literacy and Numeracy Strategy (NIELNS)

❖ Indigenous Education Strategic Initiative Program (IESIP)

❖ English as a Second Language for Indigenous Language Speaking Students (ESL-ILSS).

(www.dest.gov.au/sectors/indigenous_education/policy_issues_reviews/national_indigenous english_literacy_and_numeracy_strategy.htm#Summary. Retrieved 17.6.05)

The objective of the National Indigenous English Literacy and Numeracy Strategy is to achieve English literacy for Indigenous children at levels comparable to those achieved by other young Australians. In order to meet this objective, it aims to increase the proportion of the Indigenous 3 to 5 year old population in preschool education and ensure those children are confident and competent to enter primary school. In the 2004 Child Care Census only 2% of children attending long day care services were reported to be from Indigenous families (ABS, 2005). Two of the key objectives of the IESIP are to improve literacy across all age ranges and to specifically improve preschool educational outcomes for Indigenous children.

The language and literacy needs of children who speak English as an additional language are also seen as important and the National Agenda for Multicultural Australia (2004) has identified three objectives in the area of language policy and communication. The first objective is aimed at promoting increased proficiency in English through the extension of intensive English as a second language tuition; the second objective is aimed at helping children to maintain and develop their home/community language through the mainstream and ethnic schools systems; and, the third objective is aimed at ensuring children have opportunities to develop cross-cultural understanding. Early Childhood education is seen as having an important role to play in achieving these aims (http://www.immi.gov.au/multicultural/_inc/publications/agenda/agenda89/language.htm retrieved 2.11.05).

Clearly, the importance of recognising and building on diversity is also embedded in the Quality Improvement and Accreditation System (2005). One of the indicators of quality child care is defined as striving to 'accommodate children's diverse abilities and their social, linguistic and cultural backgrounds' (Principle 1.4, p.5) and Principle 4.3 states that home languages should be supported, as they are integral to individual identity. In addition, Early Childhood Australia has outlined several language and literacy policy principles; these include the need for early childhood educators to 'respect the child's home language and culture and use that as a base on which to build and extend children's language and literacy experience' (retrieved from www.earlychildhoodaustralia.org.au/abtus_pol_literacy.htm 7.2.05).

At a state level identifying, valuing and including linguistic and cultural knowledge in the curriculum is an underlying principle within early childhood initiatives and curriculum documents. For example, the principles underpinning the ACT 2002–05 Education Plan, include 'equality' as a key element and the Tasmanian Essential Learnings Framework (2002) is guided by a core set of values that includes 'equity'. The Northern Territory Curriculum Framework (2004) and the Western Australian Curriculum Framework (1998) both name 'inclusivity' as a key principle. In Victoria, the importance of building the future by 'building common purposes and values and by promoting mutual responsibility and trust in a diverse socio-cultural community' is part of Essential Learning Standards (2002, p.4). The NSW Curriculum Framework for Children's Services (2002) identifies that one of the major obligations of practice and provision is to honour diversity (p.16); and in South Australia 'diversity' is one of the learning areas identified in the Overview of Key Ideas and Developmental Learning Outcomes: Birth to Age 3 (2002). The New South Wales Curriculum Framework for Children's Services (2002) argues that 'the importance of maintaining the child's first language cannot be over estimated' (p.58).The Early Years Curriculum Guidelines (2004) from Queensland states that 'Diverse cultural heritages, including those of Aboriginal peoples and Torres Strait Islander peoples, are valued, respected, acknowledged and reflected in the preparatory curriculum' (2004, p.1). The Northern Territory Curriculum Framework (2004) makes reference to English as a second language and includes outcomes for Indigenous language maintenance and revitalisation (p.4). In the 'Communication' strand of the Tasmanian Essential Learnings Framework (2002), the 'importance of communicating in languages other than our own and learning to understand intercultural exchanges' is seen as a way of appreciating linguistic and cultural diversity (p.20). It can be seen, that within and across states there is a commitment to inclusivity, in which the language and literacies that children are engaged in are recognised and extended from the earliest years of pre-school education.

The importance of recognising and building on cultural and linguistic diversity cannot be underestimated, therefore, although policies and practices discussed in this book are deliberately broad, and encompass different contexts and different community needs, we recognise that there may be additional important considerations in relation to linguistic and cultural diversity. For example, literacies are learned through patterns of interaction that differ according to the social and cultural events in which they occur. Thus children come to early childhood centres with different experiences and understandings of literacy. Jones Diaz and Harvey (2002) point out that 'the literacy practices that children may engage in, such as narrating or story telling and representations of the worlds and "self" are constituted differently within different cultural and linguistic frameworks' (p.184). This has important implications for policy, planning and practice in early childhood and references to language and literacy throughout the book encompass the following aspects of diversity and are adapted from Jones Diaz and Harvey (2002, p.190):

❖ Professionals recognise and value the skills, knowledge and understandings that children have about language and literacy and where possible build on these.

❖ Where possible bilingual educators are employed who are familiar with the linguistic and cultural background of the children.

❖ Children's progress in language and literacy is documented in their English in ways that take account of the use and influence of children's home languages.

❖ A variety of texts in children's home languages are provided and used throughout the environment and across different curriculum areas.

❖ Environmental print represents the scripts and print conventions of the children's home/community languages.

❖ Children are given opportunities to take part in language and literacy activities with children and adults who speak the same language.

❖ Professionals are aware of the differences between home languages and English (both spoken and written conventions), and the way in which this may influence language and literacy development.

In sum, literacy in early childhood education is now viewed as a crucial part of the National Agenda for Early Childhood, the National Literacy Plan, the National Indigenous Literacy and Numeracy Strategy, the National Agenda for Multicultural Australia, the Quality Improvement and Accreditation System and the Commonwealth Literacy Projects.

Taking these major initiatives into account, while the primary school system is where children formally learn to read, early childhood education centres are now regarded as among the key institutions for building the foundations of early language and literacy by families, communities and government. There is evidence (Snow, Burns & Griffin, 1998) to support the view that a broad repertoire of oral language uses, including phonological awareness and vocabulary, provides an important connection between oral language use and the ways in which children access school literacies. Acknowledging and building on the language and literacy practices that children are using in their families and communities enables educators to make links between the known and the new. Research shows that opportunities for young children to retain and extend their home languages/dialects has significant emotional, social, educational and political consequences. In addition, recent evidence suggests that it is also important to take into account the different learning styles that reflect children's social and cultural backgrounds, in order to ensure that children are engaged in learning in meaningful ways. Concerns are often expressed about the place of literacy in the early childhood curriculum and many educators have been unsure as to whether it should form a part of their program, or how to incorporate it in appropriate ways. Research over the last 30 years has increasingly highlighted the importance of a wide range of early childhood experiences in supporting early reading acquisition, and it is now recognised that many literacy practices form part of early childhood centre programs. The debate, in the main, has now shifted from whether we should incorporate literacy, to how to incorporate literacy in appropriate ways.

The aim of this book

The aim of this book is to provide early childhood educators (and others interested in early childhood literacy) with the *theoretical* rationales for sound literacy policy development and debate, and the *practical* frameworks to ensure appropriate and relevant literacy practices in early childhood contexts. Because of the complex nature of the administration and regulation of early childhood provision and practice in Australia, there are numerous policy and curriculum documents that include debate about language and literacy in prior-to-school settings at both national and state level. This book aims to augment these documents rather than provide an alternative framework. It is important for early childhood professionals to develop thorough literacy policy that meets the needs of their centre community and which is also based on relevant theories and methods appropriate for early childhood. When this occurs, literacy practices in the centre are likely to be rigorous, well integrated into current centre practice and also seamlessly embedded in its early childhood curriculum. We assume throughout this book that children's literacy experiences are embedded within the more general, rich language environment of the centre.

When this is the case, informed professionals are able to deliver sound literacy practices, justify their literacy approaches, and deal with the area of literacy in early childhood education *on their own terms*. Without such an approach, early childhood educators are more vulnerable to externally imposed programs and practices that may, or may not, meet the needs of their centre community. Early childhood professionals who develop sound literacy policies and practices can critique these external pressures, support their centre community, and provide high-quality literacy experiences for their children that will stand them in good stead throughout their educational lives and later in broader society.

To clarify our approach, this book is not about 'teaching children to read' (although this may be a likely outcome if a child is embedded in rich literacy environments for a substantial period of time), or setting up 'skill and drill' lessons (though we do consider capitalising on informal learning opportunities), or about running special preschool literacy groups for 4-year-olds (although many of the ideas presented would be useful here), or about presenting a range of simple literacy recipes (though we discuss plenty of straightforward ideas), or about helping centres imitate school practices (though, where helpful, we do highlight appropriate links between terminologies and what schools do). Instead, this book aims to ensure that all infants, toddlers and young children engage with a broad-based, rich literacy environment founded within sociocultural theory.

How do we define literacy?

There are many different definitions of literacy, from more narrow approaches (such as just looking at actual reading and writing achievement), to broader language and literacy approaches that include e-literacy (e.g., computer, information and network literacy); scientific, mathematical or technological literacy; and civic literacy (e.g., economic, political and social literacy). Both of these have their own literature, approaches, methodologies and theoretical bases, and reflect the differing social, political, cultural, economic, technological, pedagogical and philosophical viewpoints of a particular historical juncture.

While there are strengths and weaknesses in both of these approaches, in this book we will be considering more practical ideas for incorporating literacy into early childhood centres and hence we have chosen to take the middle path, which considers that language and literacy learning for children in centres converge through a range of socially constructed cognitive experiences. This approach recognises and values the contribution of the diverse range of language experiences in which children engage in early childhood centres, and these aspects form the backbone of this book. It places the location of children's language and literacy learning experiences within a broader sociocultural framework that allows us to highlight the many valuable experiences and practices in early childhood centres and families that underpin and support children's early literacy development. This book views children's literacy knowledge and experiences as being developed and influenced by the social and cultural contexts within which children operate. These contexts might include the child's immediate learning environments, such as their early childhood centre or their home, but also include a consideration of the broader influences on those environments, such as curriculum, government policy and culture.

This sociocultural model may be well known to the readers of this book; as already suggested, the Quality Improvement and Accreditation System and several of the state curriculum frameworks recognise the importance of valuing and building on children's diverse social, linguistic and cultural understandings. In relation to the application of a sociocultural model to children's literacy learning, Barratt-Pugh and Rohl (2000) have identified six important elements:

❖ children learn about literacies and how to 'do' literacy through participating in a range of activities in their family and community;

❖ literacy practices are carried out in culturally specific ways and contribute to children's developing sense of identity (i.e., literacy is not only socially constructed but culturally specific);

❖ children have different understandings about what counts as literacy and how literacy is done (i.e., children's learning about literacy depends on the differing experiences they have had with literacy in differing contexts);

❖ literacy practices are carried out in specific ways for particular purposes (i.e., literacy is used for differing purposes and has many different forms);

❖ the pattern of literacy learning differs between children, as they become relative experts within different literacy events (i.e., children don't necessarily develop in the same way and each child learns about literacy differently depending on the diverse nature of their literacy experiences);

❖ literacy practices are valued differently in different social and educational contexts (i.e., different social and cultural settings engage in differing literacy experiences and children learn which of these are valued over others in these contexts).

However, we also acknowledge the need for early literacy educators to work with the resources children bring to their early years contexts and to move children into accessing mainstream literacy practices as well as those of their own sociocultural contexts. Clay (1998) summarises these elements neatly when she argues that children come to learn about literacy 'by different paths'.

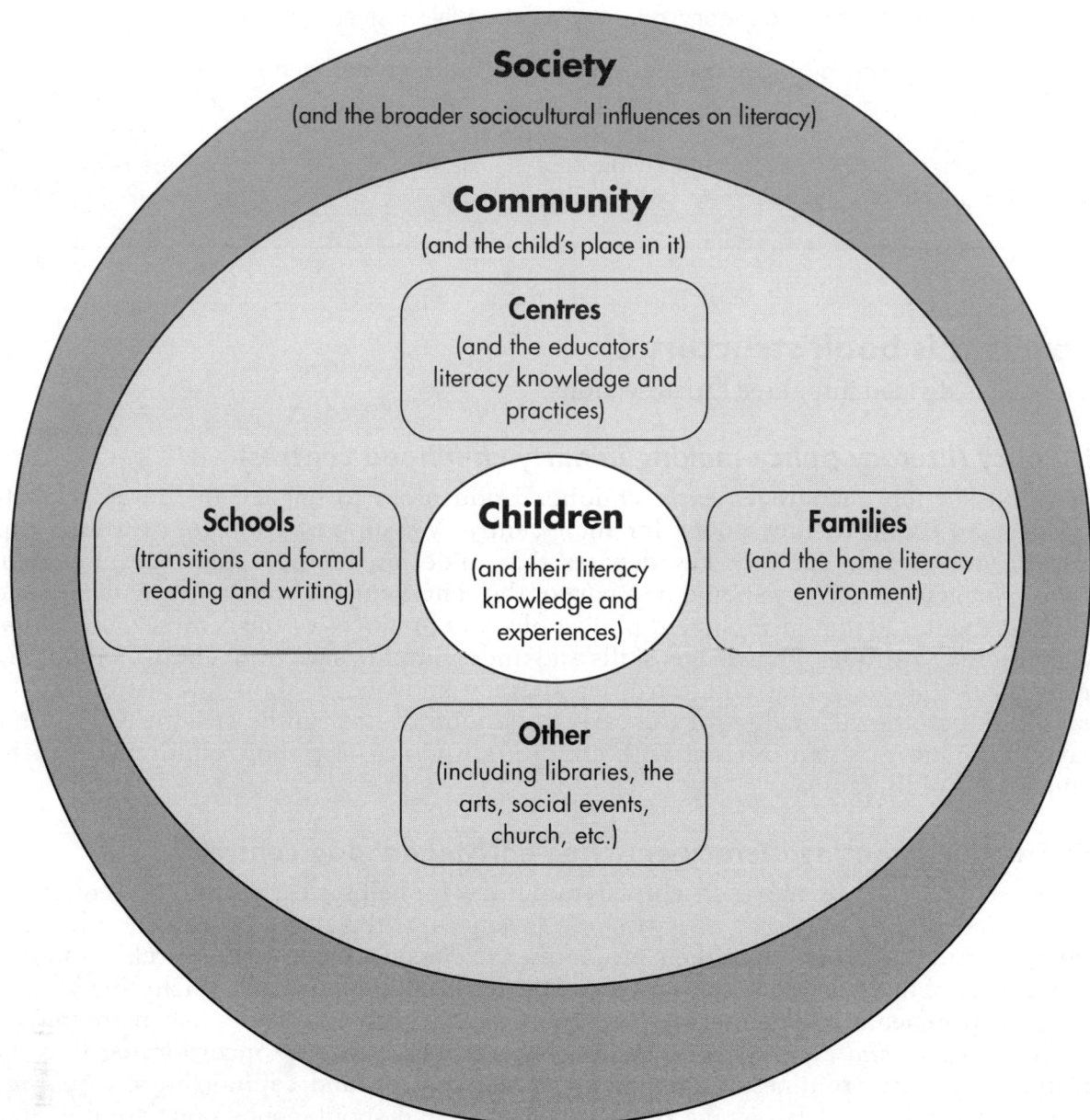

Society
(and the broader sociocultural influences on literacy)

Community
(and the child's place in it)

Centres
(and the educators'
literacy knowledge and
practices)

Schools
(transitions and formal
reading and writing)

Children
(and their literacy
knowledge and
experiences)

Families
(and the home literacy
environment)

Other
(including libraries, the
arts, social events,
church, etc.)

Figure 1: A sociocultural model of literacy learning

Hence, a sociocultural model of literacy learning (see Figure 1) at least comprises three broad areas of focus (this model draws heavily on the work of Bronfenbrenner (1979) and McNaughton (1995 & 2002)):

   i) *Children*, and their literacy knowledge and diverse experiences

   ii) The *community*, and the child's place in it, and this includes:

      ❖ Centres, and the educators' literacy knowledge and practices

      ❖ Families, extended families, community elders and the home literacy environment

      ❖ Institutions/other areas, including schools, libraries, social events, church etc.

      ❖ The child's transitions within each of these community areas, and also the literacy (and other) interrelationships between these areas

   iii) *Society*, and the broader sociocultural influences on literacy.

> In this book we have defined literacy, and particularly in this case early literacy, as:
>
> The experiences, practices, attitudes, skills and knowledge engaged with in their early years across a diverse range of settings which contribute to children understanding, engaging with and using oral, visual and written language and symbols of their own and other cultures to express their individual identity and allow them to become active participants in a literate society.

How is this book structured?

The book is divided into three broad sections.

(i) Policy (literacy policy-making in early childhood centres)

This first section encourages early childhood educators to engage in literacy debate and develop sound literacy policy for their centre. We support educators through this process and canvass the four key debates that underpin literacy policy development: *philosophical* (why literacy should be a part of the centre curriculum at all and where and to what extent it fits into the current philosophy and practices of the centre); *curriculum* (what literacy attitudes, knowledge, skills and understandings we want children to learn); *pedagogical* (the ways that children learn literacy knowledge, skills and attitudes, the ways in which the curriculum of the early childhood centre can be structured, and the ways that educators can interact with children); and *learning* (how children learn the foundations of literacy).

(ii) Practice (creating literacy-enriched early childhood centres)

This second section provides both a broad framework for helping early childhood educators analyse and structure literacy activities and practices, and a range of literacy ideas that educators can incorporate into their programs. We consider three key interrelated topics: the weaving of literacy *resources* throughout the early childhood centre (including literacy tools, environmental print, literacy-focused resource centres and books); planning for literacy *routines and experiences* (including where literacy can be incorporated into the existing day-to-day routines and planning of the centre); and capitalising on *informal literacy opportunities* (such as the often 'unplanned' and spontaneous opportunities that occur during children's everyday play).

(iii) Topics (special topics in literacy)

This final section canvasses three key aspects of literacy in early childhood education: approaches to *book reading* (including a range of practical strategies and techniques for both formal and informal book reading); highlighting *phonemic awareness and letter–sound knowledge* (including practical ways of supporting children's rhyming, syllable awareness, onset/initial sound knowledge, alphabet letter–sound knowledge and phonemic awareness in general); and highlighting children's *writing*.

Use of the term 'centre'

We have used 'centre' throughout this book as a generic term. The ideas relating to policy, planning, resources and so on are designed for the range of early childhood settings including long day care centres, playgroups, mobile children's services, community-based services, kindergarten, preschool, pre-primary, preparatory, reception and transition.

We would like to hear about your literacy ideas and practices

The development of strong literacy policies and practices in early childhood centres is a relatively new and exciting area of focus for educators. We have been fortunate to have been contacted by a number of enthusiastic educators wanting to share their experiences and knowledge with us for which we have been very grateful. Their ideas and material have been used throughout this book. In addition, the authors would love to hear from early childhood educators and others who have comments about this book as well as useful literacy ideas and practices (including examples of centre literacy policies). Please contact us at c.barratt_pugh@ecu.edu.au.

We hope that you find this book useful and we would appreciate your feedback on it

Section One

Literacy Policy-making in Early Childhood Centres

> The evaluation process (to inform program decision making) requires staff to develop an openness to change, a culture of reflective practice, an acceptance of discussing diverse points of view and a commitment to continuous learning.
>
> (QIAS, 2005, p.14)

This first section of the book comprises four chapters that are designed to encourage debate about a number of important areas of literacy. This debate within the centre community can inform centre literacy practice but can also be used to underpin literacy policy development in a centre. While all centres engage in some form of literacy-related practice, a literacy policy ensures that such practices are consistent, appropriate and underpinned by sound rationales, literacy theory and effective teaching principles. While the development of a written literacy policy can have many advantages, it is critical that first there be a sustained debate within the centre community on these key areas.

This section provides a detailed discussion of the key philosophical, curriculum, pedagogical and learning debates in relation to literacy and concludes with a step-by-step account of how a centre can go about turning this debate into a sound literacy policy. Before we move on to the key literacy debates, it is important for centres to consider why they should develop a literacy policy and engage in a literacy debate at all.

Why develop a literacy policy for your centre?

There are various reasons for a centre to develop a written literacy policy and to engage in these broader literacy policy debates. There may be requests from parents, professional development queries or government initiatives of one form or another. We have listed a range of possible reasons for developing a literacy policy and we recommend that centres consider the advantages and implications of these carefully.

a) **Literacy is a crucial area.** It is an area that is gaining increasing prominence in education and in society. Early childhood, and early childhood education, is now viewed as an important opportunity for children to learn about a range of areas that contribute to literacy development and school success.

b) **A literacy policy will provide a constructive response to increasing pressure for literacy in centres.** Recognition that literacy begins at birth and is fostered through everyday events in families and communities has led to a number of national and state government initiatives that place literacy at the centre of early learning. Parents, schools, communities and governments are looking to early childhood education to provide the foundations of children's literacy learning.

c) **A literacy policy will provide an opportunity for centres to debate core aspects relating to literacy.** Centre communities need the opportunity to debate why literacy should be a part of the centre, where it fits into the curriculum, and what pedagogical implications may be involved.

d) **A literacy policy will encourage the development of effective centre literacy practices based on sound theory.** The development of a literacy policy provides centres with the opportunity to rethink, evaluate and enhance their literacy practices and the theoretical underpinnings of those practices.

e) **A literacy policy will help centres provide a more coherent and planned approach to literacy in the centre.** The creation of a literacy-enriched early childhood centre environment does not happen by accident. A literacy policy can outline how literacy resources and practices can be built into the centre environment in a coherent and planned way.

f) **A literacy policy will formalise existing centre literacy practices.** In all early childhood centres there are, already, practices occurring which contribute to the development of children's early literacy. It may be obvious, such as storybook reading and alphabet songs; or less obvious, such as nursery rhymes, the retelling of stories, and a generally rich language environment. A literacy policy helps to formalise and recognise those practices already occurring in the centre.

g) **A literacy policy will improve the quality of centre literacy decision-making.** A sound literacy policy helps educators to make sound, fast decisions about literacy in their centre.

h) **A literacy policy will enhance the professional image of educators.** A sound literacy policy that is developed in a consultative way shows the centre community that educators can deal with complex issues in a professional way, and this will enhance the image of the educators and the centre.

i) **A literacy policy will inform prospective parents.** A literacy policy when made explicit to prospective parents will allow them to make informed choices about which early childhood centre will best meet the needs of their child.

A sound written literacy policy has many advantages for a centre both educationally and politically. A strong policy enables the centre to justify its practices, enter into rigorous debate about those practices and avoid the dangers of prepackaged literacy programs and products, aspects of which may not be appropriate for the centre community. It is also a logical and concrete outcome of sustained literacy policy debate within the centre community. The development of a sound literacy policy can also have some important spin-offs for professional development, centre relationships and the quality of the overall learning environment in the centre.

This section of the book considers the four core theoretical debates that underpin the development of sound literacy policy in early childhood centres and, accompanying this, the importance of developing strong literacy partnerships with parents, schools and the community. These four literacy debates are philosophical, curriculum-related, pedagogical and concerned with literacy theory. There are no simple answers to these debates and in order for educators to incorporate literacy in consistently appropriate, relevant and effective ways, they need to engage in serious and ongoing discussion, reading, reflection and consultation about these areas.

This process of critical debate about matters of importance for the centre community is one that is built into the aims, goals, principles and anticipated outcomes of the National Agenda for Early Childhood (DEST, 2004), and into the code of ethics outlined by the Early Childhood Australia Association. Community involvement and debate is also central to the National Indigenous English Literacy and Numeracy Strategy, which aims to increase the proportion of Indigenous 3–5-year-olds in preschool education through the continuing development of partnerships with the Indigenous community that take into account the aspirations and preference of that community (www.dest.gov.au/schools/indigenous/niels. htm. Retrieved 27.5.04). It has also been emphasised in the QIAS (2005), for example, in Quality Area 2: Partnerships with families, the importance of encouraging family members to participate in the centre's planning, program and operations; and in Quality Area 3: Programming and evaluation, developing a centre philosophy and evaluating programs on a regular basis have been identified as a key principles. The more that early childhood educators understand these areas the better they are able to develop and implement sound literacy policy and practice. Only *informed* literacy professionals are able to rigorously defend the literacy policies and approaches that best suit the children with whom they work.

Chapter 1

The Philosophical Debate

Developing a literacy policy in an early childhood centre inevitably involves some serious philosophical debate. While this may sound daunting, it is a critical part of any policy development. The philosophical debate includes a consideration of *why* literacy should be a part of the centre curriculum at all and *where* and to what extent it fits into the current philosophy (and practices) of the centre. This chapter aims to support centres in working through these two philosophical areas in a straightforward way but without providing simple answers that might undermine the integrity of the centre's own policy development process. Engaging the community in this philosophical debate will enable parents, along with staff to raise issues and contribute to the values and beliefs that will inform policy and practice.

Why should literacy be a part of the centre curriculum?

Asking the centre community why literacy should be part of its curriculum will elicit a range of responses that can provide the justification for the centre literacy policy, the centre's emphasis on literacy, and also assist the centre to further reflect the values, needs and aspirations of the centre community and society. These responses can be grouped in a number of different ways and we would encourage the centre policy writers to develop their *own* categories based on the answers they receive. For example, such groupings might be 'government, community, service, centre, family'; or 'intrinsic and extrinsic to the child or centre'.

Following on from the discussion and Figure 1 in the Introduction (which outlines a sociocultural model of literacy learning), the reasons why literacy should be a part of the centre curriculum initially involve an examination of a range of community settings, including the family, the centre, the school and other places and events within the local community. However, each of these community settings is affected by, and shaped to, different extents by a diverse range of broader sociocultural influences.

The beliefs, ideologies, values and aspirations of a society not only impact on every aspect of public and private life but such perspectives can change fairly dramatically over periods of time. Government policy, curricula, literacy theory, views about how children learn, views about how children should be taught, the economy, social changes (such as gender equity), theories on children's development and so on, are all influenced by the educational, social, cultural and political contexts of the time.

This is particularly so of literacy, where even over the last 30 years there have been major upheavals in theory, policy and practice. In summary, we cannot ask why literacy should be a part of the centre curriculum, or develop literacy policy (and practice) in any community setting (such as schools, families and centres), without first taking broader sociocultural influences into account. Figure 1.1 introduces some of these societal influences and contexts.

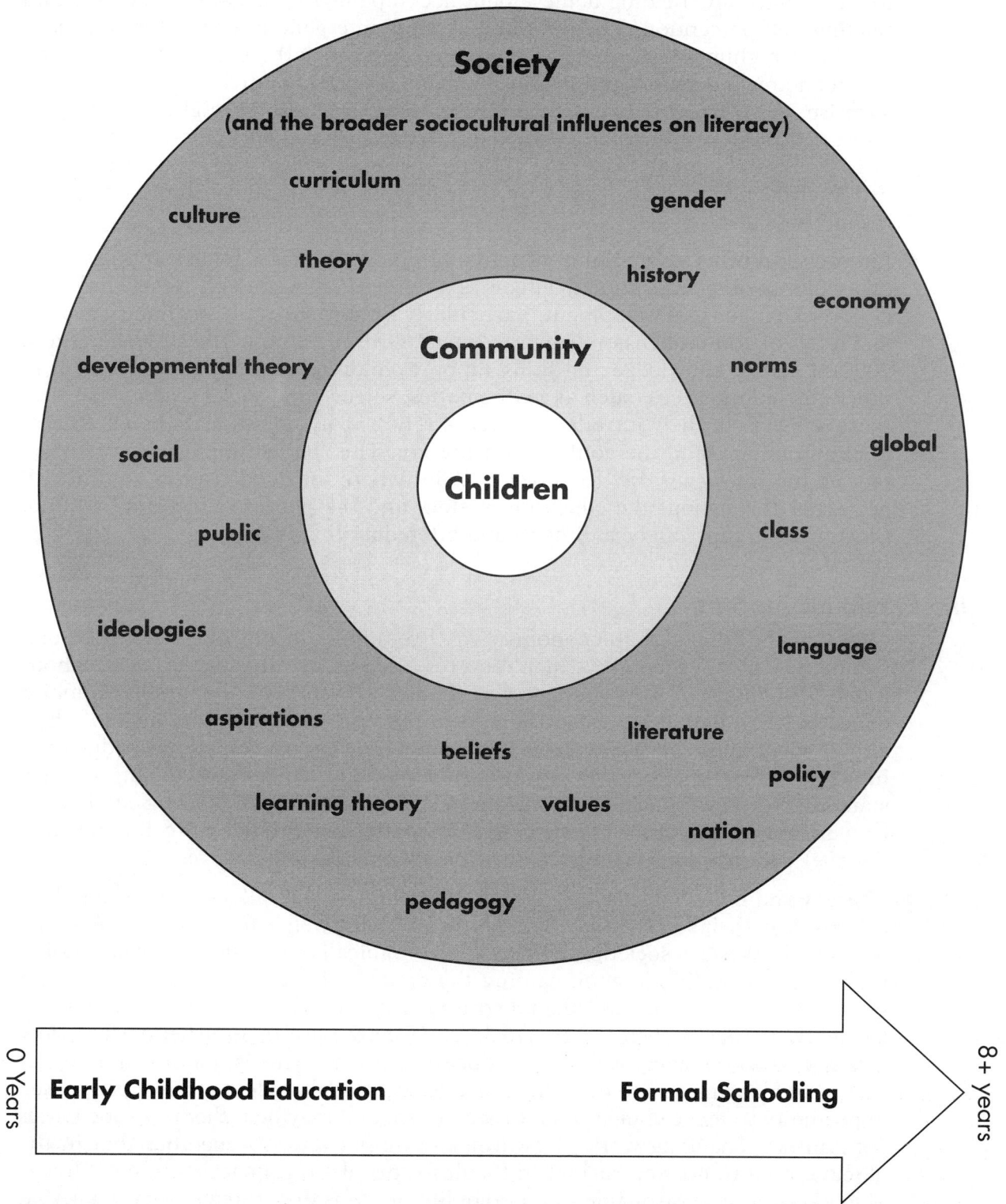

Figure 1.1: Society and the broader sociocultural influences on literacy

As an example of how a centre might group the likely diverse responses to this question, we have organised into four broad areas a representative selection of reasons worth considering: educational, economic, social and cultural, and personal.

(i) Educational reasons

❖ **Literacy and school success.** Education in Western countries is primarily based around literacy knowledge and practices. It would be difficult, if not impossible, to do well in any Western education system without being able to read or write. Consequently, often those who are most successful in the education system are those who are most literate. Those who 'fail' in the education system have been found to have low reading achievement accompanied by negative academic and reading self-perceptions. Adult illiteracy and intergenerational illiteracy have also been highlighted as major educational (and social) issues in Organisation for Economic Cooperation and Development (OECD) countries. It comes as no surprise, then, that literacy and numeracy have become the highest priority in almost all Western education systems in recent years and particularly in the early years of formal education. Young children who fail to learn to read early find it extremely difficult to 'catch-up' with their peers and require substantial help and resources to do so.

❖ **Literacy and other educational benefits.** Literacy also has a 'bootstrapping' effect on a range of other educational outcomes. Literacy achievement is closely linked to children's language development, particularly on measures of vocabulary growth and levels of comprehension (e.g., see Burns, Griffin & Snow, 1999; McNaughton, 2002). Literacy knowledge and skills support children's academic achievement in other curriculum areas (such as mathematics, science and social studies) because these subjects in their introductory years rely heavily on students being able to read and understand the content information. This 'bootstrapping' idea is often termed the *Matthew Effect* (Stanovich, 1986) where the good readers continue to get better throughout the education system and the poorer readers fall behind. Closing these gaps can be a difficult and often daunting task.

(ii) Economic reasons

❖ **Literacy and the global economy.** We live in an increasingly complex and competitive global economy which requires a highly literate and educated labour force. Virtually every OECD country in the last 10 years has embarked on major educational initiatives to raise the educational and literacy standards of their populations. These initiatives have involved increasing participation in education in all the educational sectors (from early childhood to tertiary), raising literacy standards with regional and national literacy strategies, and refocusing curriculum frameworks to emphasise more market-oriented subjects (such as technology and science). Literacy achievement is at the heart of all these initiatives.

❖ **Literacy and financial success.** Additionally, parents generally want their children to 'do well' in their society, and often this means doing well in terms of their financial position. In Western societies, doing well economically in most cases means doing well in the education system, gaining the credentials necessary for entry to the better-paid professions, and demonstrating high levels of literacy. Families are keenly aware that for their children to do as well as themselves (and better) in society generally involves doing well in the education system. This is not only a financial issue, but also an issue to do with choice. Educational credentials give people the opportunity to make choices about their future and may help them to cope better with an ever-changing world. However, it is important to remember that in the global economy, it is increasingly difficult for people to gain access to most forms of work without a reasonable standard of literacy. It is therefore not surprising that many parents have a strong interest in their children's literacy development, and many recognise clearly the importance of early literacy learning.

(iii) Social and cultural reasons

❖ **Literacy and cultural transmission.** Literacy lies at the heart of our cultural traditions. It is generally through written (and to a lesser extent oral) means that Western societies pass on their cultural knowledge from one generation to the next. Books, journals, magazines, popular culture, the Internet and other written sources are consistent and stable ways of learning about the past, the social sciences, the arts and literature, the sciences, social values and the large body of knowledge that a society accumulates over time. No other source provides such detailed, constant and easily accessible information about society. However, one needs to be reasonably literate to access and understand this information.

❖ **Literacy and cultural identity.** Literacy and language are also at the heart of cultural identity, and this, of course, applies to the Indigenous and minority groups of a society as well. The importance of acknowledging and building on the languages and literacies of Indigenous and ethnic communities has been identified by research and endorsed by federal policy documents (Department of Education and Training, 1991) and state policy and curriculum frameworks. There is a wealth of evidence that suggests children's home languages and literacies have a positive effect on learning a second language, as children are able to use (consciously and subconsciously) what they know in one language to help them learn a second language (Barratt-Pugh, 1997; Gregory, 1996; Jones Diaz, 1999; Milne & Clarke, 1993; Siraj-Blatchford & Clarke, 2000). In addition, research shows that there are significant linguistic, intellectual, social and cultural advantages to becoming bilingual/biliterate (Barratt-Pugh, Breen, Kinder, Rohl & House, 1996; Cummins, 1993; Edwards, 1997; Harris, 1990).

❖ **Literacy and democracy.** Democratic participation in society benefits from a literate and educated population. As each election nears, political parties try to persuade us that their party, their policies and values, and their vision of society deserve our votes. To understand fully what each of these parties is offering, one needs to read, understand and critique their literature and the various commentaries on it. Without literacy, democratic choice can easily descend to being based on political parties' and leaders' levels of persuasion, their looks or the slickness of their advertising. Democratic participation at the community level also often involves negotiating a minefield of written material, lengthy submissions and agendas.

(iv) Personal development reasons

❖ **Literacy and self-fulfilment.** Literacy provides many important opportunities for children to express themselves and develop their own interests. For example, children orating stories, the writing and making up of stories and poems (usually with adult assistance) and the reading of books which link to children's own interests provide important opportunities for children to develop personally. The confidence and literacy skills that children acquire not only contribute to their self-esteem (particularly their academic and reading self-concepts) and identity but also give young people the ability to become lifelong learners.

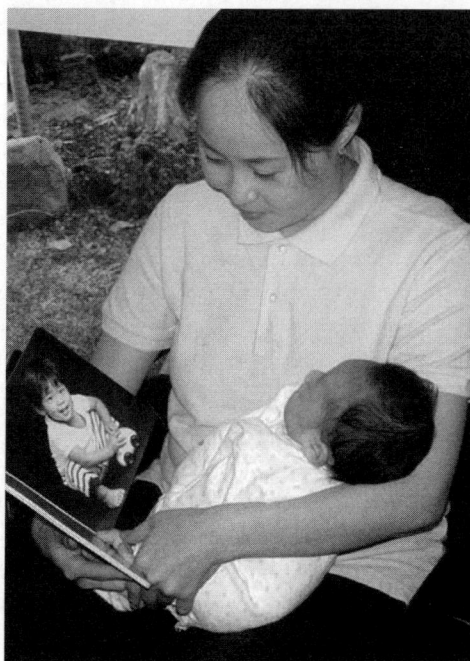

Literacy begins very early

❖ **Literacy and social participation.** Literacy also helps children to become participating members of a literate society. This not only includes being functionally literate (i.e., being able to fill out government forms or read telephone books) but assists in helping individuals to become full participants in their own social and cultural contexts. People with lower literacy skills in the Western world are often excluded from a wide range of areas (such as literature) or hindered in their ability to participate (such as getting a good job or knowing their consumer rights). Literacy in this context is a personal gatekeeper.

❖ **Literacy and emancipation.** Finally, being literate can have an emancipatory role. By being literate, and reading about the nature of the world, people can be more aware of their own social location. Literacy makes a major contribution to the ability to understand and deal constructively with such important equity areas as gender, ethnicity, socioeconomic location, disability and age. Social justice, and the redressing of social and cultural grievances, in most Western societies is often dependent on fairly advanced literacy skills and being aware of the injustices that may be occurring to oneself or one's neighbours. Therefore, an important part of being literate is being able to critically evaluate the messages and images represented in texts (such as books, magazines, television, and advertising). This includes under-standing that all texts portray only limited representations of the world that may or may not reflect the realities of people's lives. Texts also send out messages about what and who is good or bad, right or wrong, normal or not. Developing critical literacy skills helps people to question and challenge the obvious and more subtle images and messages texts present. For example, in today's society, it is becoming increasingly important to be able to critically evaluate popular text and advertising because of the increasing inundation of those texts in our lives, and the strong and often limited messages they deliver about the world.

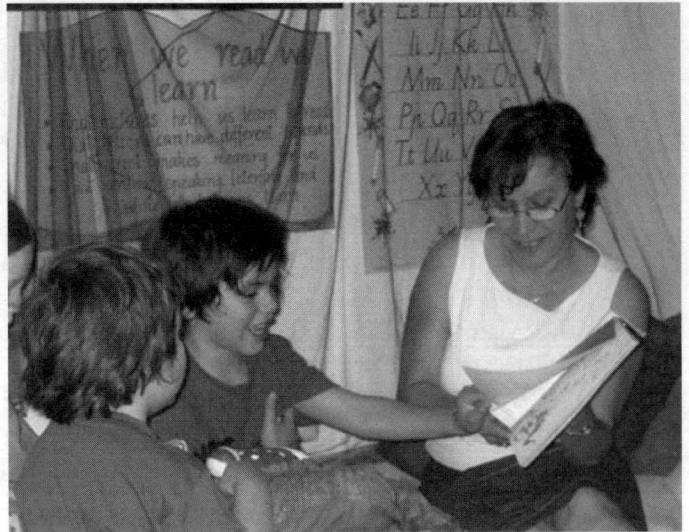

Small group discussion about different families

In conclusion, it is for these sorts of reasons that parents, businesses, governments and the community are increasingly looking to the education system to raise the achievement of all children (especially in literacy). This pressure is now, more than ever, 'trickling down' to the early childhood sector in a variety of forms, including parental requests for more academic and 'school-like' programs, increased expectations from schools, government initiatives (e.g., early childhood centres on school grounds, raising educator qualification benchmarks, targeted funding initiatives, parent education programs), community suggestions (e.g., calls for compulsory early childhood education) and changes to teacher education programs and requirements.

In what ways is literacy supported by the philosophy of the centre?

The majority of early childhood education centres will have a philosophy statement of some kind that outlines the key beliefs underpinning all aspects of the centre's operations. A centre's philosophy usually articulates the centre's purpose and direction, what it believes the children will gain from the centre, its beliefs in relation to children's learning and development, and the place and role of families and the community. Where a centre's philosophy has been developed and regularly reviewed in consultation with the centre community, that philosophy is likely to be clearly reflected throughout the policies and practices of the centre.

Once the centre community has begun debating the reasons why literacy should be a part of the centre curriculum, it is important to also consider this debate in relation to the centre's philosophy. This process involves considering how the centre's views about the importance of literacy are already reflected in its philosophy as well as how the centre's philosophy might impact on or shape these views. Such an evaluation exercise might involve a consultation process comprising various individuals and groups from within the centre community.

A useful exercise for early childhood education centres to undertake is to write down the ways in which the centre's philosophy currently supports its views of literacy. This could then be added to and revised as centres continue to examine the literacy debates discussed in this book. Such an exercise will assist centres in ensuring that their final literacy policy is consistent with and clearly reflects the centre's philosophy. As a model, Table 1.1 provides some examples of common areas of centre philosophies and the implications they might have for a centre's literacy policy and practices.

Table 1.1: The influence of centre philosophy on literacy policy

Common areas of centre philosophies	Literacy policy
Family and community	Centre literacy practices and resources reflect the integral role of literacy in children's home lives and community experiences.
Resilience	Centre literacy experiences empower children (both now and in the future) to develop personally, educationally, economically, socially and culturally (see social and cultural reasons earlier in this chapter).
Development	Centre literacy experiences provide a wide range of opportunities through which children can holistically learn, develop and experience the world.
Connection	Centre literacy experiences provide a range of opportunities through which children can engage in responsive and reciprocal relationships with people, places and things.
Health and safety	Literacy experiences can be woven into the everyday health and safety aims and practices of the centre.
Educators	Literacy provides many professional opportunities for educators to develop their pedagogical and curriculum knowledge.
Equity	As an example, centre literacy practices might seek to redress observed differences in access to literacy experiences for boys and girls.
Bicultural/multicultural	Centre literacy practices and resources reflect the bicultural and multicultural heritage of children and their families.

Concluding comments

- The development of a literacy policy should begin with debating the reasons why literacy should be a part of the centre curriculum.

- Consultation is an important step in ensuring that any literacy policy reflects the values, needs and aspirations of the centre's community and society.

- Each centre's reasons for including literacy will be unique. The reasons (and grouping of these) will vary from one centre to the next.

- Any literacy policy needs to be grounded in each centre's philosophy statements.

Chapter 2

The Curriculum Debate

Curriculum for early childhood in Australia

In Chapter 1 we considered why literacy should be a part of the centre curriculum and to what extent literacy is supported by the current philosophy of early childhood centres. In that chapter aspects of wider society were considered, particularly in relation to the role and importance of literacy in society and the influence of broader sociocultural areas on the place of literacy in early childhood education. In this chapter we look at the early childhood curriculum, which represents one of the mechanisms through which the state and community influence the nature of what goes on in early childhood education. Thus, it is important to debate the place of literacy in such documents. As mentioned previously the curriculum in the years 0–8 is complex, reflecting the relationship between state, federal and community policies and practices discussed in the Introduction.

Literacy policy and practices in Australia have been influenced by a range of social, cultural and economic values, aspirations, visions, beliefs and ideologies. Nowhere is this more evident than in curriculum documents which are social and political constructs of a particular time in history. As McCulloch (1992) points out, curricula have always been:

> a contested arena in which different social, cultural and political groups have sought their own ends. This process has encouraged negotiation, mediation, and a continual shifting of unstable and transient alliances at the same time that it has led to particular kinds of assumptions about what is 'basic' or fundamental knowledge. (p.11)

Literacy policy and practices in Australia are influenced by a range of curriculum documents developed by each state and territory, as listed in Table 2.1. It is worth noting that these cover different age ranges and service types (e.g., preschool and childcare) in each state of Australia.

Table 2.1: Curriculum documents that influence literacy policy and practices

State/territory	Curriculum document	Age range	Departments responsible for all other child care
Western Australia	*Curriculum Framework* (1998) Department of Education & Training	K–12	Department of Community Development
New South Wales	*Curriculum Framework for Children's Services* (2002) Department of Education & Training	Birth–5	Department of Community Services
Victoria	*Curriculum & Standards Framework* (2002) Department of Education & Training	Prep–10	Department of Human Services
Queensland	*Early Years Curriculum Guidelines* (2004) Department of Education & the Arts	Prep	Department of Families, Youth & Community Care
South Australia	*Curriculum, Standards & Accountability Framework (SACSA)* (2004) Department of Education, Training & Employment	Birth–12	Department of Education, Training & Employment. Curriculum document links the SACSA to QIAS
Tasmania	*Essential Learnings Framework* (2002) Department of Education	K–10	Department of Education
ACT	*Curriculum for ACT* (2001) Department of Education and Community Services	P–10	Department of Education and Community Services
Northern Territory	*Northern Territory Curriculum Framework* (2005) Department of Education	Trans–10	Department of Health and Community Services

Although the curriculum documents for preschool education and care vary from state to state, reflecting the diversity and needs of the communities they serve, there are a number of common elements. All of the curriculum documents identify language and literacy as central components of the curriculum. Many states have affiliated documents that address the needs of Indigenous learners and learners who speak English as an additional language. For example, South Australia has developed a number of companion documents to the SACSA, and these include 'Australian Indigenous Languages' and 'ESL Scope and Scales Moderated Evidence', as well as a document designed to help educators link the SACSA to the Quality Improvement and Accreditation System (for Long Day Care Centres). The importance of integrating literacy through the early childhood education program and environment is also highlighted across documents. The specific pattern of integration in each setting will depend on the nature of the early childhood service, program, philosophy and location. For example, the way in which each early childhood setting meets its literacy-related goals will vary depending on its specific goals and priorities.

However, 'reading', and to some extent 'writing', has not always had a large role in early childhood education because traditionally formal instruction was seen to begin in the compulsory education system. Recent research, which suggests that literacy begins at birth, has led to a broader notion of literacy, and the wide range of practices that contribute to the development of the literate child sits comfortably within the curriculum documents developed across Australia. This view is encompassed in Principle 4.3 of the QIAS, which states 'staff promote each child's language and literacy abilities' (p.19), in which reading and writing are identified as key components of the early childhood program. In addition, while literacy is often viewed as just being located in specific areas of the curriculum (e.g., English, communication, language and literacy), we argue that the areas that comprise literacy have a much broader foundation which span the whole of the curriculum. Again, the QIAS endorses this view, suggesting that language and literacy should be integrated throughout program planning and program documentation (p.19).

The curriculum debate that we ask centre communities to reflect on, then, is where does literacy fit within their early childhood education curriculum framework? The answers to this question have important implications for centre literacy policy, literacy planning and how and where literacy should be integrated into the early childhood setting. A more holistic approach to literacy also ensures that literacy is not viewed or implemented in a more narrow 'skill and drill' way.

Guiding principles

In order to facilitate debate about the place and content of literacy in early childhood settings, we have identified a number of guiding principles that are reflective of both curriculum documents from states and territories and some of the QIAS principles (2005). Each principle is followed by specific examples of practice that form part of an integrated and holistic approach to literacy in early childhood education.

Finding out about home literacy practices

(i) Family and community

This principle highlights the need for building strong connections between children's home, communities and schools. With regard to literacy, educators need to build upon the literacy practices already occurring in families. This can occur through the provision of literacy resources as well as routines, activities and events that reflect the diverse experiences of children. Developing partnerships with parents/carers and the centre community also supports a two-way sharing of knowledge and understanding between the child's centre, home and community contexts (see, for example, Cairney, 2002; McNaughton, 2002). Some examples of literacy practices reflecting this principle include:

❖ Home literacy routines can be reflected in centre routines (e.g., meal/snack times, stories at nap-time).

❖ Literacy resources, tools and events used throughout the centre can reflect different genders, cultures, languages and abilities (e.g., books and posters of girls doing carpentry).

❖ Literacy resources and events can reflect children's families (e.g., books that reflect children's culture, language and relationships, charts depicting names of family members including skin names and nicknames as well as English names). In addition, educators can assist children and families to question and challenge literacy texts that conflict with or ignore the realities of their own lives (e.g. questioning the lack of minority groups in story books).

❖ Children can regularly take part in familiar community literacy activities (e.g., trips to the library, shopping).

❖ Emotional and physical health and safety literature can be shared between home and centre (e.g., providing pamphlets for parents on a range of issues).

❖ Centre rules can be written and illustrated for children and their family to see (e.g., children and staff write and illustrate centre rules, parents have easy access to centre policies, access to policies in home/community languages).

Making links with community practices

❖ Literacy tools can allow children to try out familiar literacy-related events in their play (e.g., shopping, filling in forms, 'reading' the newspaper).

(ii) Resilience

This principle is about recognising strengths and maximising potential, leading to self-confidence, self-respect and greater independence. When viewed in relation to literacy, this principle supports the provision of literacy resources, routines and activities that reflect the diverse interests, experiences, home backgrounds and cultures of children and result in a sense of wellbeing based on a culture of optimism. It also highlights the need to support children to develop the skills, knowledge and attitudes needed to question and challenge those literacy texts which may either ignore or present as 'wrong', 'unnatural' or 'bad', the world-views of some (often minority) groups, while presenting the world-views of other (often majority) groups as 'right', 'natural' and 'good' (Bertanees & Thornley, 2001). In addition, this principle highlights the need to provide an environment where children can participate in literacy activities in ways that are most meaningful to them. Some examples of literacy practices reflecting this principle include:

❖ Literacy resources, tools and events can assist children to feel valued and important (e.g., books and posters that reflect children's cultures, languages and home lives; shared reading allowing children to take an active role in one-to-one and group literacy activities).

❖ Teaching strategies such as questioning and problematising, that can assist children to see themselves and their lives as recognised and valued, by questioning the images of children and their families portrayed in different texts (such as challenging the image of the two-parent family presented as the 'norm' in a storybook or advertisement).

❖ Literacy-related resources and routines can support children's emotional development (e.g., reading and recording stories about events and feelings children experience).

❖ A wide range of literacy-related tools can allow children to make their own literacy-related play choices (e.g., pens, paper, books, toy phones, stamps).

❖ Literacy resources can provide children with opportunities to try out and explore their literacy skills and knowledge (such as pretending to write).

❖ The provision of a wide range of literacy-related tools can allow children to actively explore and develop their literacy understandings both individually and with others.

❖ Children can actively use literacy as they engage in health and safety routines (e.g., adding names on a list to record who goes next, signs that remind children to wash their hands).

❖ Literacy can be used to reassure and comfort children (e.g., a favourite story read to settle a child).

(iii) Development

This principle focuses on the importance of recognising what children can do and using this as a starting point for new learning. This includes using information about children's diverse prior learning experiences and the various learning contexts or real life situations with which they are familiar. Recognition of different ways of learning and different rates of development are important considerations in recording progress and informing program planning. Development is dependent upon opportunities to interact in language and literacy events that extend the repertoire which children bring to the centre; thus interaction with educators and peers is an essential part of further learning. Some examples of literacy practices reflecting this principle include:

❖ Children's understanding of environmental print can be used to further develop their knowledge of the alphabet, words and whole texts.

❖ Rhymes and poetry can be used to develop phonological awareness prior to explicit sound–symbol relationships.

❖ Children's oral language can be monitored in order to extend the purposes for which they use language (e.g., extending language to include explaining and predicting).

❖ Literacy tools and activities throughout the centre can be used to support children's play and exploration in a wide range of curriculum areas (e.g., children's understanding of shape and design can be supported by drawing plans).

❖ Centres can provide opportunities for small groups of children to take part in literacy-related activities (e.g., two or three children listening to a story or creating a group poster).

❖ Regular trips and visits can be used to engage children in the wider literate world creating opportunities to build on and extend literacy learning through meaningful activities (e.g., visits to or from local storytellers, librarians, community elders).

(iv) Connectedness

This principle relates to a model of literacy learning that links experiences and meaning in different contexts. This suggests that literacy should be woven throughout the environment, activities and practices of the early childhood setting. This principle supports a broad view of literacy that is reflected in the integration of literacy throughout regular routines, play, activities and events. In addition, this principle emphasises that literacy is not restricted to certain ages and stages of development but is equally important for infants, toddlers and young children. Some examples of literacy practices reflecting this principle include:

❖ Literacy-related experiences can support all areas of development (e.g., rhyme play and book reading can support language development, drawing can support fine-motor skills).

❖ Literacy resources can support children's exploration and develop understanding of their wider world (e.g., reference books can provide information on a wide range of topics).

❖ Children and educators can use literacy tools and resources (e.g., books, pens, paper) to communicate and express a wide range of ideas with each other such as through art, song, stories and play.

❖ Children can be creative and expressive through literacy (e.g., drawing with pens, creating stories, exploring language sounds).

❖ Children's names can be used to promote a sense of belonging (e.g., named cubbyholes for each child).

(v) Communication

This principle highlights the importance of both oral and written communication in the early years. Oral language: enables the development of a range of personal, social and political meanings; constructs as well as conveys meanings between individuals and social groups; and provides the means for informing, persuading, questioning, explaining and engaging in a range of different contexts. Communication also involves an understanding of the symbol systems used to communicate meaning. These include words and images in print and new communication technologies, such as computer literacy. Children need opportunities to move from non-verbal to verbal communication and to extend the range of purposes used to communicate with others. The environment needs to be carefully planned in order to provide a variety of opportunities for interaction with others in different contexts that will facilitate the development of language and literacy practices and help children to develop an appreciation of linguistic and cultural diversity. Children can be engaged in using both written and oral genres that they have not previously encountered, in order to support the further development of language and literacy skills and knowledge. Some examples of literacy practices reflecting this principle include:

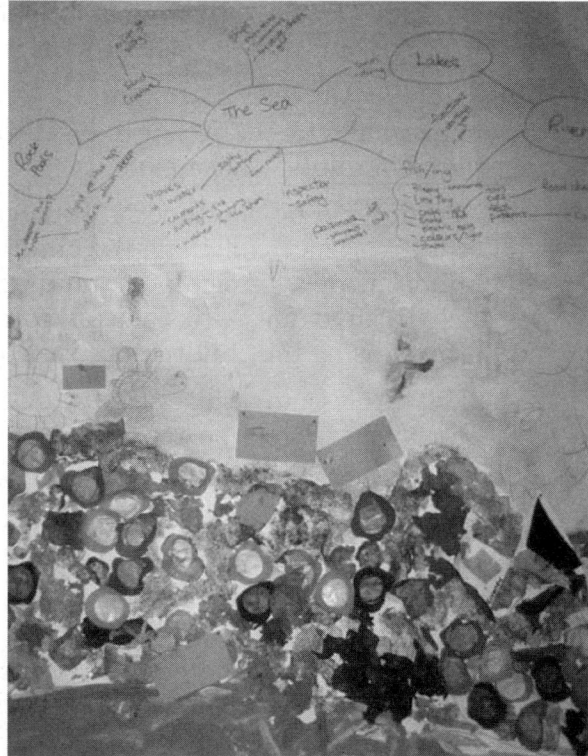
Sharing the brainstorming process

❖ Educators can build on children's oral language to develop written texts, making links between oracy and literacy (e.g., scribing children's words onto different types of texts created by the child, narrative, description, instruction).

❖ Educators can record children's experiences and stories (e.g., using language experience texts about a gardening project, photographing and recording children's explanations of a block construction).

❖ Educators and children can share stories and symbols from their own and other cultures (e.g., recording children's holiday stories, telling folk tales and myths).

❖ Children can be involved in writing letters to family and community members (e.g., writing thank-you letters to the library or cards to relatives).

(vi) Thinking and building knowledge

This principle highlights the importance of focusing on the processes of enquiry and reflection in the activities and contexts provided in early childhood centres. In addition, it recognises that knowledge is a social and cultural construct developed in specific contexts for transfer to new contexts. This includes the need to support and encourage children to build on prior knowledge and make links to prior learning. This principle also supports children developing their understandings that information presented in texts can be questioned and challenged, and that differing views of the world are an important part of living in a diverse and ever-changing world. Some examples of literacy practices reflecting this principle include:

❖ Literacy can be used to support children's understanding of physical and emotional health and safety issues (e.g., books and posters about health and safety information are read and discussed).

❖ Literacy can be used to promote children's understanding of wider social issues (e.g., reading and discussing stories about consequences).

❖ Literacy can be used to help children learn that people have different views and experiences of the world (e.g., through reading stories that reflect the lives and views of minority groups).

❖ Literacy can be developed through the use of language experience texts based on real experiences in which the children have been engaged. Such texts can support children's developing understanding of concepts of print and book knowledge and help them to make links between oracy and literacy (e.g., an excursion is made into a book using the children's representations and written ideas).

❖ Centre rules can be discussed and depicted in written form that children can access (e.g., 'wash hands' posters in the bathroom).

❖ Children can consider ways of managing health and safety routines and actively engage with literacy tools and resources during routines (e.g., writing their name on a list, creating a 'keep quiet' sign for the sleep room door).

(vii) Scaffolding and support

This principle recognises the need to support students with a range of strategies such as modelling, sharing, guiding and strategic prompts in order to support learning as children progress towards independence. This includes enabling children to participate and collaborate within purposeful learning contexts. Such contexts create an environment in which children feel safe and are provided with modelling and formative feedback through both explicit and integrated teaching strategies. Some examples of literacy practices reflecting this principle include:

❖ Frameworks that provide guidance and support such as using small group activities to introduce different purposes of literacy (e.g., News time 'When, where, who, what', About me 'I like …', Health and safety routines 'We always …').

❖ Modeling strategies for critically engaging with different literacy texts (e.g., 'I wonder why she did that?', 'Is that what you would do?', 'What's another way this story could have ended?').

❖ Use of information and communication technology to support a move towards independent literacy learning (e.g., interactive storybooks, word processing, supervised Web activities).

❖ Literacy tools can be provided that support children to use them successfully (e.g., 'fat' pencils and paper taped to the table make drawing easier for small hands).

❖ Educators can use illustrations to tell stories or give a message (e.g., picture books with no words, a 'wash hands' sign with a picture of soapy hands under a tap).

❖ Educators can become literacy resources themselves (e.g., singing rhymes, highlighting language sounds and rhythms).

Concluding comments

• The guiding principles outlined above build on and augment those outlined in many state curriculum documents and the QIAS (2005).

• The principles reflect a sociocultural view of literacy, in which language and literacy learning occurs through a range of cognitive experiences and socially and culturally constructed events, guided by explicit and implicit teaching.

• The principles provide a basis for sound and appropriate literacy policy development and sociocultural teaching practices.

Chapter 3

The Pedagogical Debate

The pedagogical debate is linked to the previous curriculum debate, and relates to the ways in which the curriculum of the early childhood centre can be structured, and the ways that educators can interact with children to facilitate their learning of literacy knowledge, skills and attitudes. The early childhood curriculum is underpinned by a sociocultural approach to pedagogy that complements and, to a growing extent, supersedes previous behaviourist and cognitive/Piagetian conceptions of how children learn. This chapter will primarily focus on this sociocultural model of teaching. The core elements of these sociocultural debates will be canvassed in a question and answer format to assist the centre community in facilitating discussion, and we specifically highlight its importance and relevance to literacy policy-making and practice. Finally, we consider some key aspects of sociocultural theory relevant for literacy policy, including the importance of linking literacy meaningfully to children's experiences, facilitating appropriate literacy interactions and considering the literate child as being a part of a broader community and focusing explicitly on the skills of literacy as they arise in children's experiential learning.

It is helpful to distinguish between the pedagogical debate in this chapter, which is primarily concerned with how to *teach* literacy, and the learning debate in the next chapter, which focuses on how children *learn* literacy. An examination of each area separately highlights differing questions, literatures and debates; although, you will notice that we are, at times, looking at the same or similar overlapping concepts and ideas, albeit from different directions.

What is the educator's role in early childhood education?

The nature of teaching is influenced by a range of factors. The theories of teaching and learning evolve and change, sometimes fairly radically, and recent developments in sociocultural theory have had a significant impact on the conceptions of the educator's role and on curriculum developments. This section will briefly consider both of these aspects.

(i) Changing conceptions of the educator's role

Throughout history theories of how children learn to read and write have influenced the way in which literacy is taught. Today the influence of sociocultural theories of language and literacy can be seen in the development of policy and practice in several states across Australia, as literacy has been incorporated into the early childhood curriculum. However, at the beginning of the 1900s it was believed 'that children could only learn to read when they had reached a particular mental age, brought about through a process of biological maturation' (Barratt-Pugh & Rohl, 2000, p.2). It was believed in relation to reading, that children needed to be maturationally 'ready' before reading instruction could begin (hence the term 'reading readiness'). This maturational view was largely superseded by behavioural approaches from around the 1950s.

From the 1950s, Cullen (2001) points out that:

> As theories have developed and changed, the focus of research on learning has moved from learning as a change in behaviour, to a cognitive view of learning characterised by the learner's cognitive ability 'in the head', to the study of learning in social contexts (Bereiter, 1990). The three phases in research on learning identify learning in different terms: learning as behaviour that can be controlled by external events; learning as individual cognitive activity; and learning as a social construct. (p.47)

Cullen (2001) noted that each perspective of learning viewed the role of the educator in different ways. *Behaviourist* approaches in the 1950s and early 1960s viewed the educator as active, particularly in controlling and manipulating events in the environment to facilitate learning, while the learner was seen as a relatively passive recipient of this structured knowledge. *Cognitive/Piagetian* approaches, dominant in the 1970s and 1980s, viewed learners in a more active light where they 'constructed' knowledge and the educator's role was to arrange a rich and stimulating environment for the learner to make sense of in their own time. Recent *sociocultural* approaches (heavily influenced by the work of the Russian developmentalist Lev Vygotsky) view the learner and the educator as co-constructing knowledge together in a more collaborative model of learning. Both educator and learner are seen as being active participants engaging with the range of cognitive 'tools' provided in the learning environment. For a more in-depth coverage of the changing perspectives on learning, Cullen's (2001) chapter titled 'An Introduction to Understanding Learning' provides a useful overview of the changes that have led up to the rise of the sociocultural model.

In addition, critical literacy, which draws on both sociocultural theory and critical theory, has become increasingly influential in Australian education. Gilbert and Taylor (1991, in Bertanees & Thornley, 2001, p.5) explain critical literacy as 'grounded in the belief that readers should be encouraged to critique and challenge through in-depth analysis and investigation, the ways in which language and texts function to advantage or marginalise social groups'. A critical literacy emphasis fits well within a sociocultural approach to early childhood education as both are based on an understanding of the inter-relationship between language, culture, social practice and learning. Sociocultural theory, as with critical literacy, is founded on the view that language is a social practice, and that through language we both understand and construct our world (Knobel & Healey, 1998). Thus, from this approach the role of the teacher in early childhood is to 'examine the way patterns of inequality are constructed and maintained and explore ways of teaching literacy which expose and challenge this inequality, as part of children's developing literacy competence' (Barratt-Pugh, 2000, p. 4).

(ii) The implications of key principles for the educator's role

Although Australia represents a diverse range of communities, there are some key principles that have emerged from curriculum guidelines from different states and are also evident in the QIAS (2005). Many of these have been influenced by sociocultural theories as evidenced in both their theoretical perspectives and practical outcomes. We explore the implications of the principles embedded in many of these documents and identified in the previous chapter for the educator's role.

(a) Family and community

The principle of family and community emphasises the importance of educators respecting children's home lives and communities and reflecting these in their teaching practices. It is important for educators to be aware of the social, community and economic lives of children and their families, and to acknowledge and take account of the variety of family groupings and ways of teaching and learning within families. In order to do this, it is important that educators know each child well and that they continually build their knowledge of children's experiences outside of the early childhood education environment. When educators view children's home and community literacy experiences as relevant, purposeful and meaningful to children, they can provide a positive basis from which to motivate children and co-construct shared literacy meanings. They are then also able to assist children to question the ways in which their own and others' lives are portrayed in various texts. In addition, this principle encourages educators to include the family and community in centre literacy practices and in debates concerning literacy policy.

(b) Resilience

The principle of resilience emphasises the importance of educators seeing each child from a positive, rather than a deficit perspective, that children (and their families) may have differing, but equally valid, ways of viewing the world, and recognising that children are different in their approach to learning literacy and their capacity to persist in the face of any difficulties they may encounter in either their home or school contexts. A positive view of all children's literacy knowledge, skills and experiences supports educators in seeing these as assets from which literacy skills and meanings can be further developed. This allows educators to view infants, toddlers and young children as active participants in a literate community. Educators can also empower children by mediating children's literacy experiences, supporting their successful participation and explicitly focusing attention on particular aspects of language and literacy as they arise within these experiences.

(c) Development

The principle of development helps educators to view literacy as a broad concept involving a range of literacy knowledge, skills, attitudes and dispositions. Such an approach leads to a literacy-rich early childhood environment that makes provision for children's differing needs according to their level of development. This implies the need for educators to be able to recognise what children already know about literacy and what they can do with literacy, and can provide appropriate activities or explicit direction for further development. It also emphasises the need to recognise that children learn in many different ways and that the sequence of literacy development differs between children. The sequence of development is influenced by cognitive as well as sociocultural factors. These differences need to be taken into account when assessing and planning literacy learning.

(d) Connectedness

The principle of connectedness emphasises that literacy is not a discrete body of knowledge that sits outside of or on top of the contexts in which it is used. Rather, literacy is viewed as a broad concept that is constructed through social negotiation and exists within a social context. In addition, it acknowledges that images and messages may or may not reflect children's own lives or views of the world, and that these images and messages can be questioned and challenged This principle guides educators to work with and alongside children to help them to develop increasing literacy understandings, meanings, narrative abilities and skills. This principle also highlights the importance of educators providing a literacy-rich and socially stimulating environment that gives children ample opportunities to engage meaningfully with a wide range of literacy tools. Regular, planned routines and events, both within the early childhood setting and in the wider community, are also supported by this principle.

(e) Communication

The principle of communication helps educators to recognise how the range of social purposes used to communicate with others, including communicating in other languages and dialects, conveys meaning between individuals and social groups. It also demonstrates the importance of learning to decode the symbols systems used to communicate meaning which may include letters, words, images and communicative technologies. As well, it emphasises the importance of developing and building the oral language use of children as a vehicle for making links with early literacy skills and understandings.

(f) Thinking and building knowledge

The principle of thinking and building knowledge makes the connection between language and literacy development and cognitive development. The importance of this principle cannot be underestimated as the interrelationship between language, literacy and cognition is inextricably interwoven. The implications of this principle relate to the need for educators to provide experiences that facilitate the construction of knowledge required for understanding the range of texts that children use, as well as the ability to critique the messages these texts contain. It also emphasises the importance of ensuring success in early literacy, because children who struggle to read in their first years of school have limited access to the knowledge that is being constructed through written texts and is available to their more successful peers.

(g) Scaffolding and support

This principle recognises the need for educators to utilise a range of strategies such as modelling, sharing, guiding and strategic prompts in order to support literacy learning as children progress towards independence. The principle relates to thinking and building knowledge and critical skills that will enable children to compose, comprehend and critique texts effectively. The implications for educators are the need to provide frameworks, guidance and support that enable children to access literacy at an appropriate level in a safe and supportive environment.

Learning together

What do educators need to know about a sociocultural model of literacy learning?

Building on the previous introduction to sociocultural theory and the implications for the educator's role, educators and the centre community need to be aware of the underlying nature of a sociocultural model of literacy learning in order to be able to fully debate the policy and practices of literacy in their centre. In this section we frame this discussion within the sociocultural model of literacy learning initially discussed in the Introduction and in Chapter 1.

The role of the educator in an early childhood education centre that is planned and organised around a sociocultural model is distinctive and involves a range of specialised knowledge and practices. When reviewing the pedagogical issues around literacy it is clear that learning to be literate is a highly complex process (Adams, 1990; Freebody, 1992). Factors related to the society in which children are located, the family and community in which they live, and the early childhood centres which they attend all influence the ways in which children take up literacy. In Figure 3.1 we outline the knowledge and practices of educators that we cover throughout this book, with a specific focus on early childhood education centres. On first looking at this diagram it may be hard to understand how this seemingly disparate list of terms and ideas fit together and how they relate to literacy policy and practice. However, the following section aims to systematically unpack some of the complexity associated with sociocultural theory and literacy learning, through a question and answer format that can be used to facilitate discussion on these topics. The answers, although thorough, are not intended to be definitive and in centre community discussions additional questions and answers are likely to emerge. This material is based on, or refocused from, Cullen (2002) and Wink and Putney (2002) and is adapted to concentrate solely on literacy, and what educators need to know about a sociocultural model of literacy learning.

3

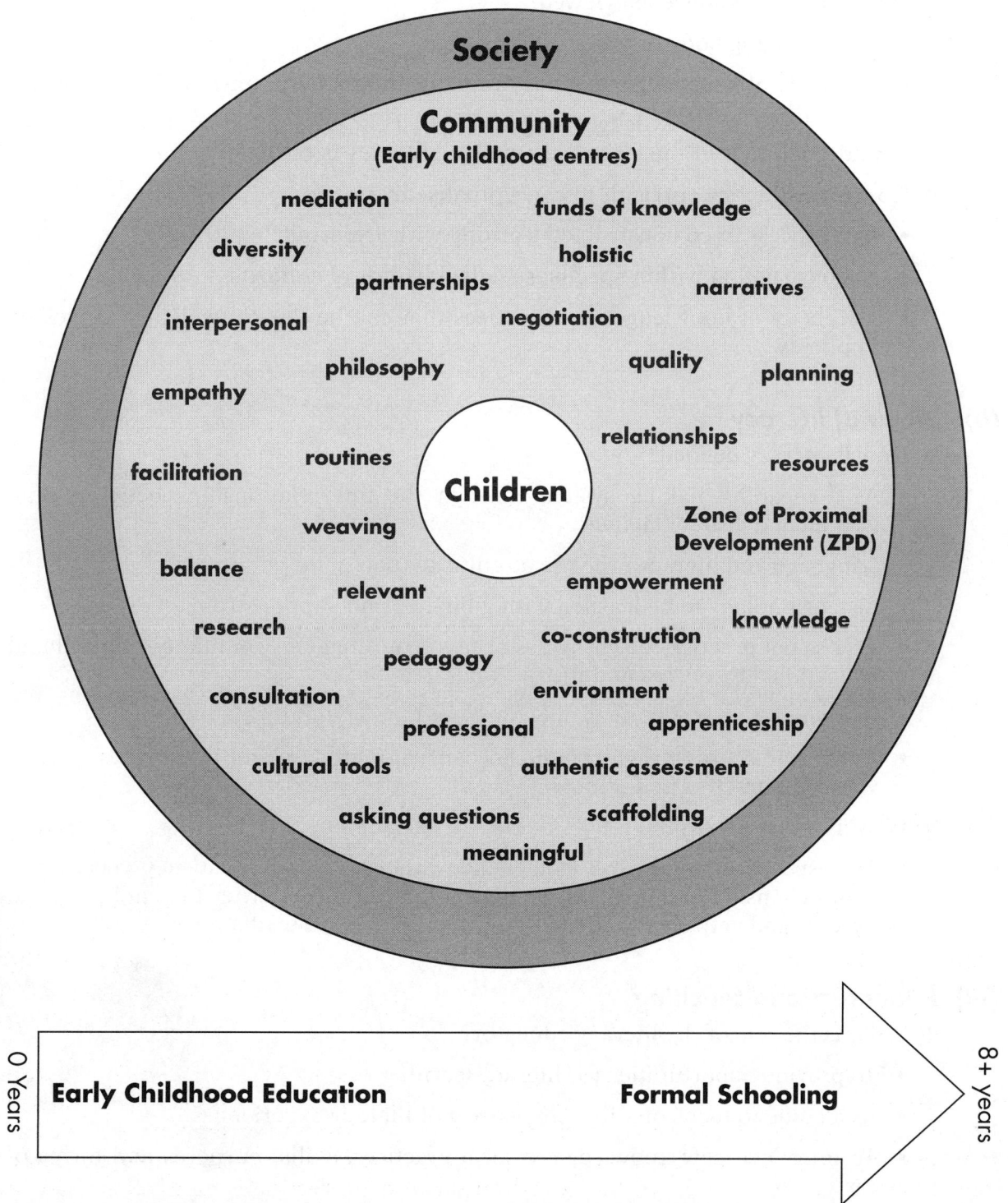

Figure 3.1: Centres and the educator's literacy knowledge and practices

(i) Education and curriculum

❖ What is the purpose of literacy education?

- To create new understandings about literacy
- To help students learn strategies to support literacy learning
- To prepare individuals as active social members of a literate society
- To provide students with expanding literacy repertoires of appropriate ways for interacting in a literacy-based society
- To provide students with knowledge about how literacy is shaped by different contexts for different purposes.

❖ How is literacy knowledge viewed?

- As a changing body of literacy knowledge
- As a body of knowledge which is mutually and socially constructed with others
- As a body of knowledge and skills that is systematic and governed by underpinnings of the language on which literacy is based.

❖ How is the literacy curriculum conceptualised?

- As a process of co-constructed learning with 'experts'
- As construction within specific social and cultural contexts
- As a body of knowledge and practices that can be taught explicitly as well as implicitly.

(ii) Views of literacy

❖ How is literacy defined?

- As a meaning-making system through the interrelationships between oral, written and visual language
- Language and literacy are seen as cultural tools
- As a technology to be learned with guidance and support from an expert
- As a social practice that provides access to a range of community, cultural and educational resources and institutions
- As shared literacy interests, meanings and understanding
- As a means through which we can construct, understand and express world-views of ourselves and of others.

❖ What is a literacy skill?

- The aspects of literacy (phonological awareness, decoding, fluency, vocabulary, comprehension and critical practices) required by a learner to enable them to process and actively engage with written, visual and media texts.

(iii) Educators and teaching

❖ What is the role of the literacy educator?

- To provide opportunities for literacy learning
- As a guide to focus on different aspects of literacy experiences
- To introduce new knowledge, critical practices, skills, purposes and forms of text
- To teach specific concepts about literacy at text, sentence and word level.

❖ What are the methods of teaching literacy?

- Creating opportunities for students to interact with meaningful literacy activities and texts

- Reviewing children's understanding of literacy and providing opportunities for connecting new concepts of literacy to what is known

- Explicitly teaching specific aspects of literacy that are timely and appropriate for a student's level of development

- Constructing literacy knowledge and skills with students by sharing literacy expertise and understanding

- Constructing opportunities with students for interacting with meaningful literacy ideas, materials and others.

(iv) Learners and learning

❖ What is the role of the literacy learner?

- To actively participate in the literacy activities and events provided

- To actively engage with expert adults, peers and siblings

- To generalise knowledge and understanding to other contexts

- To be an active literacy thinker, explainer, interpreter and enquirer

- To be an active social participator in literacy experiences.

❖ What motivates the literacy learner?

- Being able to connect literacy learning to their knowledge and understanding of the world

- Successful literacy learning experiences

- Appropriate purposes for participation in literacy-related activities

- Gaining pleasure and enjoyment from literacy experiences

- Empowerment through successful socially constructed literacy experiences.

❖ How do literacy students view themselves?

- As active sense-makers, challengers, problem-solvers and socially appropriate members of a literate community.

(v) The learning environment

❖ What is important in the literacy learning environment?

- Authentic, meaningful literacy experiences

- Print-rich environments, which include explicit examples of how literacy works

- Socially constructed literacy experiences

- A knowledgeable literacy expert to guide and support literacy learning.

❖ How is evidence of literacy learning collected?

- Through ongoing authentic literacy assessment throughout the centre

- Through ongoing authentic literacy assessment across a range of community settings

- Through assessments designed to identify particular components of literacy

- Through a process of literacy enquiry
- Through socially competent literacy participation in the centre community
- Through literacy performance, such as explanation of reasoning and social performance.

❖ What role do literacy peers play?
- Helping to create, mediate and construct literacy learning contexts
- Helping to create and define opportunities for literacy learning.

Key sociocultural literacy practices educators should know about

We have covered a range of sociocultural areas in the chapter so far, and this section now discusses in more depth some key practices that make significant contributions to this pedagogical debate and centre literacy policy and practice. Three areas in particular have been highlighted in the literature as being important for educators and centre communities to reflect on: providing meaningful literacy experiences for the child, facilitating appropriate literacy interactions with children, and acknowledging the literate child's place in the broader community. The ultimate goal for educators, as McNaughton (2002) puts it, is to facilitate a 'meeting of minds'.

(i) Providing meaningful literacy experiences for the child

When incorporating literacy into early childhood centres, the sociocultural literature suggests that the literacy experiences provided should have meaning for the individual children in the particular contexts in which they are engaging. Makin and Groom (2002) argue that educators 'need to set in place ways of learning from all families about their children's home and community literacy experiences ...' (p.75). Educators can then use this knowledge to develop ways of extending literacy learning for the children in the centre. For example, Hanlen (2002) suggests that for Indigenous children teaching 'should reflect the cultural focus on concrete examples... and provide opportunities to experiment, practice and gain competency ...' (p.229).

It is important to remember that oral language forms an important base for the development of literacy. Making opportunities for children to develop an increasing repertoire of oral language structures and linking these with literacy practices is central to creating meaningful literacy experiences. Embedding oracy and literacy within the everyday life of the centre is one way of making literacy meaningful and purposeful. This includes enabling children to use their home language and being aware of differences between standard Australian English and Aboriginal English.

Taking these differences into account, literacy can be made more meaningful for children when it is integrated purposefully within day-to-day centre life and linked to oral language. The early childhood centre provides many opportunities to achieve this. Literacy can be modelled in purposeful ways by adults, such as writing shopping lists with children, using children's names frequently to label belongings, writing down children's stories, and demonstrating how phone books work. In order to enable children to progress, specific aspects of literacy can be explicitly introduced within these meaningful activities, contextualising knowledge at text, sentence and word level. Similarly, literacy opportunities and props can be provided that allow children to explore and use literacy for different 'real-life' purposes in a range of centre contexts, and in ways that are helpful and extending for children. Literacy experiences in early childhood environments, then, are more meaningful for children when they link and enhance children's interests and experiences and when they are integrated into the everyday life of the centre. The implications for early childhood educators are many. For example, instead of imposing externally derived literacy 'programs' or prepackaged materials on children and their environments, educators can support children's literacy development more appropriately by building centre-developed literacy tools and experiences more seamlessly into the child's everyday life while at the centre. This more authentic approach to literacy better reflects the broader nature of the literacy experiences and practices the child meets in the wider community.

(ii) Facilitating appropriate literacy interactions with children

Educators also play a vital role in supporting children's literacy learning in the day-to-day life of the early childhood centre. The planned environment provides the broader framework for supporting literacy, including the literacy resources, routines and activities. Within this structure, educators have a critical part to play in facilitating literacy interactions, developing children's narrative abilities, being literacy models and setting up 'literacy apprenticeships'. In other words, young children's learning about literacy is mediated by the adult in social learning situations. As Neuman (1998) reminds us, 'literacy is a profoundly social process that enters children's lives through their interactions in a variety of activities and relationships with other people' (p.8). Not only do children learn to use language for different purposes in different families and communities, but they also learn to use language in different ways. For example, key differences have been identified between Aboriginal English and Standard Australian English, in that in Aboriginal English asking direct questions is regarded as impolite, whereas answering a question is seen as optional, being explicit is potentially offensive and being direct is associated with hostility (DEET, no date).

Thus, there is no simple recipe for ensuring effective literacy interactions with children in early childhood centres. To some extent, the quality of such interactions is dependent on the educator's level of knowledge about literacy, their understanding of the languages used in the centre and is also linked to the quality and depth of the literacy planning and environment provided. Each aspect works together to ensure that a strong literacy framework is in place. As Neuman, Copple and Bredekamp (2000) note, such contexts need to facilitate 'positive nurturing relationships with adults who engage in responsive conversations with individual children, model reading and writing behavior, and foster children's interest in and enjoyment of reading and writing' (p.16). It is through these social processes that children can actively engage in and make meaning about their world. However, children come to the centre from a range of diverse backgrounds and experiences, and consequently educators need to utilise a variety of strategies, materials and teaching approaches to facilitate their language and literacy development (Neuman, 1998).

While educators may relatively easily set up a literacy-rich environment, as Nutbrown (1997) cautions, 'simply giving children literacy related materials and the opportunity to play is of limited use unless they also have some sense of *how* to use them' (p.7). In this context, educators can use a range of teaching strategies to help children actively engage with literacy in the learning environment. For example, when children are engaged in dramatic/structured play adults can support them to use literacy tools which are close to hand such as using phone books, writing shopping lists, reading menus in restaurants and so on where it is relevant to what the children are trying to do. As Hall and Robinson (2000) point out literacy and structured play make powerful companions, 'they both involve experiences in which people make choices, relate to a range of purposes, involve different audiences, handle complex webs of areas of knowledge and orchestrate equally complex responses' (p.104).

Environmental print throughout the centre in forms such as labels, signs, names and so on can be either static and barely noticed by children, or dynamic where the educator draws it to the attention of children, often in purposeful contexts, and where educators work co-constructively with children to design and contribute to the environmental print. When reading, rather than simply reading the book to the children, the adult can highlight different aspects of books, such as covers, directionality, letter–sounds and so on, and can help children engage with the meaning of the text in such ways as encouraging children to predict the storyline ('what do you think happens next?'). They can also model strategies that support children to develop critical literacy practices such as identifying the assumptions and messages in stories and exploring alternative, and equally valid viewpoints. In short, as Pellegrini (2002) argues, 'literacy is something that must be taught either implicitly or explicitly' (p.55). For example, educators need to support children to move from recognition of whole words (logographs) to being able to analyse these words using the alphabetic principle.

There are many opportunities for embedding literacy into the everyday play, interactions and activities of children. As Whitehead (1999) summarises, informed educators can support this by taking on a range of pedagogical roles – literacy informants, demonstrators, role models, constructors, facilitators of opportunities and materials, setting up literacy apprenticeships and managers of tools, places, materials and things to do. However, adults just need to be mindful that such approaches are not just imposed on children, but are introduced in ways that help children to see literacy as having a purpose and meaning in their lives. Such experiences should aim to empower children to learn, use and develop their literacy skills and knowledge so that they come to view themselves as active members of a literate society.

(iii) Acknowledging the literate child's place in the community

It is this recognising that the literate child is a part of a broader community which is fundamental to sociocultural approaches. Children live in a range of formal and informal family and extended family situations that are located within communities. Children also participate in a number of local social organisations which reflect those communities, such as early childhood centres, schools, libraries, mosques and so on. In addition, children regularly engage in a wide range of social events both on a regular basis and in one-off situations. Children come to know their place in the world initially through their family but, as they grow older, also from their participation in these other aspects of the local community.

Relating this to literacy experiences, children operate in a number of different settings (also known as contexts or microsystems) and they are exposed to and engage with a wide variety of cultural tools and artifacts. There is a diversity of literacy practices across these settings and children see and participate in a wide range of real-life literacy experiences. In addition, in these contexts children have the opportunity to participate in a range of often informal expert–apprentice literacy

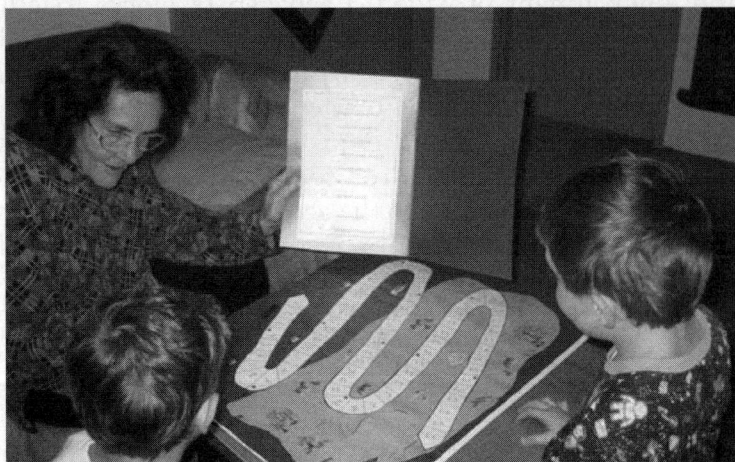

Valuing home literacy practices

learning opportunities with parents or other members of the community. Each setting has its own 'funds of literacy knowledge' which have an important part to play in the child's literacy development.

For example, children's main contexts are usually the home and one, or sometimes more, early childhood centres. As Anstey and Bull (1996) suggest, 'different literacy practices arise from the range of contexts in which individuals participate. Each context requires different ways of behaving and interacting in both oral and written modes' (p.152). Each setting, then, provides a number of differing literacy experiences for young children that the educator can build on.

The challenge for educators is to actively construct links between the literacy experiences of the children in the early childhood centre and other valued institutional settings where specific literacy practices are needed in order to participate in the broader community. As Rivalland (2000) suggests, unless educators can make links with children's home and community practices 'some children will be unlikely to connect into the literacy practices offered in childcare, preschool, school and wider institutional settings' (p.33). One way of achieving this connection is by identifying the sociocultural literacy practices in children's other settings and adapting pedagogical approaches and the early childhood environment to build on these (McLachlan-Smith & St George, 1999). This might mean reading stories to children before they go to sleep, or setting up shops, restaurants and libraries that enrich children's dramatic play and which reflect literacy aspects of the other settings that children encounter regularly outside of the early childhood centre. By following such approaches, educators can build on this diversity and develop stronger links across community settings, especially between the home and the centre. Besides enhancing literacy learning for children, such approaches can also strengthen many other areas of the centre program.

However, the messages presented in the various texts children engage with will not always reflect their, or their families' experiences, their ways of doing things or of seeing the world, and this is particularly true for children from minority groups. Such texts can send subtle but pervasive messages about who and what is, or is not 'normal', 'right' and 'good'. Therefore, in addition to highlighting connections between literacy experiences and children's lives, educators can also support children to identify and question those texts in which their own views of the world are excluded and to learn that they do not necessarily need to accept the images, world-views and messages presented in texts. In order to support children to develop these critical literacy practices educators can build their own knowledge and understanding of the social, cultural, economic, political and historical contexts of children, their families, and their communities; and utilise strategies such as modelling and scaffolding critical practices when engaging in literacy experiences with children.

Children move between community settings frequently within a short space of time (such as from the home environment to the early childhood centre) or in a more staged way (such as the transition between the centre and school). The sociocultural literature is especially interested in the nature of children's transitions and in the similarity (or not) between these settings. In addition, the structural interrelationship between the settings themselves is an important part of this category, such as centre and school policies and practices concerning transitions between the two settings.

There is now a large body of literature which considers sociocultural approaches to literacy that we recommend the readers of this book follow up on. For example, Barratt-Pugh and Rohl (2000), Clay (1998, 2001), Cullen (2002), Gee (2002), Hamer and Adams (2002), Jackson and Adams (2002), Lee and Smagorinsky (2000), McLachlan-Smith and Shuker (2002), McNaughton (1995, 2002), Makin and Jones Diaz (2002), Neuman, Copple and Bredekamp (2000), Roskos and Christie (2000), and Wells (1999).

Concluding comments

- Sociocultural theory is currently an important aspect of pedagogical approaches in early childhood education, and educators and the centre community would find it useful to debate the implications of this model for literacy policy and practice.

- The sound teaching of literacy, based on sociocultural theory, recognises that:
  - children's literacy learning needs to be understood as occurring across a range of broader social and cultural contexts
  - when links across home, community and educational contexts facilitate ongoing development of literacy, children experience little discontinuity in their literacy learning
  - literacy learning for children is a collaborative process of negotiation, scaffolding, and guided participation with 'experts'
  - literacy learning occurs best through meaningful and authentic experiences
  - literacy learning involves explicit as well as implicit teaching within purposeful activities.

Chapter 4
The Learning Debate

A sociocultural model of the literate child

The theoretical debate in relation to literacy learning is probably the least understood by many early childhood educators. As we noted in the previous chapter, the pedagogical debate is concerned with how to teach literacy, and what educators can do to teach literacy better. Conversely, this chapter is primarily concerned with how children learn about literacy, and what goes on in their heads cognitively. As you will note from our approach to this chapter, the two debates are inextricably linked, and the sociocultural/contextual theme of this book runs through both chapters, but with important differences in emphasis.

Exactly how children learn the foundations of literacy has a rich theoretical literature. In the main, this debate seeks to reconcile three key areas:

❖ the broader sociocultural contexts (society) that indirectly influence every aspect of a child's life (including their literacy development)

❖ the more immediate contexts (community) within which children operate where they encounter more specific literacy experiences and practices (e.g., the family, centre, school and other shorter- and longer-term community-level events, experiences and activities)

❖ the cognitive aspects of learning which support individual children's literacy acquisition (such as comprehension, decoding and motivation).

While different theories of literacy learning arising from a number of academic disciplines emphasise varying aspects of these three key areas, on the whole these theories are interrelated or overlapping in many of the core understandings about how children acquire literacy. For example, there is a substantial amount of anthropological and cross-cultural work in the area of literacy learning, there is a strong sociocultural tradition that builds on the work of Vygotsky (the Russian developmentalist), there are insightful analyses that are concerned with political and sociological research, there is a large body of literature that focuses on the cognitive processes of literacy learning (from Piaget to metacognitive theories), and there is a significant body of literature on the area of critical literacy. Each discipline focuses on how children learn to become literate from different intersecting perspectives on literacy learning.

Our model seeks to reconcile these different perspectives by providing a holistic framework for understanding and acknowledging the different views and the relationship between them. Consequently, Figure 4.1 outlines a sociocultural model of the literate child, which builds on the sociocultural model of literacy learning that we considered in previous chapters. There we presented diagrams and an overview that placed children (and their literacy knowledge and experiences) in their community and societal contexts.

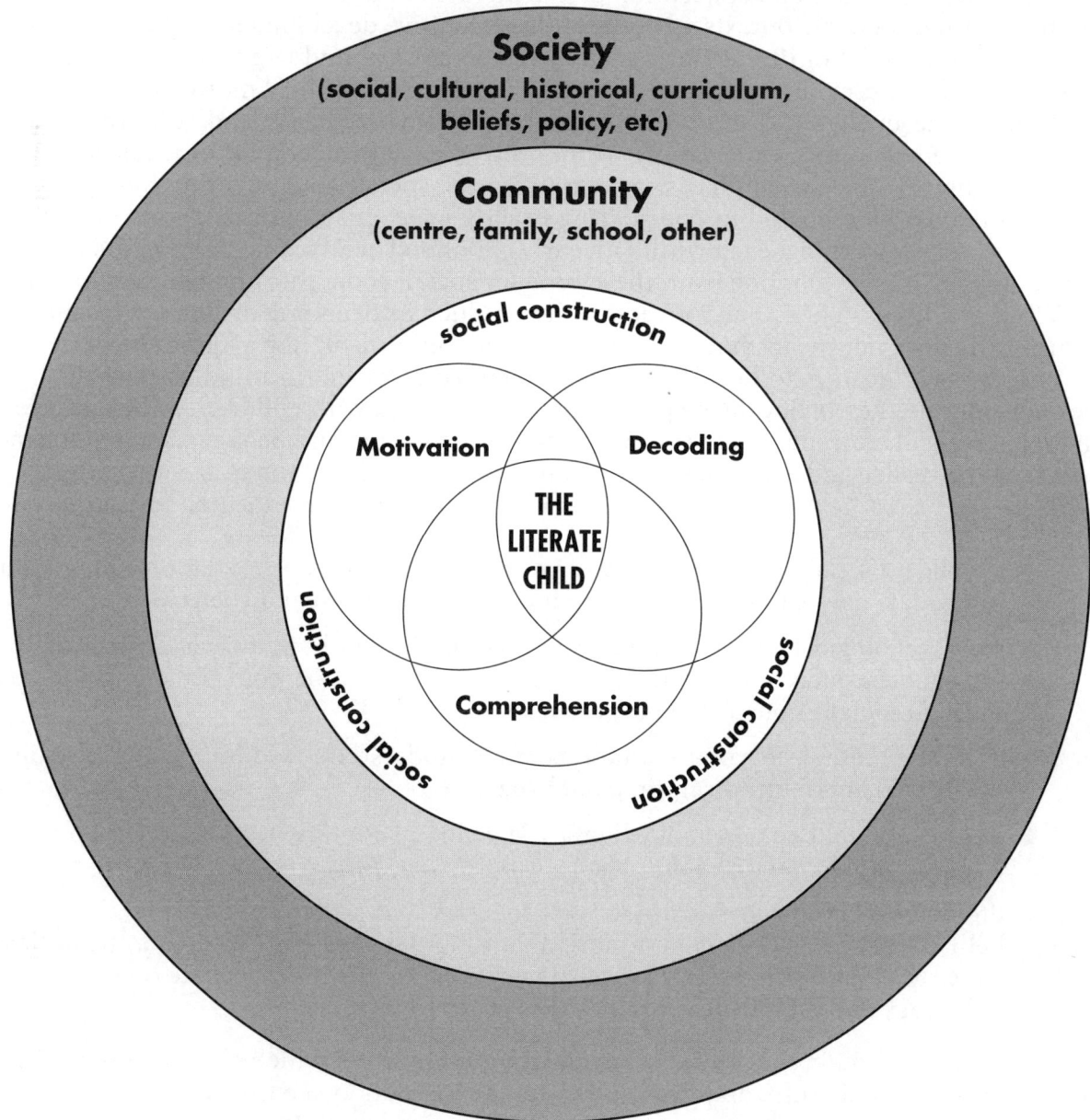

Society
(social, cultural, historical, curriculum, beliefs, policy, etc)

Community
(centre, family, school, other)

social construction

Motivation   **Decoding**

THE LITERATE CHILD

social construction   social construction

Comprehension

Figure 4.1: A sociocultural model of the literate child

Drawing on this model, the theoretical perspectives concerning how children learn to be literate can be grouped into two broad, interactive and inseparable areas which are linked through social construction:

a)   the contexts of literacy learning (community and society)

b)   the literate child.

The contexts of literacy learning involve an examination of the child's immediate settings and also the wider contexts within which those settings are embedded. *The literate child* examines those cognitive aspects of learning (and their social construction) that support children's literacy acquisition. In particular, we will examine the areas of comprehension, decoding and children's motivation. Combined, we can call these two areas the child's literate world. This chapter will follow this two-part structure, with a larger emphasis on the literate child as the contexts of literacy learning (community and society) have been discussed in depth in previous chapters.

The contexts of literacy learning

This book argues for a broad conception of 'the literate child' which integrates the broader community and societal contexts with the child's cognitive development and learning into a sociocultural model of literacy learning. These contextual and cognitive aspects are so interwoven that we cannot examine any aspect (such as a child's motivation), without considering the quality of the literacy interactions, environments and resources being provided; whether in the home, centre, or in other areas of the community. Likewise, we cannot outline the recent emphasis in many Western societies on creating more literate adults in the workforce without considering exactly what this might mean for individual children's literacy learning, even within an early childhood centre. Early childhood centres and educators are not immune from these broader social, economic and political forces.

While we discuss particular concepts or areas (such as decoding or literacy resources) in turn, this does not mean that each should be viewed in isolation – quite the opposite. We encourage educators to keep the broader contextual model in mind as they read, as they consider literacy policy development and as they work with children in their centres. The separating of concepts or areas is a conceptual, academic and pedagogical tool for the benefit of the reader and is not meant to imply that these areas stand alone.

Therefore, a contextual model of literacy learning asks the educator to understand that:

❖ a child's literacy learning cannot be fully understood in isolation from their immediate contexts and the wider contexts of education and society

❖ the psychological and contextual aspects of children's literacy learning cannot be viewed separately – they are like two sides of the same coin, inherently linked through socially constructed experiences

❖ a child's literacy learning cannot be fully understood without taking a multi-theoretical and multi-disciplinary approach

❖ the theoretical debates about literacy learning are interwoven and overlap more than they conflict with each other

❖ literacy concepts, ideas, frameworks, theories and so on are conceptual tools to help the educator understand more about literacy learning. Each is a theoretical construct that forms part of a larger ever-changing historical debate on the nature of literacy and literacy learning.

In practice, the main immediate contexts of literacy within which children operate are in the early childhood centre and the family. The early childhood centre provides a learning environment where there is a range of literacy resources which facilitate, encourage and provide numerous opportunities for children to incorporate literacy into their everyday lives at the centre. Four areas of literacy resources are examined in this book – literacy tools, environmental print, literacy-focused resource centres and books.

This literacy-rich environment (or context) is one where literacy is also planned for and made explicit within regular social routines, activities and events. Such formal planning ensures that all children have consistent and regular exposure to all aspects of literacy. In addition, we also examine later in the book the importance of informal literacy opportunities, which are often 'unplanned', responsive, incidental and spontaneous and can be both adult or child initiated. These sorts of spontaneous literacy opportunities arise during children's everyday play and are therefore focused on what children are immediately interested in. This is where the child's context is at its most powerful – in short, it is both relevant and meaningful for the child, where the child impacts on and influences their own environment and where the child's own voice becomes a critical part in the development of their own literacy expertise. Contextual approaches, then, are a two-way street linked through social interaction.

During the development of the centre literacy policy we encourage debate on this contextual model of literacy learning and the highlighting of the important role that centres, families, schools and the community have in children's literacy development. In particular, the continuity of literacy approaches, resources, practices and environments between these settings needs considerable discussion as well as the importance of transitions between the settings specifically in the area of literacy (particularly from centre to school). In addition, the implications of the strengthening of a literacy-enriched early childhood context (such as we detail in Sections Two and Three of this book) needs further debate, particularly in terms of resourcing, planning considerations, theoretical understandings and the professional development of educators.

In summary, this book argues that educators need a strong knowledge base about literacy learning in order to provide sound literacy experiences for children. A sociocultural model of literacy learning involves educators in thinking about: children's immediate and broader contexts of literacy learning (such as the literacy experiences provided in their early childhood centre or family environments or government policy concerning literacy); and the cognitive aspects of individual children's literacy learning (such as comprehension, decoding and motivation), and how these are socially constructed. An early childhood literacy setting based on creating a rich literacy environment will support the development of literate children and their capacity to participate in the school system and a literate society.

The literate child

What does it mean to be 'a literate child'? A more narrow definition would view a literate child as one who is able to read and write successfully. On the other hand, a wider definition highlights the importance of being able to be an *active participant* in society and of knowing and engaging with the diverse range of knowledge that underpins our social, literary and cultural heritage. This conceptualisation moves beyond literacy as being just the acquisition of a set of reading and writing 'skills', essential though they may be.

A literate child is a product of ongoing interactions with their

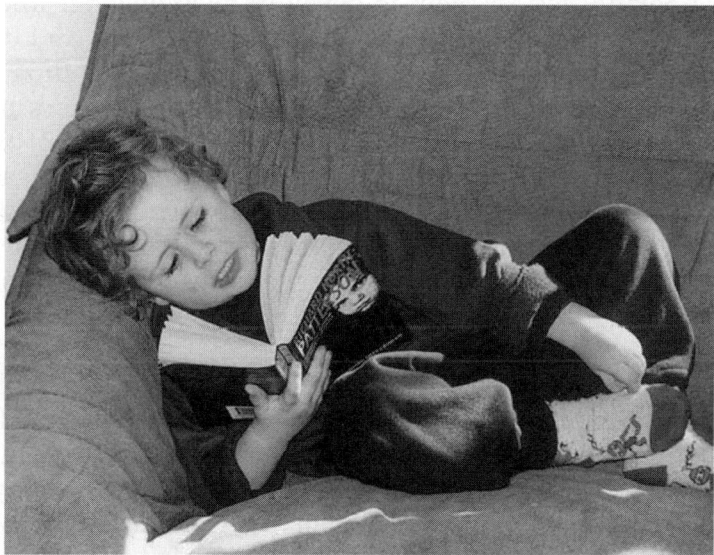

An active participant in a literate society

immediate and broader social contexts. In such environments as early childhood centres, children are exposed to a range of literacy-related activities, resources and practices and they learn about three core literacy areas in particular, which are key components of all mainstream theories on how children learn about literacy:

❖ knowledge that underpins their *comprehension* of texts

❖ knowledge that underpins letter and word *decoding*

❖ the development of positive *attitudes* and self-constructs about literacy and reading.

These three key strands should underpin individual children's literacy learning in early childhood centres, and generally, each is socially constructed and enhanced through conversations with children. As McNaughton (2002) argues, in order for children to comprehend the content of any texts (whether spoken or written) they require a wide range of background experiences, knowledge and skills that provide a basis for helping children engage with the specific content of the texts, using information from across a variety of texts, and providing an understanding of the specific vocabulary of the texts. In addition, learning the prerequisites of decoding written text is a non-negotiable critical foundation of early reading, including the functions, structures and literacy forms of books. Finally, it is important that children develop enduring positive attitudes towards literacy and reading. After all, if children want to read, and find literacy-related activities enjoyable and personally fulfilling, their chances of learning to read well will be greatly enhanced.

The idea of individual children learning about both comprehension and decoding draws heavily on the cognitive literature (such as Hoover & Tunmer, 1993; Tunmer & Chapman, 2003; Whitehurst & Lonigan, 2002) and the sociocultural literature (e.g., see McNaughton, 2002), while the inclusion of children's motivation, attitudes and self-perceptions about literacy is a recent powerful theme that is being widely discussed across the literacy literature. We believe that these three theoretical strands not only complement each other but help overcome the limitations of considering each area in isolation.

In other words, we see 'the literate child' as learning knowledge about comprehension and decoding, along with positive attitudes towards literacy, within a range of broader literacy contexts, rich language environments, and through positive interactions with informed and enthusiastic educators.

(i) Comprehension

Comprehension is a real strength for most young children. Well before starting school, children have grown up in family and community environments that provide many opportunities for them to develop the knowledge and language to engage with the world. Early childhood centres augment these home and community experiences with a range of more specific learning opportunities, including a variety of language and literacy experiences that ultimately help extend children's understandings about the world and about literacy. This includes, as McNaughton (2002) explains, 'conceptual knowledge about events and scripts for ways of acting and, specifically in literacy, ideas about different types of text structure. This set of knowledge and skills enables children to construct ideas about literacy and ways of using writing' (p.167). These sorts of language experiences have ensured that children's oral language and comprehension on starting school is considerably stronger on most measures than their concepts about print and simple decoding-related skills.

Comprehension, then, in relation to literacy, involves being able to understand what is either said or written (Hoover & Tunmer, 1993, p.8). In other words, listening and reading comprehension is viewed as the ability to answer questions about text that has been read or heard (McNaughton, 2002, pp.164–5). For example, a child may bring with them a wide range of experiences which help them to comprehend a book about pets (e.g., they may have a pet at home). Their knowledge and understanding of pets can then be further extended as they discuss the book's content and share their knowledge and experiences with others, including educators and their peers. A stimulating and language-rich early childhood environment provides this broader range of opportunities and experiences that are so vital for supporting comprehension. Educators, then, can help children 'hone' their comprehension skills by appropriate and focused questioning, encouraging children to retell stories and develop their narrative skills, and the modelling of a range of self-checking strategies (such as prompting children to query that what they hear and say does make sense). In addition, providing strategies that children can use to pick up information additional to the text, such as information from pictures, unwritten assumptions, meanings or messages, and focusing on the narrative structures of stories is also useful for developing comprehension.

Further, as Luke and Freebody (1997) explain, 'all texts are motivated – there is no neutral position from which a text can be read or written' (p. 193). Therefore, comprehension also involves being able to critically analyse texts in order to identify the world-views presented and those that are ignored, and to consider the impact this has on oneself and others. Early childhood educators can support children to develop the expectation that texts can (and should) be critically examined, along with some of the skills to begin doing this. For example, children can be encouraged to consider the positions texts ask them to take and to the possibility of other positions, such as examining gender stereotyping evident in advertising brochures (Jones Diaz, Beecher & Arthur, 2002).

Besides these broader language comprehension skills, young children also need more specific support in understanding the functions, structures and literacy forms of texts. Different types of texts have different purposes, provide different kinds of information, use different kinds of language and have a variety of structures. For example, shopping lists contain items you buy at shops, reference books provide information about specific areas, recipe books give ingredients and tell you how to cook different foods, and storybooks have main characters, plots and a range of structures. A rich literacy environment provides these sorts of experiences for children.

Moreover, children also require an understanding of the more functional and mechanical aspects of texts, such as book knowledge and broader concepts about the nature of print. There is a wide variety of book knowledge that young children need to learn – for example, that books have a front and back, a cover, an illustrator, and an author; books are read from left to right, we turn pages one at a time and in order, and that books are read from front to back; and that written words have meanings, pictures provide cues for and illustrate the plot, and book events occur out of real time often in a fictional world (Clay, 1998). In addition, as Roberts (1998) points out, children need to be aware that text is constant – it remains the same from one reading to the next, the events stay in the same order, and 'the reader does not simply make it up as he or she goes along' (p.43).

In sum, language-rich early childhood environments build on and validate children's broader understandings about the world. Centres also provide more specific literacy-related knowledge and skills which help children understand spoken and written texts, which elaborate on the functions, structures and literacy forms of texts, which assist children to critically examine texts, and which explore the more functional and mechanical aspects of texts. These areas combined underpin the development of children's comprehension (and specifically understandings about literacy) and are essential precursors for children's beginning reading achievement. Many centres already have a great deal of strength in these areas.

(ii) Decoding

While much of the literature relating to literacy in early childhood has concentrated on promoting positive attitudes and language comprehension expertise there has always been a struggle with introducing aspects that lead up to and promote the decoding process. Put plainly, if children cannot decode, they will not be able to read. Decoding is generally broadly defined as the ability to read print by attaching sounds to written letters and words (Hoover & Tunmer, 1993, p.6). Consequently, all mainstream theories of how children learn to read place a strong emphasis on the ability of children to decode written text. Of course, decoding is a little like a wire fence around a beautiful playground – you must be able to scale it to fully engage in all the wonderful benefits that being literate provides. As McNaughton (2002) argues, insufficient levels of expertise in decoding can 'constrain the ongoing effects of the skills and knowledge that children have about their world' (p.167). In other words, decoding and comprehension have a critical reciprocal relationship with regard to children becoming literate.

Hoover and Tunmer's (1993) 'Simple View of Reading' model follows much the same argument from a more cognitive perspective. Hoover and Tunmer also argue that *both* decoding and comprehension skills are critical reading skills, and a child cannot read text without both being in place. An imaginary child who can decode but understands nothing is not viewed as a reader, nor is the child who knows everything but cannot decode. Somewhere in between these two extremes a child is viewed as being a reader. This model consequently argues that *individual* differences in being able to read are related to these two areas of decoding and listening comprehension. It is suggested by Gough and Tunmer (1986) that these areas (and their interaction) account for more than 90 per cent of the variance in reading comprehension performance. Tunmer and Chapman (2003) and Whitehurst and Lonigan (2002) develop this argument. Whether some children learn to read well (or not) is closely related to these two areas.

How does this discussion of decoding relate to early childhood educators? Centres can provide a range of language and literacy experiences that ultimately will help facilitate children's decoding (reading written text). While only some children in early childhood settings are able to fluently read (or write) text, many children can be expected to read some letters (particularly in their own name) and most children can develop knowledge and skills in a range of important prerequisite decoding areas, such as phonological awareness, which will provide a solid foundation for their reading progress in primary school.

McNaughton (2002) suggests there are three key areas that have been linked to successful decoding: linguistic awareness, print principles and writing skills. We cover writing extensively in Chapter 10, and print principles (including the conventions of print) both in that chapter and throughout this book. In this section we will consider two aspects of linguistic awareness: phonological and phonemic awareness, and knowledge of the letters of the alphabet and their sounds (known as the 'alphabetic principle').

The first aspect of linguistic awareness that underpins decoding is phonological and phonemic awareness. While phonological and phonemic awareness are often used interchangeably in the literature, *phonological awareness* is generally seen as a broader understanding of the sounds of a language, and has been defined as 'the explicit knowledge of the sounds of language that enable children to break down words into component sounds, put individual sounds together to form words, and order and sequence the sounds of words' (Adams, 1990, cited in Bergen & Mauer, 2000, p.45). This includes an implicit awareness that a spoken word can be divided into smaller pieces such as syllables (e.g., tel/ e/phone), onset and rimes (e.g., b/at, c/at); and individual phonemes (e.g., b/a/t). The term *phonemic awareness* is often more specifically used when referring to those smallest units of sound that make a difference to the meaning of spoken words; for example, the /b/ sound in 'bat' (if it were a /c/ it would be cat) (Adams, Foorman, Lundberg & Terri, 1998).

Phonological and phonemic awareness are language skills that involve children's growing awareness of aspects of spoken language (*not* print at this point). In order for children to 'play with language and to think about it as a system', they need to be able to mentally 'stand back from their own talk and reflect on it' (Nicholson, 1999, p.11). This 'meta' approach to language involves moving children beyond their unconscious implicit knowledge of language to a conscious and explicit understanding of spoken language. As Nicholson (2000) concludes, 'children have to go through stages of understanding where they realise that spoken language is made up of sentences, that sentences are made of words and that spoken words are made up of phonemes' (p.184). This is where early childhood educators can play an important role in children's early literacy development through such sound-related practices as reciting nursery rhymes. (Chapter 9 has a range of specific practices which can help educators develop children's phonological awareness.)

Recent literature has found strong links between this phonological awareness and reading and writing. Burns, Griffin and Snow (1999) indicate that children with good phonological awareness are likely to become better readers in the early years at school. Nicholson (1999) also cites research that demonstrates that 'phonemic awareness at school entry was the best predictor of later reading success, even after taking into account many other variables including age, intelligence, and home background' (p.14). It is worth noting that children's phonological awareness also continues to develop as they learn to read and write.

However, the development of phonological and phonemic awareness is *not* necessarily viewed as a natural process, because children 'do not attend to the sounds of phonemes as they produce or listen to speech. Instead, they process the phonemes *automatically*, directing their active attention to the meaning and force of the utterance as a whole' (Adams, Foorman, Lundberg & Terri, 1998, p.1; emphasis added). The challenge, for educators, is to find ways to get children to notice these various components of spoken language. The difficulty for children is that they have to 'ignore the meaning of a word and focus on its form. The child has to think about the sounds in words, not meanings of words' (Nicholson, 2000, p.200). Simply reading with children and discussing stories is not sufficient for this sort of linguistic awareness to develop; children need to experience an environment where such knowledge is actively encouraged, and these aspects are covered in later chapters.

The second aspect of linguistic awareness that underpins decoding involves helping children gain a knowledge of the letter names of the alphabet and their sounds, known as learning the 'alphabetic principle'. With an understanding of phonological and phonemic awareness, children are more readily able to learn the letters of the alphabet and their sounds. As Nicholson (2000) notes, knowledge of the names and sounds of the letters of the alphabet is an important component of the foundations of learning to read. He describes it as the solution to one part of the puzzle, allowing children to focus on other parts. Many letters of the alphabet have names that correspond closely to their sound, which assists children in learning letter–sound relationships (e.g., s, m, p, l, v). In addition, learning the alphabet and the letter sounds helps young children more easily learn that the written alphabet corresponds to units of spoken sound and vice versa in a similar way (Roberts, 1998). This is a fundamental aspect of the decoding process.

When children develop these core underpinnings of decoding, linguistic awareness (including phonological and phonemic awareness, and letter–sound knowledge), basic print principles and simple writing skills, they are well on the way to being successful readers and writers. Many early childhood practices underpin these areas (along with comprehension and motivation) and when children formally start to learn to read at primary school this knowledge will help them to learn to read more quickly.

(iii) Motivation

Accompanying these comprehension and decoding aspects, children's motivation to engage in literacy experiences is viewed as being crucial. It is not sufficient, as Chapman and Tunmer (2002) argue, for children to just have literacy knowledge and skills - they need to know they have them, want to use them, understand how and when to use them, and believe that their use will actually make a difference. In addition, it is important that children experience literacy as empowering rather than disempowering. In other words, children's literacy attitudes, their enjoyment of literacy, their self-perceptions, dispositions and beliefs about literacy are just as important as the development of their comprehension and decoding knowledge and skills. (For an in-depth review of this area please see Chapman & Tunmer, 2002.)

In order to support children's motivation to be literate, educators can again draw on a sociocultural model of literacy learning. A child's motivation to be literate is enhanced when they see literacy as valued, useful and important within their community. This can be supported through literacy experiences that reflect children's various community experiences, including their home literacy practices. As White (1998) explains, literacy experiences (such as reading books) that reflect the realities of children's lives can engage and empower children. However, they can be equally disempowering when children find no links to themselves in the literacy resources and practices of the early childhood education centre.

In addition, motivation includes the child's literate self-perceptions, which comprises literate self-concepts and self-efficacy. *Self-concepts* are defined by Chapman and Tunmer (2002) as the 'perception, knowledge, views and beliefs individuals hold about themselves' (p.264). In relation to literacy, self-concept relates to the development of a child's 'literate identity' (Dunn, Beach & Kontos, 2000), where children come to see themselves as active and capable literacy participants, regardless of their level of knowledge and skills. In addition, developing a critical approach to literacy can also support children to feel positive about who they are, their culture and ways of viewing the world. *Self-efficacy* relates to the 'judgements that people form of their ability to organise and carry out the actions that are needed to accomplish specific learning tasks' (Chapman & Tunmer, 2002, p.267). This aspect of a child's literacy motivation refers to the extent to which they see themselves as capable of actively taking part in the literate world and capable of learning literacy-related skills and knowledge. Children's sense of literacy self-efficacy can be enhanced by providing opportunities for children to engage successfully in a range of positive, meaningful and authentic literacy experiences that will help them to master relevant literacy skills and knowledge, and by assisting them to develop effective literacy strategies.

Sharing portfolios helps reflection on literacy learning

Lastly, but certainly not the least, motivation includes the development of a life-long love of literacy. When children have enjoyable, warm, relaxed and relevant literacy experiences they are more likely to grow up with a love of reading and writing, want to engage in a wide range of literacy experiences, and be motivated to learn more complex literacy skills and knowledge.

The competent reader

To help gain an idea of how all of these different components of the literate child (comprehension, decoding and motivation) combine in a competent reader, this final section brings together the cognitive processes involved in reading. When thinking about how children learn to read, it is important to understand the cognitive processes used by skilled readers to make meanings from texts. These cognitive processes are part of the bigger picture of what it means to be a literate child. These cognitive processes are also shaped by the larger sociocultural influences experienced by children.

Put briefly and simply, effective readers scan, select and sample print from the text (left to right and top to bottom in English). They use decoding (matching sounds with letter/s) and their vocabulary knowledge to pronounce words and attach meanings to those words. This information is stored in the memory while in-head or previously stored knowledge about language, grammar, word knowledge and the reader's sociocultural experience is used to help process the text and arrive at meaning (Roller, 1998, p.24). So readers must at the same time use information from the text and information they already have in their heads in order to decode print and arrive at appropriate meanings.

This process then continues with a skilled reader automatically scanning and selecting the next part of the text, to take in further information from the text. As this is done the reader checks to see if this meaning is consistent with the gist of the meaning constructed so far, by confirming and using predictions about the meaning of the *whole* text. If meaning is lost, then the reader re-reads, corrects and confirms. This process is iterative and continues until the text has been fully sampled and cohesive meaning has been constructed. These processes will break down if readers do not automate them, that is, use the processes described above without thinking consciously about any part of the process.

Of course when readers are learning to read they often read more slowly as they learn to match sounds to the letters and pronounce words. When they do not use information they have stored in their heads they may easily make errors as they try to decode. So it is important when working with young children to encourage them to think about the meanings of the text as they struggle to learn how to 'crack the code'.

Understandings about the reading processes have always been contentious. Most of the arguments revolve around how the sources of information are used. For example: Is decoding more important than using the in-head information stored in the memory or are the print or pictures on the page more important than the general meaning of a text? The evidence points to the fact that both can cause problems for readers if they are not being used effectively. Any problems with decoding or with using the information stored in the memory will cause an overload and thus a loss of comprehension. Often young readers will struggle to decode the words and read so slowly that they forget what the overall meaning is about. On the other hand, some young readers will find decoding so difficult that they will try to guess what the words are by relying on the overall meaning of the text. In either case it is likely that the young reader will have difficulty unless they learn to use both decoding and in-head knowledge to confirm meanings.

Others argue about which sources of information help readers recognise words – the sounds, the print or the general meaning of the text. The answer is that skilled readers use both sound codes and visual codes, and they do this quickly so that they can save their predictions to deal with comprehension of the whole text. The research suggests that sounds, letters and words are all important and that children need them to effectively process texts (Roller, 1998, p.33).

We also know that the processes described above require motivation and self-monitoring by the reader. The context of situation, the cultural background of readers and the motivation of the readers will affect the efficiency of the reading processes and the capacity of readers to comprehend texts. The influence of these factors may also differ with various forms of text. Readers who are familiar with particular text structures and are motivated by the topic of the text will be more likely to process a text efficiently than when the form of the text is unfamiliar, the text has unfamiliar concepts or the topic is of no interest to them.

In summary, learning to read is not easy; the inclusion of literacy within early childhood education is not necessarily to teach children to read, but to provide children with a strong foundation in relation to comprehension, decoding and motivation. It is important to provide children with a wide experience base that builds their knowledge, attitudes and skills in all three areas (comprehension – lots of exposure and experiences with oral language and written texts, as well as experiences of the wider world; decoding – lots of exposure to different sounds and language play; and motivation – lots of positive, enjoyable and meaningful experiences with literacy, as well as the opportunity to develop interests), before focusing on the formal teaching of literacy skills.

Concluding comments

- In this chapter we develop a sociocultural model of the literate child that integrates the different contexts of literacy and the literate child.

- The chapter focuses on three core language and literacy areas in particular which are components of all mainstream theories on how children learn about literacy: knowledge that helps their comprehension of texts; knowledge that supports letter and word decoding; and the development of positive attitudes and self-constructs about literacy and reading.

- Being 'a literate child' involves more than just a narrow focus on being able to 'read and write' successfully. It highlights the importance of the child's voice, of being an active participant and of knowing and engaging with the diverse range of knowledge that underpins our social, literary and cultural heritage.

Finalising the Literacy Policy for Your Centre

We recommend that a written literacy policy should be the logical and concrete outcome of the literacy debates that have occurred throughout the centre community. This literacy policy development can be developed and implemented in a robust manner taking into account the current philosophical, curriculum, pedagogical and learning debates regarding literacy. If policy-making is underpinned by these aspects, educators can be confident that they can explain, justify and defend the contribution of their literacy practices to young children's literacy development. Without such an approach, early childhood providers may find themselves open to criticism that they are not doing the best they can for young children and their future school success. By being informed literacy professionals, early childhood educators can demonstrate that their literacy policy and literacy practices are credible, based on recent research and have the backing of their centre community.

The structure of this first section has aimed to support centre staff and the centre community in their development of a literacy policy that takes into account the unique context of the centre and an understanding of early literacy learning, in consultation with families and where possible the broader community. Hence, we have discussed the sorts of philosophical debates that should be considered, the curriculum debates and the place of literacy within the curriculum, the pedagogical debates and what educators need to know about a sociocultural model of literacy learning, and the learning debates concerning how we help children to become literate in both the narrower and broader senses.

However, it is not sufficient to engage in these debates in isolation. The debates at this point, we would argue, should also lead to written literacy policy development (or perhaps changes to existing literacy policies where they exist) and flow on to planning for changes in literacy practices in the centre. The process of literacy policy development is not always an easy one and we have endeavoured to make the previous chapters as easy to follow and presentable to the centre community as possible. To conclude this section on literacy policy development we provide some information on the actual process of developing a written literacy policy.

How to develop a literacy policy

The following information is designed to complement a centre's existing policy writing procedures, including the consultation processes which the centre community already has in place. As an overall guide we have drawn on the Australian Early Childhood Association (1995) booklet entitled 'The Policy Handbook', which provides a range of helpful general policy development guidance. Adapting its generic flow chart, we suggest the following procedure as a starting point for developing your literacy policy. Bear in mind that each centre will work through this process in its own way, adapting it to meet the needs of its own centre community.

1. Why develop a literacy policy?

New or updated policy development in the centre usually comes about for a reason. Through the philosophical debate encouraged in Chapter 1 there should emerge a wide range of reasons for developing a centre literacy policy.

2. Setting up the process

Management and educators need to discuss at this early stage how the literacy policy development process will proceed. In other words, a range of areas should be considered such as:

❖ who will do what and when

❖ who will be the policy researchers and writers

❖ how consultation will be undertaken and what the timeline will be

❖ how consultation will include parents/carers and community members from diverse linguistic and cultural backgrounds

❖ who will implement the policy and how it will be implemented

❖ what in-service training will be needed

❖ how the policy's outcomes will be evaluated.

3. Research and initial consultation

We suggest that you finish reading this book before initiating your literacy policy development. The policy and practice sections of this book are designed to help inform your policy and make policy-making easier.

Collecting information before developing any policy is important. For example:

❖ your next staff meeting might discuss the process and policy ideas

❖ you may wish to contact other centres and look at their literacy policy if they have one or discuss the issue of literacy policy with them

❖ if parents/carers haven't initiated the literacy policy you may wish to consult with them now about why literacy should be a part of the centre and what they might want to see included

❖ community/government agencies may be able to provide additional literacy information

❖ professional development/in-service training support may be available.

4. Centre stocktake

A critical aspect of the information-gathering process is to consider the implications of the literacy policy on the centre philosophy, other policies, the curriculum and centre practices. In addition, professional development needs can be identified.

5. Evaluate the information

Steps 3 and 4 will have provided a range of information that needs to be sifted and sorted. This 'brainstorming' process may be best delegated to a policy subcommittee comprising a broad representation (e.g., parents, staff, management etc). This group can basically sort out the key policy information and identify the broader issues in preparation for the first policy draft.

6. Write the first draft

Policy writing is an ongoing process of organising and refining. You may have a generic policy structure which all your centre policies use or you may wish to start from scratch.

These steps may be helpful:

❖ organise the information under key headings and use short bullet points

❖ check that the overall focus of the literacy policy is consistent with your centre philosophy statements

❖ check that the literacy policy contains an aim and reasons or explanations for the policy

❖ check that the policy has clear goals or statements on how to put the policy into practice in the centre under some simple headings such as those used in this book:

- literacy resources

- planning for literacy routines and experiences

- capitalising on informal literacy opportunities

- book-reading approaches

- developing phonemic awareness and letter–sound knowledge

- supporting children's writing

❖ check that the policy looks at working with parents/carers, schools and the community

❖ check that the policy has a statement that relates to the implications for staff, such as professional development needs, books required for the centre library etc

❖ edit the policy so that it is easy to read and understand for both educators and parents/carers

❖ the policy goals may well be written in a staged format – some to achieve this year, some to achieve the next year and so on

❖ check that unresolved issues or areas that need further thought during consultation are highlighted.

7. Consult and seek feedback

Distribute the draft policy to the centre community (including parents, staff, management committee and other interested parties) and provide them with sufficient time for feedback. Open feedback should always be requested even if you are not able to add all the requests to the policy. Make sure you create ways of enabling all parents/carers to give feedback.

8. Finalise and distribute the literacy policy

Incorporating the feedback on the first draft, develop and refine the final policy (possibly with some further or more selected consultation), ratify the document and distribute the literacy policy to the centre community. This may involve publishing your policy in languages other than English in order to ensure that all parents/carers can read the policy.

9. Putting the policy into action

Once the policy is finalised educators can develop a plan for putting the policy into practice. This might involve a 'stocktake' of current practices (drawing on Sections Two and Three of this book) and the setting of a range of staged goals covering the sorts of areas we consider here.

We wish you well in developing your literacy policy and we would be very interested in seeing your finished policies.

Section Two

Creating Literacy-Enriched Early Childhood Centres

Weave all kinds of literacy experiences into the children's daily lives.

(Reynolds 1998, p.159)

The focus of this second section is to consider practical ways in which literacy can be appropriately integrated into early childhood centres. The overall aim for educators is to develop a rich literacy culture within their centre that reflects the wider society, as well as the child's contexts of their community and home, by creating as many purposeful and meaningful opportunities as possible for children to engage in literacy. In this way all children develop the knowledge, skills and attitudes to become active participants in a literate society. In order to achieve this, it is necessary to underpin centre policy and practice with a sociocultural model of literacy learning. As we discussed in Section One, this means having a clear understanding of why literacy should be a part of the centre program, taking a wider holistic view of the place of literacy in early childhood centres and providing sound literacy teaching opportunities, experiences and environments in order to support the development of literate children in the broader sense.

Because of this broad view of literacy, we have not used such terms as 'literacy programs' as this may give the impression that literacy should be 'bolted on' to existing programs and environments. Instead, this section will argue that it is more pedagogically sound to integrate, incorporate and infuse literacy practices more holistically *throughout* the early childhood centre. Initially it may seem easier for educators to pick up a pre-prepared literacy package (of which there are many), especially if they do not feel confident about the area of literacy. However, more benefit for children and educators will be gained by centre staff becoming better informed literacy professionals. Such educators are then in a position to more meaningfully and effectively integrate literacy in their centre by weaving literacy resources throughout the centre, planning for literacy experiences in centre routines and practices, and creating and building on informal literacy opportunities. Literacy, then, should be woven through the whole centre program in an ongoing way by a team of literacy experts. The day-to-day benefits for all children of this latter approach are very clear in the literature.

In this section we provide a three-tier framework to assist educators in providing an enriched environment where children encounter a broad range of literacy experiences, practices, attitudes and knowledge. There is a wide range of equally valid approaches for enriching literacy in early childhood settings. We have chosen a straightforward framework that is easy for educators to work with, which reflects the way many centres analyse and improve their own centre practices, and is underpinned by a sociocultural model of literacy learning. In Chapter 5 we first focus on developing literacy resources, in Chapter 6 on the building of literacy into centre routines and experiences, and in Chapter 7 we consider informal literacy opportunities such as the social interactions with educators and peers through which children learn to be literate. We argue that alone each area is important but there is also an ongoing reciprocal relationship between each of them. While we discuss each separately, it is intended that these three areas be viewed and implemented as part of an integrated, centre-wide literacy approach.

Children and their literacy knowledge and experiences

In the previous section we outlined a sociocultural model of literacy learning that highlighted the importance of viewing literacy learning in its societal, community and centre contexts. We also placed the development of 'the literate child' firmly within that model. Drawing on this model, and the four guiding principles mentioned below, this section of the book will focus specifically on the various ways in which centres and educators can create a literacy-enriched early childhood centre. Through a literacy-enriched environment that provides ample literacy resources, interactions and opportunities, children learn to become literate.

Figure 5.1 summarises the scope of the literacy knowledge and experiences that we wish children to learn and engage with, and which we will cover in depth throughout the three chapters in this second section. This is a fairly comprehensive list of literacy knowledge and experiences, and educators may feel daunted by it. However, most early childhood centres, to differing extents, already provide these experiences, in some cases without realising they are doing so. It is not until one sits down and considers the varying literacy interactions, opportunities and experiences that occur in the centre that the full picture starts to emerge.

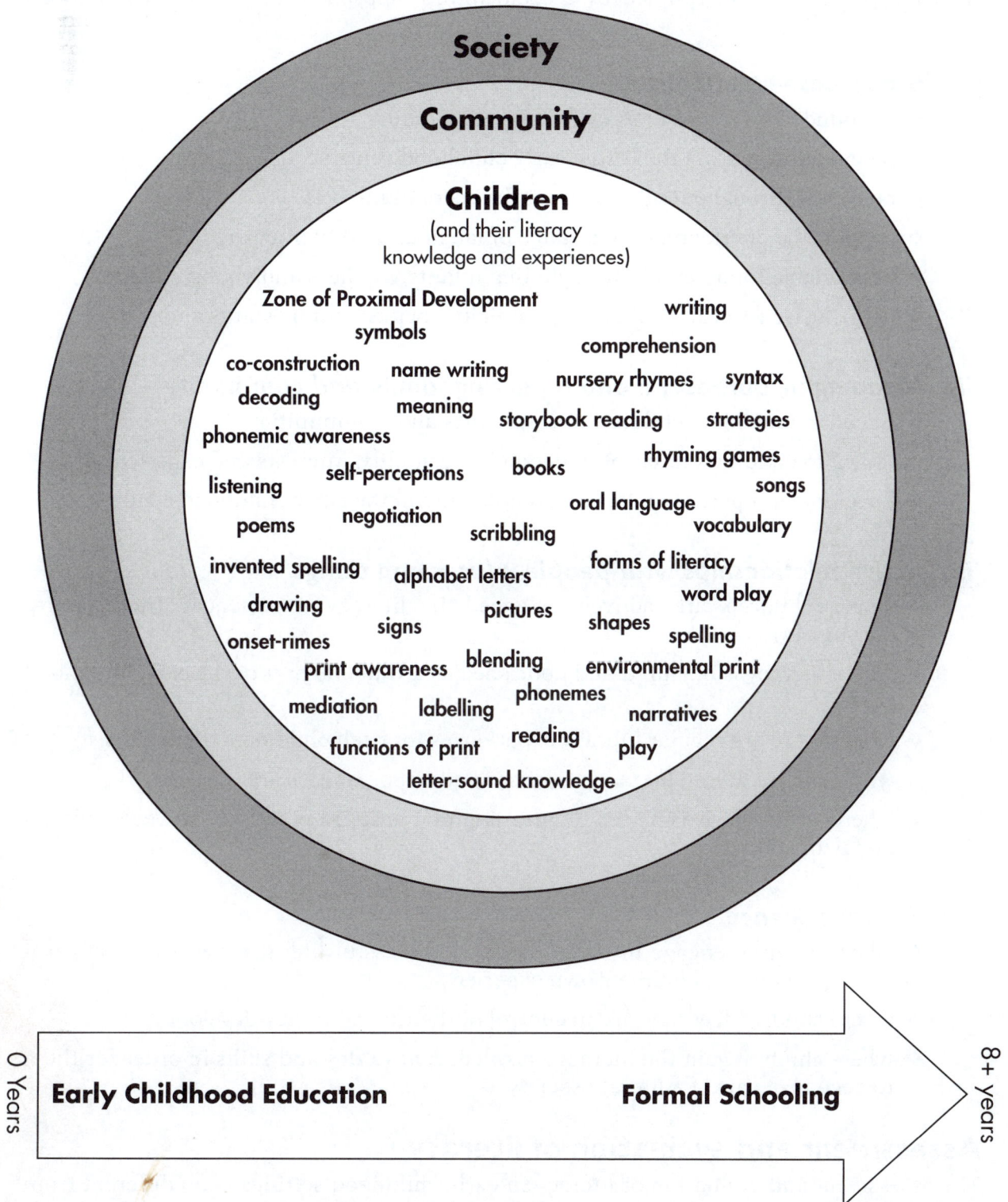

Figure 5.1: Children and their literacy knowledge and experiences

Core principles for creating a literacy-enriched early childhood centre

This second section of the book assumes that the reader has reflected on the broader policy aspects, canvassed in Section One, which are intended to guide literacy practice. In reviewing the first four chapters of this book, there are four important *principles* that should inform the process of creating a literacy-enriched early childhood centre. These four principles broadly reflect and support the principles outlined in many of the state curriculum documents and the QIAS (2005).

Consider the following principles to help you identify the components of a rich literacy environment that is underpinned by a sociocultural approach, in your early childhood centre.

(i)   Broad-based and holistic
   ❖ be founded on sound literacy policy and planning

   ❖ be integrated across the whole early childhood centre

   ❖ be woven throughout all aspects of the curriculum

   ❖ support the development of a range of language and literacy areas

   ❖ be available for all children (including infants, toddlers and young children)

   ❖ be inclusive regardless of ability, ethnicity, socioeconomic status and gender.

(ii) Meaningful, purposeful and reflecting family and community
   ❖ linked to individual children's lives, homes and communities

   ❖ linked to children's levels of understanding, ability, interests and experiences

   ❖ be an integral part of children's everyday life in the early childhood centre.

(iii) Active relationships with people, places and things
   ❖ where children are actively engaged in literacy experiences (not passive consumers)

   ❖ where literacy is nurtured and nourished as a valuable part of the early childhood centre

   ❖ where there are regular literacy experiences for each child on a daily basis

   ❖ where many varying literacy resources and opportunities are created

   ❖ where an emphasis is placed on meaningful literacy interactions between children and with adults.

(iv) Foster resilience
   ❖ where children engage in rewarding and successful literacy events and achievements, which build on their own experiences

   ❖ where children feel they are in control of their own literacy development

   ❖ where children gain the literacy knowledge, attitudes and skills in order for them to become a part of a literate society.

Assessment and evaluation of literacy

The assessment and evaluation of literacy in early childhood settings is no different from that of any other area in the centre program. Such processes seek to answer five broad questions: why do we teach this area; where does it link to the curriculum; what should the children learn; how should we teach it; and how should we celebrate our achievements? Literacy assessment and evaluation cannot begin without the centre community coming to some consensus about these areas, and this is one reason for encouraging the literacy debates, as outlined in Chapters 1 to 4. The answers to these questions can be found in the philosophy, goals and policy statements of the centre.

Throughout this book we encourage an inclusive and broad sociocultural model of literacy learning that provides us with a clear foundation for assessing and evaluating literacy. Using this reciprocal contextual model, we cannot separate the *assessment* of individuals and groups from broader *evaluations* of the contribution of the centre and the community. Hence, assessing literacy is not just about individual literacy learning alone but also the quality of the literacy learning contexts that children are embedded within.

Assessment and evaluation should also be carried out regularly because the centre community and environment is constantly changing. For example, different infants, toddlers and young children are moving through or within the centre; the mix of children is changing and peer friendships are in flux; staff move around and are constantly upskilling; parents/carers are learning more about literacy and their circumstances can also change quickly; and children are maturing, developing and generally learning more about literacy outside of the centre. This means that literacy needs to be monitored through an ongoing program of group and individual assessment, and centre and community evaluation.

For the centre, this might involve an evaluation system which ensures that *on a regular basis* the centre: reviews centre literacy policy; discusses the way that literacy is conceptualised and placed within relevant curriculum documents; enriches the educators' literacy knowledge; expands the centre's literacy resources; further integrates literacy within the day-to-day routines and planned experiences of the centre; broadens the range of strategies and techniques for capitalising on informal literacy opportunities; and enhances the gathering, using and celebrating of information on the developing literacy expertise that children are learning in the home environment and the community. For long day care centres registered with the National Child Care Accreditation Council this would also involve ongoing evaluation for continuing quality improvement as outlined in the QIAS (2005).

Accompanying these broader evaluations of the centre, educators should assess individual children and groups. The overriding focus or aim of this assessment should be on: ensuring that *all* children in the centre engage in a broad range of authentic, relevant and meaningful literacy experiences and practices on a regular and systematic basis; and, that educators monitor, document and then extend children's literacy learning over time based on this assessment process. Carr (1998) suggests, as part of the centre's regular planning cycle, that these areas can be assessed through a process which might involve *describing* (learning and monitoring what the children are doing), *documenting* (gathering evidence to learn what the children know and demonstrate), *discussing* (sharing and consulting with children, educators, parents) and *deciding* (using the information for the benefit of children's further learning). This same assessment cycle would also be useful to further develop the family–centre literacy partnership by specifically involving parents/carers in describing, documenting, discussing and supporting children's literacy experiences in the home (e.g., home languages, favourite songs or rhymes, literacy routines, special interests). This two-way collaboration would be beneficial for the whole centre community.

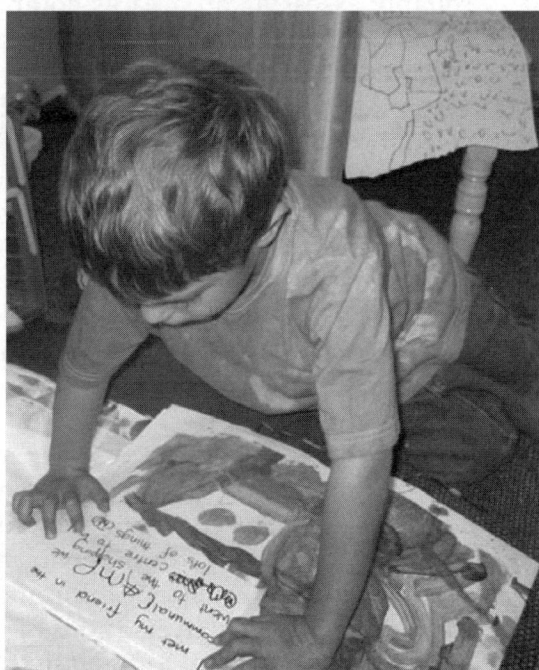

Selecting favourite samples of work for a 'learning journey' discussion

Centres will already have their own established systems for assessing children's learning based on their existing practices, goals and philosophy. QIAS (2005) highlights the importance of regular reviews to maintain and develop a quality service: 'it is essential that staff keep a range of documentation for each child that profiles their learning, development and interests and to which all staff, children and families can contribute' (p.14). Assessment and evaluation is at the heart of state curriculum documents, where assessment is seen as a central part of the 'plan, do, review' cycle. When assessing literacy, centres may wish to expand or adapt their assessment systems to also incorporate aspects that we highlight as significant in this book.

Once it is clarified what areas of children's literacy are to be assessed, educators can use a range of techniques and methods for assessing individual and group literacy learning; centres already use many of these in their assessment of other areas of their programs. Carr (1998, 1999), Crooks (2000) and Jones Diaz *et al.* (2001), for example, outline a number of principles which should guide the use of these techniques and methods:

❖ the main goal is to achieve maximum educational benefit for each child

❖ we should use ways that allow children's growth to be seen and celebrated

❖ procedures should be fair, thorough and representative

❖ learning should be assessed in the child's contexts

❖ gender, social and cultural areas should be considered

❖ assessment should be an integral part of the centre planning processes

❖ no child or area should be neglected

❖ reflect the holistic way children learn

❖ quality information is more important than quantity

❖ educators should avoid unnecessary and unproductive approaches

❖ there should be a sense of partnership between educator, child and parents/carers.

Taking these principles into account, we recommend the use of multiple techniques and methods which can yield the depth and breadth of information required for more reliably assessing an area as complex as literacy (bearing in mind that children's literacy learning is not a linear developmental sequence; e.g., see the comments in Chapter 10 on the growth of children's writing expertise). The information gathered needs to be dated, systematically filed and stored so that during the discussion and deciding phases a broad selection of children's literacy achievement is quickly to hand (the ambit of digital and computer technology has a role to play here). Clay (1998, 2001), Fleet and Lockwood (2002), Hamer (1999), Johnston and Rogers (2002), Lee and Carr (2002), Salinger (2002) and Tayler (2000), for example, discuss the importance of one or more of the following approaches: collations (e.g., of centre children's stories or lists); conversations and informal interviews; environmental print created by children (e.g., displaying children's maps or signs); literacy diaries for individuals (e.g., a cumulative record of book knowledge); photographs (e.g., of children's writing); portfolios (e.g., wide-ranging samples of children's literacy selected by adults or children over a period of time); profiles (e.g., cumulative record of the children's literacy interests/choices/experiences); question logs (e.g., a record of the sorts of questions a child asks about books, print, writing etc); running records (e.g., of literacy experiences); self-assessments (what kind of writer are you?); sound recordings (e.g., children reading to a doll, retelling stories, playing together); transcripts (e.g., of children's stories); video recordings (e.g., group of children playing in a literacy resource centre); written narratives (e.g., of children's conversations or self-talk); and 'learning journeys' where children choose samples of work over time and review each item with parents, peers or staff. A careful selection of these approaches will enable educators to gather the broad range of literacy information they need for all the children in their centre.

3 – Way Conference

Dear Family

A Conference time for us to discuss

_____Chè_____ 's (child's name)
progress has been booked for
____7.00____ (time) on _Tuesday_ (day)
the _29th_ (date) of _June_ (month).

Please let me know if this time is not convenient for you.

Yours sincerely

_____Denise_____ (Class Teacher)

Please note that each Conference is only

20 minutes long.

BE PREPARED - SEE OVER

3-Way Conferences - Purpose & Process

The conference provides an opportunity to focus on specific areas of learning. In a supported discussion we will review progress in many learning areas, reflect on how learning has been achieved and review and set goals. Your child will take on the role of facilitator as autonomously as they can. Parents and teachers should encourage and support the child in open and honest dialogue through questioning, constructive commenting and promotion of meta-cognitive skills (thinking about thinking).

Sample questions may include:

- How have you grown as a reader? What will you do now to improve?
- In which areas have you achieved the greatest improvements? Why?
- How have you enjoyed working in groups? How successful were you as a team member?
- Why did you choose this piece of work for your portfolio? What goals will you set for future learning?

The 3-way conference and learning journey give us opportunities to take ownership of our role in the learning process. They build and strengthen partnerships between all those involved.

Centre literacy assessment and evaluation should provide answers to two distinct but interrelated questions:

❖ To what extent is the program 'literacy enriched' and based on sound policy and practice, and how can it be improved to better support children's literacy learning?

❖ What literacy knowledge, skills and attitudes do children have and demonstrate, and in what ways can educators use this information to extend children's literacy learning?

Chapter 5

Weaving Literacy Resources Throughout the Early Childhood Centre

A literacy-rich environment is one where there is a range of literacy resources that facilitate, encourage and provide numerous opportunities for children to incorporate literacy into their everyday lives at the early childhood centre. Literacy resources are a fundamental component of a centre's literacy environment and provide the backbone for both planned and informal literacy experiences. By weaving literacy resources throughout the early childhood centre, children and educators have close at hand the tools and props with which to engage in meaningful literacy experiences. This environment should be built on and reflect the children's real-life literacy experiences. In this way children will come to see literacy as meaningful and relevant to them, and to their everyday lives.

Children in early childhood centres become literacy apprentices where they are able to observe and explore their literacy understandings with the support of informed educators. When given the appropriate resources, experiences and opportunities, children also develop their self-concept as literate persons. Literacy involves more than the specific skills of reading and writing. In this chapter we will consider a diverse range of literacy resources and how to ensure that these are spread widely across all areas of the centre and through the entire centre program, including four broad areas: literacy tools and props, environmental print, literacy-focused resource centres, and books.

Literacy tools and props

One way of creating a literacy-enriched environment is to ensure that a broad range of literacy tools and props are provided in as many areas as possible throughout the centre, are freely available and that children are encouraged to use these in their everyday activities. Many books on literacy provide long lists of tools and props which we recommend as a useful source of additional ideas (e.g., see Arthur & Makin, 2001; Nel, 2000; Neuman, Copple & Bredekamp, 2000; Reynolds, 1998).

The wide variety of literacy tools and props that can be included within early childhood education centres can be grouped as writing tools and props and reading tools and props. Writing tools and props can be used for a range of purposes such as compiling lists, sending messages, writing stories, sending cards and filling in forms. Writing tools and props can be categorised as writing implements, writing materials and writing equipment. Conversely, reading tools and props can be used for gaining information and exploring different forms and purposes of literacy. These include a wide range of general reading tools and props, storybooks, picture books and posters, reference books and instruction books.

Incorporating literacy tools and props necessitates consideration of context and relevancy issues. Neuman (1998), for example, poses the following questions:

❖ Are the literacy tools and props *appropriate* for the children's age, development and abilities especially in relation to safety and ease of use (e.g., providing non-toxic, fat markers for infants and toddlers)?

❖ Are literacy props and tools *authentic*, that is, do they reflect the real literacy items that children see being used in their everyday lives?

❖ Are literacy props and tools *useful* and relevant for children in their everyday play?

Additional questions worth considering are:

❖ Are the literacy tools and props located throughout the environment in such a way that they allow and encourage children's *active* engagement with them?

❖ Are they *meaningfully* integrated into the different areas of the centre (e.g., books on woodwork in the carpentry area)?

❖ Does the selection of literacy resources *empower* (or disempower) children from different sociocultural groups (e.g., reinforcing gender or ethnic stereotypes) (Anstey & Bull, 1996)?

❖ Is there a *balance* between the real literacy tools provided and literacy props which can be used as aids for dramatic play?

(i) Writing tools and props

There is a wide range of writing tools and props that a centre may find useful, such as writing implements, materials and equipment.

Writing implements

Chalk, charcoal, crayons, felt pens, markers, pencils (plain and coloured), pens, and (naturally) fingers for sand and fingerpaint etc.

Writing materials

Booklets (ready-made of different sizes and types), cards (e.g., greeting cards for a range of festivals such as Christmas and birthday cards, postcards), coupons, diaries and calendars, envelopes, exercise books and notebooks, forms (e.g., bank slips), labels and tags, letter writing paper, notices, pads (e.g., message pads and notepads), paper and card (wide range of colours, sizes, shapes, quality), paint, signs, specialist cards (e.g., appointment and business cards) and of course, sand, concrete, walls, misty windows, fences etc.

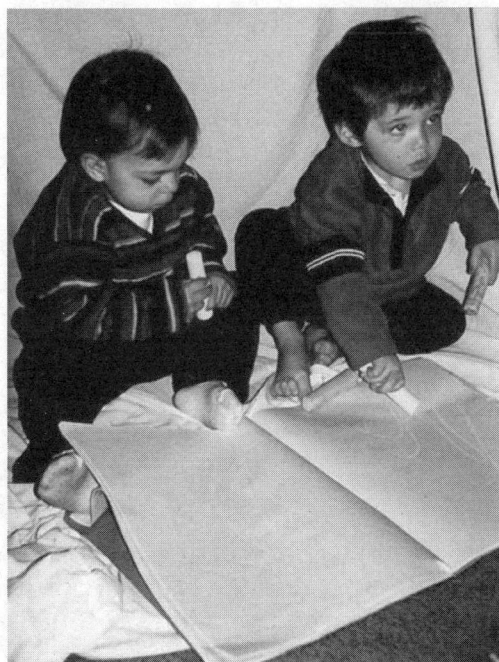
Drawing with chalk

Writing equipment

Blackboards, books, cellotape, computer (with word-processing software and email) and printer, erasers, fax machines, folders and folios, glue, hole punch, in and out trays, letters (e.g., magnetic, felt, plastic, wooden), line guides, paper clips, paper trimmer, post boxes, rubber stamps, rulers, scissors, sharpeners, staplers, stencils, string, tables and chairs (small and large), whiteboards.

(ii) Reading tools and props

Reading tools and props form a diverse group of literacy resources including: general reading tools and props, storybooks, picture books and posters, reference books, and instruction books. There are many quality books for young children that are written in children's home languages and in both English and another language (dual texts). These are an essential part of recognising and valuing diversity within the early childhood centre.

General reading tools and props

Maps and globes, phone books, address books, newspapers, magazines, junk mail, car manuals, menus, alphabet puzzles, alphabet posters, bibles, comics, felt board, grocery packets, lotto tickets, play money, calculators, price tags, receipts, recipe books, letters and faxes, computers, traffic signs, TV guides, written music, video tapes and DVDs, audio tapes and microphones.

Storybooks

Fiction and non-fiction stories both modern and traditional from a range of cultures and that depict a range of ethnicities, genders, abilities and ages; song and nursery rhyme books; joke books; poetry books.

Reading a reference book about trains

Picture books and posters

Bought or 'home-made' books depicting familiar as well as new objects, people, animals, places and things.

Reference books

There is a wide range of colourful reference books available that provide information about children's wider worlds, including animals, insects, people, places, vehicles, plants and so on.

Instruction books

Books that show how to make things, such as cooking books, woodwork and construction, arts and craft, science and technology projects, and instruction booklets that come with appliances and equipment.

Environmental print

A second way of weaving literacy resources throughout the early childhood centre is to develop a print-rich environment. Environmental print can take a variety of forms, from print on walls and surfaces, to print on objects. It can also represent the linguistic and cultural diversity within the early childhood centre, by ensuring that some of the print is written in the home and community languages. The aim is to make print a natural and functional part of the centre environment.

There is also a range of environmental print that is specifically appropriate for the development of decoding skills. For example, alphabet charts and friezes that link each letter with the picture of an object beginning with that letter (e.g., 'a' for apple) are particularly valuable as they link the letter name to the sound of the letter. For older children, jointly constructed charts can further develop graphophonic understandings, e.g., letter names are constant, but sounds vary; letters work alone and sometimes in groups (sh, th, ee); the same sound can be represented by different letters (bear, hare, stair), and different sounds can be represented by the same letters (crown, flown). Making these kind of charts to support relevant and meaningful activities already being undertaken will give children the opportunity to build on and consolidate their literacy learning. As most children's books use lower-case letters, Nicholson (2000) notes that children should focus on lower-case letters first. It is helpful to remember that there are approximately 44 sounds (phonemes), represented by 26 letters in about 140 combinations.

A particularly effective form of environmental print is the use of children's names. Children's own names are highly personal and as such are often the first words children recognise (Arrow, 2002; Davidson, 1996). Including children's names in a range of purposeful ways throughout early childhood environments and routines takes advantage of this almost guaranteed literacy interest. Individual laminated name cards with magnetic or velcro backing allow children to put their own name on objects or on themselves and can be taken to where children are playing. They can be used by children for signing in or identifying their own work. Young children often become interested in their friends' names as well. In addition, scribing children's comments about their piece of work (model, picture, painting, plan etc.) gives them a sense of ownership and helps them to make links between spoken and written language, recognise that print is permanent and gives the educator the opportunity to model a particular form of writing.

Miller (1998) provides some valuable suggestions for including environmental print in the centre:

❖ Use pictures and symbols to accompany words, particularly for labels and signs, as a way of assisting children to develop an understanding that words convey meaning.

❖ The positioning of environmental print in the early childhood centre provides children with important contextual clues as to the messages that print conveys. For example, a 'wash hands' sign that includes a picture of hands and is located above the bathroom hand basin will support children in interpreting the message being conveyed.

❖ Print needs to be at the children's eye level. While this may seem obvious, environmental print is often largely placed at adult height for adult use.

❖ Not all environmental print has to be attached to things. For example, names on laminated card allow children to take them around the centre. Or use moveable signs such as 'Work in progress', 'Please do not touch'.

The role of the adult is vital if environmental print is to play a part in supporting children's literacy development. Environmental print throughout the centre can be either *static* and barely noticed by children, or *dynamic* where the educator draws it to the attention of children, often in purposeful contexts, and where educators work with children to design, add or alter the environmental print. Where adults engage and support infants, toddlers and young children with environmental print, children will develop the understanding and expectation that print conveys useful, interesting or entertaining messages and that they can use their increasing literacy understandings, with the support of others, to explore, interpret and create those messages.

Environmental print on walls and surfaces

These can include posters at child height on walls as well as above nappy changing tables and cots, nursery rhymes, words of songs, labels, wash hands signs above sinks, large and small play road signs, 'welcome' or 'please shut' signs on gates, birthday trains, names of different areas of the centre (such as 'block corner', 'book corner'), captions under photos, documenting centre activities and trips as well as children's work and projects. For older children, charts about the rules of spelling, sentence starters, organisational frameworks for different purposes of writing and many other types of environmental print which focus on phonics, grammar and vocabulary are useful ways of helping children to become independent literacy learners (see Education Department of Western Australia, 2004).

Environmental print on objects

Labels can be added to objects, storage containers, drawers, shelves, pet cages and children's own storage spaces. Print can be found on objects such as food packets (e.g., cereal packets), menus, centre equipment and magazines.

Environmental print that supports decoding skills

Environmental print includes: alphabet charts, friezes and posters, mats and materials depicting the alphabet, alphabet puzzles and games. Charts which help children recognise high frequency words and personally significant words (names of family members, names of suburbs). Charts that help develop phonemic awareness (rhyming words, alliteration – she sells sea shells).

Using children's names

Children's names can be used to identify:

❖ each child's own space such as lockers, coat hangers or cubby holes, 'mailboxes', beds and cots, chairs

❖ children's belongings such as place mats, cups, hats, clothing, artwork and projects, plant labels.

Highlighting the letters representing the initial sound of children's names can also be useful in assisting children to identify their name and provide a focus for discussions about starting sounds (e.g., Zac starts with a /z/ sound, Philip starts with a /f/ sound, Manu starts with /m/).

Finding each other's name

Literacy-focused resource centres

In addition to weaving literacy resources throughout the early childhood centre, and providing a print-rich environment, a case can be made for the provision of more focused literacy resource centres that provide specific locations where literacy activities can occur, and where such resources can easily be located by children. A range of centres can be created, such as writing centres, information resource centres, listening-recording stations and book corners.

(i) Writing centres

Writing centres, as Reynolds (1997) elaborates, are valuable for the development of children's writing concepts and skills. Writing centres provide children with writing resource areas as well as spaces where they can engage in a range of literacy tasks. For example, a writing centre can be used to write notes, cards, messages, names or to generally practise developing concepts of writing and print. To support these activities, a writing centre should include writing equipment, materials and implements, and print models. For further information on writing centres, see Chapter 10.

(ii) Information resource centres

Information resource centres provide children with real world literacy resources in a single, easily accessible place. Centres can develop a number of these information resource centres that can support standard areas of the centre (such as block, art and sandpit areas) but could also be developed to suit more informal and unplanned experiences that reflect children's interests. Information resource centres can be developed and added to over time by children, educators, parents and members of the centre and wider community.

5

Equipment

Information resource centres can take the form of desks or boxes. They need to be solid enough to last but also be able to be moved to where the action is.

Information resource centres that support standard areas of the centre

For example:

❖ A cooking information resource centre could include cooking books, recipe cards, blank recipe cards, pens, pencils, pictures of cooked and raw food items, empty food packets, and measuring devices such as spoons, jugs and scales.

❖ A woodwork information resource centre could include reference and instruction books on different forms of wood construction, plans, paper, pens, rulers and tape measures.

Information resource centres that support children's interests

For example:

❖ An information resource centre on people of different ethnic groups could include picture and reference books, an atlas, examples of clothing, paper, eating implements, examples of writing in different languages, and crayons or colour pencils in a range of skin colours.

❖ An information resource centre on dinosaurs may include reference books, storybooks, pictures, puzzles, puppets, miniature dinosaur figures, as well as writing materials and implements.

(iii) Listening-recording stations

Listening-recording stations are also useful for facilitating and providing a range of language and literacy experiences for children of all ages. There is a wide range of quality commercial recordings available that include narrated stories, often with musical accompaniment. Having copies of books that can accompany the tapes can also be useful, particularly where children are already familiar with the book. In addition, children and educators can record their favourite songs and stories to add to this collection of resources. Where possible, recordings can also reflect the languages spoken in the centre and children can make recordings in their home languages. Listening-recording stations, as Hall (1998) suggests, can also be set up to allow children to record stories, poems, rhymes and songs that they have created. Infants, toddlers and young children will enjoy listening to a wide range of recordings as well as participating in recording themselves. Listening to recorded stories over and over again is not only enjoyable but helps children to internalise a number of important aspects of literacy.

Recording equipment

Would include:

❖ a tape deck with clear and easy to use controls and either an in-built or separate sturdy microphone of reasonably good quality.

❖ five-minute blank tapes – these make it quick and easy for children to rewind and find their recordings. They also allow children to have their own named tapes, helping avoid precious recordings being taped over by others.

❖ more recently, computers and digital tape recorders have become popular methods for recording and even be enhanced through a range of software programs that allow children to add sound effects and visual images. These recordings can be stored digitally on hard drives or copied to CD/DVDs or MP3 players.

❖ instructions for recording, rewinding and playing, both written and illustrated.

Where recording is popular, a booking sheet can be used for children to book a time to use the station.

Listening equipment

❖ A tape deck, CD/DVD/MP3 player, or computer for listening.

❖ Avoid using headphones unless you can be certain that volume levels can be controlled (such as using a volume limiter).

❖ Use copies of your original cassette tapes in listening-recording stations and remove the copy-protect tabs on the cassette to prevent them being recorded over.

❖ Include books that go with recorded stories as well as posters that reflect the content of recordings.

❖ Provide a comfortable, attractive place for small groups of children to sit and relax while listening.

Recordings

❖ These could be nursery rhymes, rhyming songs, traditional and contemporary stories, poetry, alphabet songs.

❖ Children can record their own stories, songs, poetry and jokes either individually or in small groups.

❖ Invite parents and local community members to record stories, legends and myths.

(iv) Book corners

Book corners are available in most early childhood centres. Not only do books provide a medium through which the comprehension, decoding, vocabulary and fluency aspects of reading can be supported, but reading books is an enjoyable and comforting activity that also plays a significant role in developing children's motivation to read. It is important, then, that the book corner is well presented, comfortable and welcoming in order to promote a sense of belonging and ownership for the children (and adults) who use it. It is vital that adults model the use of the book corner, including entering this area to sit and look at books alongside children. In addition, educators should read to children often and not just during planned group times.

Sharing a story in Chinese and English

5

Equipment

❖ Book corners should be inviting, cosy and comfy and include cushions, carpet, couches and good lighting.

❖ There should also be places for adults, including parents, to sit comfortably and read with children.

❖ Books should be reachable and well displayed to show covers as opposed to the spines.

❖ There should be a good selection of books (but not overwhelming numbers) that reflect the lives, experiences, cultures, languages and interests of the children who attend.

❖ Different books may be provided for different age groups but favourite books should continue to be provided for all.

❖ Books can be rotated on a regular basis, but it is also important to allow children to read the same book over and over as this helps children to understand that text stays the same.

Books

Books are a vital resource in the creation of a rich early childhood literacy environment. They can support children's literacy development in many ways, including facilitating and supporting comprehension and vocabulary, decoding and motivation. It is important, then, that the selection and range of books reflects all of these aspects and reflects the languages of the centre. This is not to say that every book should support all three aspects at once; rather, there needs to be a balance of different kinds available for children. In addition, it is also important to think about where books are kept throughout the centre.

Books that support comprehension

Storybooks can assist children to develop a sense of story that supports reading comprehension, while non-fiction books can help children to understand that books can be a source of information as well as entertainment. There are many different views on what makes a storybook irresistible or a non-fiction text highly engaging, and it is worth remembering that what appeals to one child may not necessarily appeal to another. In addition, the criteria for selecting books will change according to the cognitive level and interests of the child. The following descriptions may give you a starting point from which to create or review your own criteria for selection.

❖ *Storybooks*. A good storybook has the following elements: one main character that can be easily identified; a good, simple plot with a simple, satisfying climax; and illustrations that reflect, build on and give clues to the text.

❖ *Non-fiction books*. Non-fiction books can be provided that contain accurate but not necessarily complex information and pictures of things that interest children, such as cars and trucks, animals, insects, plants, places and people.

Books that support vocabulary

Vocabulary has been described as all the words we know, and in order to support the development of speaking, listening, reading and writing we need to continue to build children's vocabulary knowledge. Research suggests that 'children who are exposed to sophisticated vocabulary in the course of interesting conversations learn the words that they will later need to recognise and understand when reading' (Burns, Griffin & Snow, 1999, p.19). We would argue that all books have the potential to support the development of vocabulary, but it is how books are chosen and used that makes the difference to learning new vocabulary.

❖ *Baby and toddler books*. Choose books that connect to the children's lives and that include familiar and new language. When reading with infants and toddlers talk about those connections in the book, label objects and events, and provide appropriate feedback to help with new vocabulary and pronunciation. Give children the opportunity to hear and use this new vocabulary in different contexts.

❖ *Books for older children*. Choose a range of fiction and non-fiction books that can help children expand their vocabulary and knowledge and build on their experiences and interests. Older children can learn a lot of new vocabulary when they are engaged in a more sustained exploration of a topic. For example, a child's interest in caterpillars can be explored by providing first-hand experiences such as observing, drawing and discussing real caterpillars. Fiction and non-fiction books on caterpillars (e.g., *The Very Hungry Caterpillar* (Carle, 2003)) can then be provided to extend children's vocabulary, knowledge and understanding of this topic.

❖ *Using books to further develop vocabulary.* The *First Steps Reading Resource Book* (2004) suggests that before reading a book it is important to check children's understanding of key vocabulary and make links to their experiences. During reading educators can discuss the meaning of new words and their relationship to the story ('why do you think the caterpillar was very hungry?') as well as increasing awareness of words by talking about the author's choice of words. After reading, educators can extend children in a number of ways, such as retelling stories, collecting and displaying new and interesting words from the topic, writing their own books, and using reference books to help learn more about the topic (e.g., What is the difference between a moth and a butterfly?).

Books that support decoding

Books can help children develop the prerequisites of decoding and can be appropriately used with infants through to young children.

❖ Books, such as alphabet books, can emphasise the learning of letter names, letter sounds and letter shapes.

❖ Books can develop an awareness of rhymes and rhyming patterns, such as nursery rhyme, poetry and song books (as well as many children's storybooks).

❖ These sorts of books generally help children learn about the sounds of language (e.g., syllables, rhymes, onset-rimes, letter sounds and phonemes) through such linguistic devices as alliteration (e.g., 'Tiny Tim'), rhyme (e.g., 'been queen'), assonance (e.g., 'Hairy Maclary'), and phoneme switching (e.g., 'a cake for tea, a cape for me …') (Nicholson, 1999).

5

Books that support motivation

An essential ingredient of any book selection is that the books motivate and interest children, and are relevant to their everyday lives.

❖ Enjoyable books are ones that have colourful language, attractive illustrations and are funny and interesting.

❖ Enjoyable books are ones that children want to read, or have read to them time after time.

❖ Books can also include the new and different but need to be mixed with enough of the familiar for children to identify with.

❖ Book collections should also reflect a variety of cultural backgrounds that are realistic and not stereotyped, and particularly the backgrounds of the children in the early childhood centre (Fields & Spangler, 2000).

❖ Books need to be appropriate to the child's development and abilities. Different books will be more suitable for different age groups. For example, books for infants need to be safe, non-toxic, chewable and easily cleaned, as well as being very simple and containing interesting, clear, uncluttered illustrations (Fields & Spangler, 2000).

Finally, it is worth considering ways in which books can be utilised in other areas of the centre, rather than just keeping them in the book corner. For example, books can be added to family play areas where children can read them to dolls or to each other within the context of their play. To encourage children to utilise books as sources of information and/or inspiration they can be placed near other activity areas. A book stand in the art or woodwork area will hold books open at a certain page and minimise the chances of paint or glue getting on the book. The challenge for educators is to develop innovative ways of weaving books throughout the centre. We focus on book-reading approaches in Chapter 8.

Concluding comments

A literacy-rich environment is one in which there are a broad range of literacy tools and props, environmental print, literacy-focused resource centres and books:

- Literacy tools and props that are meaningfully integrated into the centre life and environment encourage children's active engagement and empower all children to be actively literate.

- A literacy-rich early childhood centre is one that contains a wide range of environmental print, including print on walls, surfaces and objects.

- Literacy-focused resource centres such as writing centres, information resource centres, listening-recording stations and book corners provide resource-rich areas in which children can engage in a range of literacy tasks.

- Books are an integral part of literacy-rich early childhood education environments and support many aspects of literacy development, including comprehension, vocabulary, decoding and motivation.

Chapter 6

Planning for Literacy Routines and Experiences

6

A literacy-rich environment is one where literacy is planned for within regular routines, activities and events. Such planning helps educators ensure that all children have *consistent* and *regular* exposure to all aspects of literacy. Planning also helps to provide consistency in the practices between staff. Building literacy into the routines and practices of the early childhood centre does not mean a total reassessment of current practice, but involves looking for the opportunities where literacy can be integrated into existing practice. This process first entails the consideration of where literacy can be incorporated into the existing day-to-day routines of the centre, the development of specific literacy routines, and then the examination of planned activities and practices, including trips and projects where literacy can play an important role. As Rivalland (2000) suggests, '... we cannot just rely on teaching at the point of need or using the "teachable moment". We also need to plan appropriate opportunities to ensure that all children in early childhood care and education contexts have the chance to engage in a systematic way with print-related play that includes scaffolding and support from a carer/teacher' (p.46). In addition, such routines and practices can be enhanced through planning for and developing strong literacy partnerships between the centre and parents/carers, schools, and communities.

Adding literacy to established routines

Integrating literacy into the day-to-day routines of a centre not only ensures literacy experiences are regular but that they are embedded in centre activities and events. These events often have a clear purpose and usually are of particular importance to children, such as arriving at and leaving the centre, meal times, organising and choosing activities and group-time routines. This supports children in seeing literacy as meaningful to them and their lives.

Thoughtful planning can ensure that many aspects of literacy are experienced on a regular basis by all children, including infants, toddlers and young children as part of their day-to-day routines.

Infants

Routines play an important role in an infant's everyday life. Many of these routines focus around meeting the needs of infants such as for food, sleep, cleanliness, stimulation and responsive interactions. Therefore, there is a lot of scope for incorporating literacy elements within regular routines of infants such as daily reading, tapes at sleep time, singing, rhymes and finger plays, as well as talking with infants about environmental print.

Toddlers

While toddlers are becoming (and wanting to be) more independent, there is still a need for strong routines. Most routines will be similar to those of infants; however, more opportunities can be provided for toddlers to make decisions within those routines, for example, choosing books, songs, rhymes, finger plays and tapes. Toddlers can also begin to play an active role in other routines. This can be either directly or indirectly at their own level such as 'writing' lists, recipes, signing in and 'reading' favourite books.

Young children

As young children develop, the possibilities increase for embedding a wider range of literacy experiences into routines. In addition, children are able to take more of a leading role in these routines. For example, children's names provide a particularly useful tool for incorporating literacy into regular routines. Regular visits to the library, helper for the day and classroom charts such as days of the week, birthdays and weather are all routines that involve meaningful literacy events.

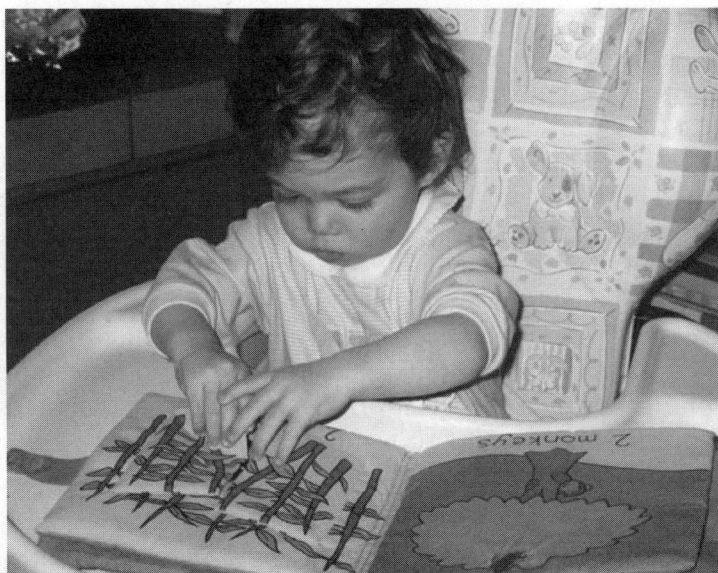

A book after lunch

How to add literacy to established routines

1. Select an existing routine (e.g., sleep time, meal time or nappy changing).
2. Outline the key elements of that routine.
3. Identify any existing literacy resources and practices.
4. Brainstorm ideas for incorporating further literacy resources and practices (take into account your knowledge of individual children here and their literacy interests). For example:

sleep time	meal time	nappy changing
Brainstorm ideas: • Reading/telling stories to children • Playing story or music tapes • Books by beds • Posters on walls • Names on beds/bedding • Mobiles (e.g., alphabet letters) • Children involved in writing up sleep charts • Building narrative skills – e.g., talking with children about what they did earlier and what they might do later	Brainstorm ideas: • Place mats with children's names on or alphabet etc. • Children's names on cups, plates, lunch boxes etc • Menu cards and names on food containers (e.g., apples) • Rosters for meal time jobs • Posters on walls • Books before or after lunch • Playing story or music tapes • Building narrative skills – e.g., encouraging discussion between children about what they did at home or plan to do	Brainstorm ideas: • Posters on walls, ceiling • Mobiles (e.g., alphabet letters) • Children's names on lockers, nappy bags etc • Signs such as 'wash hands' above sink • Singing rhymes, songs • Finger plays • Nursery rhyme charts (as reference for staff) • Playing story or music tapes • Children involved in writing up toileting chart • Building narrative skills – e.g., talking with children about daily events

5. Develop a plan for adding literacy to this routine (this might include developing or purchasing additional resources, staff development, consulting children and their parents, and some mechanism for assessing how the changes are working).
6. Trial ideas, assess how they are working, and fine-tune as necessary.

Any established centre routines can be adapted to include a range of literacy resources and practices. Following are three examples of common centre routines that can be easily adapted to include literacy – records and forms, 'signing in' and turn-taking.

(i) Records and forms

For most early childhood education centres, the filling in of dynamic records (records that regularly change) is part of the daily centre routine. These kinds of records and form-filling are examples of ongoing and everyday, purposeful uses of literacy that can often be adapted to include children. Children can either be directly involved in filling in records, such as ticking boxes or adding their name, or take on more of a supportive role, such as providing information for an educator to include.

Monday 29th April Teacher-	Trip
Tuesday 30th Teacher- Kathie	RORY
Wednesday 1st may Teacher- Althea	pallaVi
Thursday 2nd ~~3rd~~ Teacher- Bronwyn	JamES
Friday 3rd Teacher- Kathie	benjamin

Mat-time helpers

Records and forms that could involve children

Toileting charts, sleep records, food records, menus, safety checks, mat-times, attendance registers, program records, individual children's assessments, plans and profiles, helper for the day, buddy records and activity management boards in which children move their name to the next activity as they complete each one.

(ii) 'Signing in'

Signing in is an example of daily form-filling that can easily involve children. Nelson (1999) describes how sign-in procedures can provide a functional use for name writing as well as name recognition. Infants, toddlers and young children can be actively involved in the daily routine of signing in as they arrive at the centre each day. This can be done as a parallel activity to their parents' sign-in routine or as an independent activity.

Parallel signing in

❖ Children 'sign' their name in a space near or alongside the place where their parent signs them in. This allows children to observe their parent sign in as well as providing an opportunity for the child to take part.

❖ Infants, toddlers and young children can participate at their own level.

❖ Provide writing surfaces with plenty of space to sign in, such as a lined whiteboard.

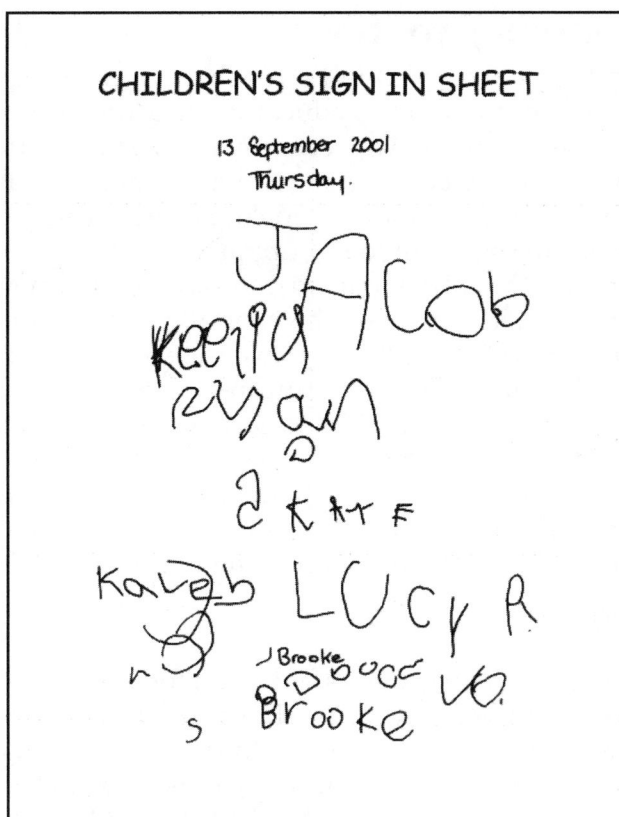

Sign-in sheet for children

Independent signing in

❖ Children can sign in on their own either by writing their name, marking off their name from a list or placing their name card on a board or in a container.

❖ Photographs of each child alongside their name give children additional cues for identifying their own name and provide opportunities for examining their peers' names.

(iii) Turn-taking

An example of a regular routine that uses children's names is turn-taking, such as the allocation of tidy-up jobs. This can be done in a wide range of ways such as using children's names on a card that can be placed next to resources to hold their place in line, allowing children to write their own names on lists, for picking children's names out of a hat for a random selection of who goes next or who does what. For example, below is a description of a job wheel that can be used to allocate daily jobs to children.

Job wheel

A 'job wheel' is a circle divided into segments with a range of jobs written onto each segment alongside a corresponding illustration. Spaces are included around the circle where children can place their names (written on laminated card).

Each day, children find their names and place them around the job wheel which is then spun to determine who is allocated what job.

The educator and children then work out whose names are next to each job. This involves discussions about children's names and job titles (Whose name might this be? What sound/letter does it start with? Which job starts with /pl/?). As Bloodgood (1999) notes, this kind of use of 'name' has the potential to involve children in using literacy in meaningful ways.

Developing new literacy routines

In addition to incorporating literacy within established routines (e.g., such as meal times, sleep times, library visits and home time) educators can look at developing new 'literacy routines' or expand on existing ones. We recommend that educators seek to develop or expand on ways to actively involve children in regular, meaningful and purposeful literacy activities. This might involve an evaluation or stocktake of existing centre practices perhaps following a process similar to that outlined in Chapter 5.

New literacy routines can be infrequent existing practices or new ideas that can easily be developed to become a *regular* part of the everyday centre routines and established practices. It is the regularity of such literacy experiences for children which cumulate to be an important foundation for children's future literacy achievement. However, such regularity needs to be planned for as it will not necessarily occur without the guidance of informed educators.

Following are five examples of literacy practices that we have observed being used as the basis of everyday centre literacy routines – message boards, letter writing, recording children's stories, reading with children, and reading to groups of children.

(i) Message boards

Message boards are common in most centres but often focus on the sharing of information between adults, such as parent notice boards. However, centres can develop new message boards that are specifically designed to involve children. Such message boards offer a venue for children to announce or record events, and share information with each other as well as with educators and parents. They also enable children and parents to record messages in home and community languages, helping children to recognise and value diversity. In addition, educators and parents can use these boards to share information with children. Messages can be in a range of forms, including illustrations, words, photos and dictated messages (Davidson, 1996; Laster & Conte, 1998–99; Neuman, Copple & Bredekamp, 2000). Message boards can also support the collection and exchange of information about home literacy practices as parents record home reading, writing and viewing events, and staff (where possible) incorporate these into their planning.

Message boards

❖ Message boards can be made from a wide range of materials, including painted or fabric-covered particle board, cork tiles, board crisscrossed with elastic or with pegs attached, metal surfaces using magnets to hold messages on (such as fridge doors), blackboards and whiteboards.

❖ Write messages that include clues as to the content, such as a child's name, a picture of a cake and a date as a reminder of a child's birthday.

❖ Photographs with brief messages attached can remind children of upcoming or past visitors, trips or happenings both in the centre and in the wider community (such as announcing the birth of a baby).

(ii) Letter writing

While message boards provide a way of incorporating literacy into the process of sharing information within the centre, writing letters can become a regular part of centre life that not only involves literacy, but strengthens children's relationships with the wider community. Enabling children to write or dictate letters in the language they feel is most appropriate reinforces the importance of diversity within the centre and community. Letter writing can involve a range of forms and functions of literacy and a variety of literacy tools and props.

Forms and functions of letter writing

Letters to friends and relatives; letters to other early childhood centres or to schools sharing information; cards or letters to say thank you, congratulations, happy birthday or get well soon; letters making requests such as to the local council, MPs or organisations; letters that voice opinions such as letters to the editor.

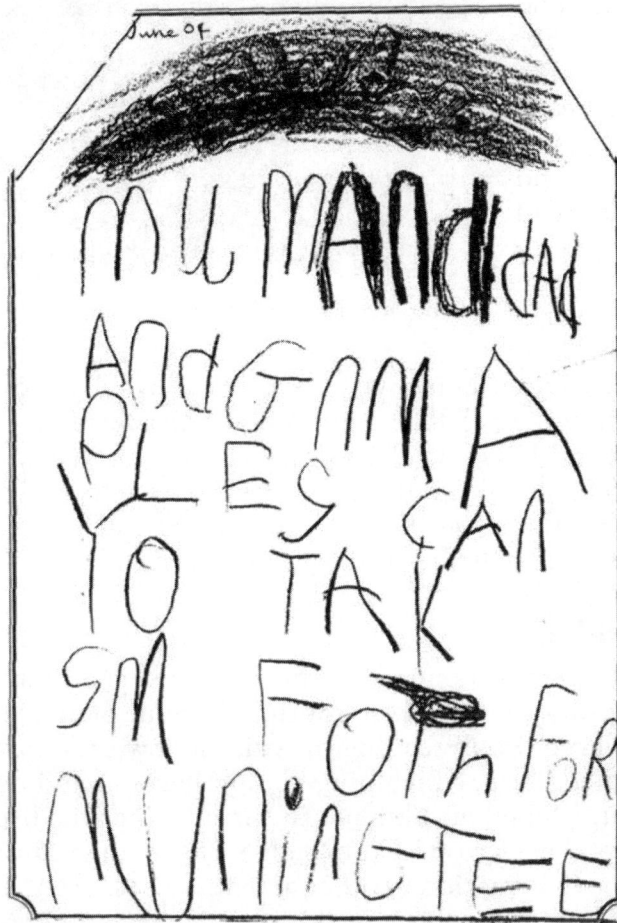

Writing a letter to send home

Tools and props of letter writing

Writing paper, cards, mail boxes, envelopes, stamps, postcards, post boxes, pens and pencils, fax machines, computers (to print or email).

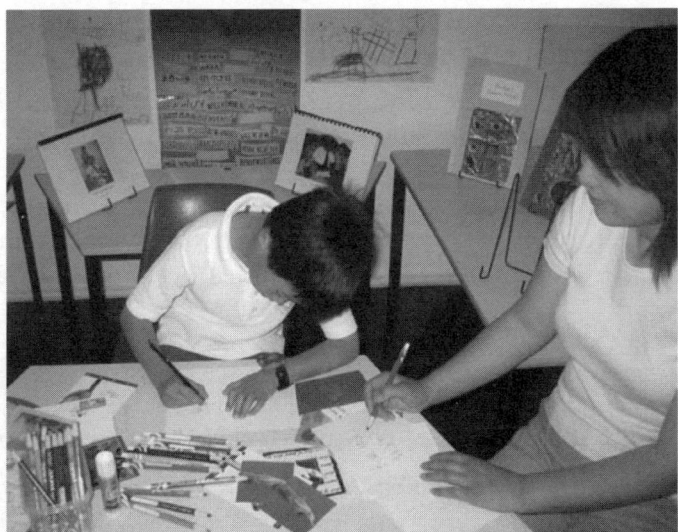

Writing greeting cards in home languages

(iii) Recording children's stories

The recording of children's stories can become an embedded part of everyday life in the early childhood centre. In some families storytelling forms a significant part of their literacy practices and has many functions. For example, in some families storytelling is used as a means of building children's cultural heritage, sharing values and teaching about rights and rituals. Thus, storytelling is an excellent opportunity to share different views of the world and introduce new concepts.

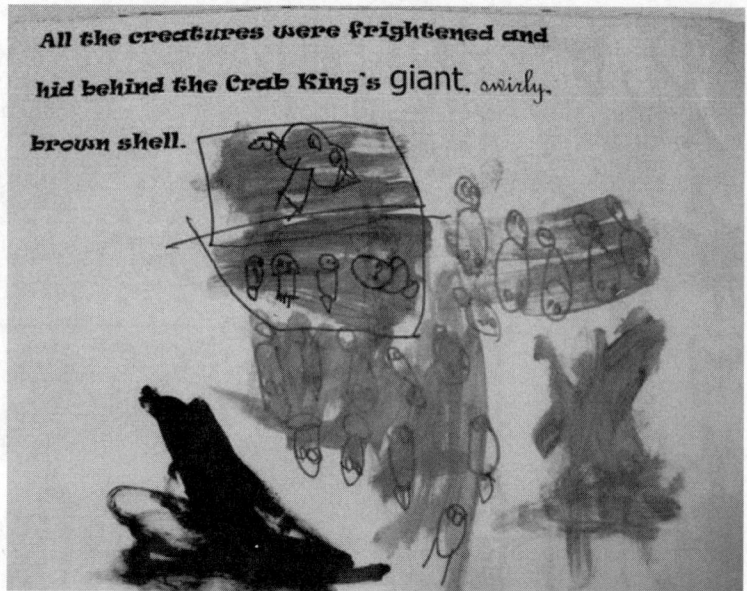

All the creatures were frightened and hid behind the Crab King's giant, swirly, brown shell.

Creating and sharing group stories

Children can draw and/or write their own stories, read or tell them to others, or dictate them to an adult or microphone. Recording children's stories provides recognition of children as storytellers or authors and allows children to explore and express their literacy knowledge, skills and understandings. It also assists children to 'see' themselves as literate. The listening-recording stations (outlined in Chapter 5) can be used as a base for this routine. Also see Chapter 10 for further information on this area.

(iv) Reading with children

Reading to children, either one-to-one or in small groups, is a literacy-related event that plays an important part in a centre's daily routine. Careful planning can ensure this is a regular event for all children. Book reading provides a powerful opportunity for children to learn about book-related literacy including comprehension and decoding. It also helps children build on and extend their vocabulary. By introducing and discussing new concepts children build their general background knowledge, which enables them to make sense of new texts and transfer the information to other activities. Because it occurs in a one-to-one or small group situation, the educator can tailor their teaching strategies to each child. In addition, the 'closeness' and individual nature of this kind of book reading supports children's literacy motivation where reading is linked to a sense of security and enjoyment. Chapter 8 encourages educators to enhance their book-reading strategies and techniques.

(v) Reading to groups of children

Reading to young children in groups often occurs during regular routines such as mat times. While group times such as this do not always provide ideal conditions for book reading, and are generally not appropriate for toddlers and infants, thoughtful planning can help ensure that these group reading events are supportive of children's literacy development. Therefore, it is worthwhile for educators to evaluate the effectiveness of this routine and their own strategies and techniques. Again, see Chapter 8 for detailed information.

How educators can capitalise on group reading

❖ Point out titles, author, illustrator and other book features.

❖ Link with children's experiences and understanding.

❖ Point out the relationship between words and illustrations.

- ❖ Introduce and talk about new vocabulary.
- ❖ Hold the book steady and so all children can see it.
- ❖ Use eye contact to include all children in the group.
- ❖ Speak clearly and vary the tempo (speed up, slow down, pause) to reflect the action in the story.
- ❖ Model and support children to formulate questions, make predictions about the outcome, respond to events and make relevant comments.
- ❖ Keep the listening period within children's attention span.

(Adapted from Fields & Spangler, 2000)

Incorporating literacy into centre planning

This section considers how literacy can be incorporated into the planning processes of the centre. The ways in which each centre plans for the learning and development of individuals and groups of children will differ. However, planning principles from several of the state curriculum documents and the QIAS (2005) suggest that an effective planning cycle should contain the following elements.

(i) Short-term planning

Below is an outline of how literacy could be incorporated into each step of the planning cycle with examples based around a short-term plan for a small group of children who have demonstrated an interest in burying and finding treasure.

6

Observe

Educators gather information on the children's learning and development through written observations and discussion with the children about what they are doing. Parents are also consulted. Particular note is taken of the literacy resources, knowledge and skills used and demonstrated by the children.

For example: The educator observes three children spending a lot of time burying treasure (shells and plastic toys, etc) but often forgetting where it was buried later on.

Interpret and analyse

Educators share the information gathered and discuss this in relation to the children's learning and development, including their interests, and literacy skills, knowledge and understandings. The children's opinions and ideas are also sought in this process.

For example: The children demonstrated an ongoing interest in burying and finding treasure but agreed that finding it was often hard. The children relied on discussion and memory, rather than literacy skills and knowledge to find their treasure.

Set learning objectives

Educators set learning objectives for the children based on their interpretation and analysis that utilises the children's interests and extends their literacy knowledge, skills and understandings. These objectives are discussed with the children.

For example: Educators decide to build on the children's interest in locating their treasure. They formulate the following learning objectives: to extend the children's understanding of treasure maps as a form and function of literacy (i.e., a means of recording information); and to extend the children's skills in the use of literacy tools (i.e., using pens, paper, rulers etc to develop treasure maps).

Plan learning experiences

Educators develop plans to meet these learning objectives. Children's ideas are also sought and included in these plans.

For example: The plan involved discussing and exploring treasure maps with the children and assisting them to develop their own treasure maps.

Develop and implement teaching strategies

Educators discuss which teaching strategies are most appropriate for providing the planned learning experiences and meeting the learning objectives. This includes the provision of literacy resources as well as the role of the educator.

For example: Educators provide examples and books on treasure maps, felt pens, paper and writing surfaces suitable to use outside. They also decide to scaffold children's map-drawing skills, using such techniques as describing, modelling and suggestion.

Evaluate results

Educators gather examples of the children's learning experiences such as written observations, examples of their work and discussions with the children. The children's learning is then discussed and assessed in relation to the learning objectives.

For example: Educators record observations of children developing and using treasure maps, and collect examples of their maps as well as photographs. Later they discuss these with the children and use this information to evaluate their understanding, knowledge and skills in the use and creation of treasure maps as a form and function of literacy.

Reflect

Educators reflect on and evaluate the overall effectiveness of each step of the plan.

For example: On reflection the educators feel the plan was effective in helping children use literacy skills and knowledge to find their treasure. To build on what the children have learned and to capitalise on their growing interest in map-making the educators decided to extend the children's knowledge of maps and map-making into other areas (such as the local community), and so begins the planning cycle again.

While this is a fairly simple example of incorporating literacy into centre planning, it illustrates that it is relatively easy to view literacy as an integral part of planning for children's overall learning and development. Such an approach is often more desirable and relevant to children's learning than decontextualised, 'bolted on' literacy programs.

(ii) Longer-term planning

As well as short-term planning, which is focused on the learning and development of a small number of children such as described above, literacy can also be incorporated into larger-scale and longer-term plans such as projects. Such planning generally follows a similar process to the planning for individuals and small groups described above.

The benefits of longer-term plans, like projects, are that they provide opportunities for in-depth investigations on topics. These longer-term investigations can be more meaningful for children, allow for a wide range of literacy activities and resources to be used, and generally involve the use of multiple symbolic forms such as talking, drawing and writing. In addition, such projects also provide opportunities for children to work together and learn from each other, and their individual strengths and interests can be utilised by developing different roles for children within a project (Neuman, 1998). An example of a longer-term plan is the buying of a new centre pet.

A project to buy a new centre pet

This project could incorporate the following literacy activities:

❖ developing questionnaires to find out what kind of pet children and educators want

❖ researching different kinds of pets, their care and housing

❖ looking through the phone book for pet stores

❖ writing questions to ask the pet store owner about the pet

❖ planning and undertaking a trip to the pet store to buy the pet

❖ naming the pet

❖ designing and helping to build the pet's home and facilities

❖ drawing up posters to introduce the new pet to the centre community

❖ developing instructions on the care and handling of the pet

❖ developing rosters for cleaning and feeding the pet.

Developing literacy partnerships with parents/carers, schools and the community

Inherent in the policy-making debates discussed in the first section of this book is the importance of early childhood centres planning to develop strong literacy partnerships with parents/carers, schools and the community; for without such partnerships, literacy policy cannot be planned and implemented effectively. Parents/carers are children's first literacy educators, and children learn about literacy and its functions within the social contexts of the family. Working with parents/carers in this area can be rewarding for the early childhood centre, the child and the parents/carers. As well, building strong literacy links with schools can be beneficial in a range of areas, from helping children's transition to school, to reinforcing educational partnerships with other professionals. The community, of course, provides a range of rich literacy opportunities and resources that the centre can use. The development of a collaborative partnership between centres and parents underpins Quality Area 2: Partnership with Families: 'The relationship between the child's family and staff is crucial to the child's wellbeing, development and progress' (QIAS, 2005, p.8).

(i) Parents/carers as literacy partners

Early childhood educators and families can work together to gain valuable knowledge about children's literacy interests, development and experiences that can then be built on in the early childhood centre and at home. Planning for this form of two-way collaboration has many benefits. There is a validation of the child's home experiences and practices and, as Neuman (1998) points out, 'communication between families and teachers built on mutual respect and the sharing of information creates bonds of continuity, purpose and consistency in children's early literacy programmes' (p.12). These aspects of continuity and consistency are important components of literacy learning.

Children bring with them literacy knowledge and skills from the home environment. Literacy practices in the home reflect the literacy language backgrounds and culture of the family. However, the forms of literacy exposure in the home can vary from that of the early childhood centre. Some home environments complement those of school to a greater degree than others, for some a mismatch exists. Sometimes parents/carers and early childhood educators hold different views of literacy and in these situations, it is important that parents/carers and early childhood educators work together to co-construct a broader definition of literacy, one where each can learn from the other for the benefit of the child (see McNaughton, 2002 for valuable insights here).

Where educators plan to provide a flexible curriculum that responds to the unique interests, strengths and experiences of children, early childhood educators not only validate children's home experiences but also provide opportunities to engage and involve parents/carers, grandparents and extended family in the early childhood centre.

> Families often have much to offer the centre and staff need to work with families to develop various strategies and opportunities for family involvement in the centre program.
>
> (QIAS, 2005, p.10)

Sharing books at home

It is also important that parents/carers are regularly informed of what is happening in the early childhood centre, and literacy areas are no exception.

Parents/carers can be informed through

❖ Pamphlets on early literacy skills, whiteboards, newsletters, flyers, communication books, photo books, information displays, portfolios, centre diaries, informal discussions, meetings and home visits.

❖ Centre-run literacy workshops can provide a useful opportunity to inform parents of the centre literacy policy and approaches, as well as provide a forum where views of literacy learning are shared and parent concerns and queries are answered.

Finally, there is a range of home literacy activities that can support children's early literacy development. Many parents/carers are keen to help their children but are unsure exactly what to do. Early childhood centres can help reinforce 'the importance of parents/carers as educators and of homes as learning environments' (Barbour, 1998–99, p.71).

Centres can support home-literacy activities through

❖ 'Books-home' schemes, a lending library, and home-literacy bags that contain books, puzzles, literacy games and literacy guides.

❖ Developing fun parent-child projects such as finding as many words as you can that mean 'big' (e.g., large, huge ...) as well as words from other languages (e.g., nui, grande ...).

(For information on creating effective home-literacy environments see Adams & Jackson (2002).)

(ii) Schools as literacy partners

There is not a great deal of literature concerning schools as literacy partners. However, there is a range of possibilities here. Early childhood centres frequently visit schools to support the young child's transition to schools. These visits can be used as an opportunity for early childhood educators to see how school literacy programs work. Junior school educators are generally chosen for their expertise and knowledge in early literacy learning, and can be very useful in providing support, guidance and resources to early childhood centres. However, what may work with primary-age children may not work, nor be appropriate, for younger children. It is here that the early childhood educator needs to use their professional knowledge in order to adapt primary school methods so that they are appropriate and relevant for the group of children with whom they are working.

Setting up reciprocal visits with local schools can also be valuable. For example, it would be useful for junior-primary school educators to view the literacy-enriched environment that the centre has in place, not only because they will be able to see first-hand the literacy experiences of the children who may move on to their school but, in addition, many of these literacy ideas may well be appropriate for children moving into Year 1. Research has demonstrated how closer links between schools, centres and parents/carers can be fruitful for all children. Partnerships between the early childhood educators and Indigenous families and children who speak English as an additional language are especially important in order to build on and extend ways of learning (Cairney & Ruge, 1998; Makin & Groom, 2002; Mullen, 2000).

(iii) Communities as literacy partners

Communities are rich in literacy resources. Besides parents/carers and schools (which have just been discussed), centres can draw on community resources in a number of ways, including bringing the literate community into the centre and by taking children on trips and excursions.

(a) Bringing the literate community into the centre

The local and wider community can be drawn on to bring community literacy experiences into the early childhood education centre. As in trips and excursions out of the centre, visitors to the centre need to be organised and planned by the educator and can either be directly related to literacy or provide broader, shared experiences for children that can later be drawn on to explore literacy within the centre. Such visits strengthen community relationships and children's sense of belonging within the wider literate community.

> ## Literacy visitors might include
>
> Poets, authors, illustrators and artists, musicians and musical groups, theatre groups, puppeteers, historians, educators (early childhood, primary and secondary), orators such as local elders, storytellers and book readers.

(b) Trips and excursions

Regular trips and excursions provide rich opportunities for literacy and strengthen links with the centre's community. Such activities need to be planned by adults, though they are often initiated by children's desires and interests and range from short walks to trips wider afield. Trips and excursions can have a specific literacy focus or provide broader experiences for children. These activities give children 'first hand experiences that expand children's vocabulary ... and exposure to various tools, objects and materials' (Neuman, Copple & Bredekamp, 2000, p.16). They create shared community experiences for children which can then be built on and explored within the centre. Trips and excursions also create opportunities for children to engage in meaningful community-based literacy experiences and reinforce the concept that 'literacy is a community endeavor' (Davidson, 1996, p.233).

Planning a trip or excursion

❖ Build in a range of literacy activities before, during and after the trip such as reading or retelling stories relating to the trip.

❖ Seek to highlight specific examples of literacy from the trip (e.g., road signs, environmental print).

❖ Make time to share and discuss ideas and understandings with children about aspects of the trip.

❖ Extend children's knowledge and vocabulary that is relevant to the trip.

(Fields & Spangler, 2000)

Trips with a specific literacy focus

Literacy trips can provide children with direct experiences of literacy activities found within their centre and wider community. Such trips may include:

❖ visits to libraries, book stores, stationery shops, post offices, publishers, illustrators, writers, printers, primary and secondary schools, community arts groups, and plays and musicals

❖ 'literacy discovery walks' looking for aspects of literacy around the local community environment (such as street signs, advertising, and car number plates).

Broader excursions

Broader excursions provide children with experiences of a wide range of places in their local and wider community that can support children's literacy development. Such excursions may include: visits to shops, restaurants, fast-food outlets, offices, farms, builders, banks, recycling centres, parks, reserves, historical sites, or significant local landmarks depicted in local legends.

6

Concluding comments

• A literacy-rich environment is one in which literacy is incorporated into the existing day-to-day routines as well as the planned activities and practices of the centre.

• Daily routines such as sleep time, meal time, nappy-changing, record-keeping, form-filling, 'signing in' and turn-taking can involve children in regular literacy experiences.

• Centres can also plan to include new literacy routines into the daily life of the centre such as message boards, letter writing, recording children's stories and reading to children.

• Literacy can be easily incorporated into the existing planning processes of the centre, including individual and group planning.

• Developing literacy partnerships with parents/carers, schools and the community ensures that children gain access to a broad range of literacy experiences and view literacy as a community endeavour.

Chapter 7

Capitalising on
Informal Literacy Opportunities

In Chapter 5 we discussed the weaving of literacy resources throughout the early childhood centre. These resources included literacy tools and props, environmental print, literacy-focused resource centres and books. In Chapter 6 we considered the importance of building literacy into the established day-to-day routines of the centre and the development of new literacy routines. In addition, we looked at how literacy could be incorporated into the centre's short- and longer-term planning, along with the strengthening of literacy partnerships with parents, schools and the wider community.

With these literacy foundations in place, the early childhood centre not only provides a literacy-rich environment but also provides children with a wealth of regular and meaningful literacy-related experiences. Such strong foundations generate numerous opportunities both for children to engage in literacy-related play as well as for educators to capitalise on literacy opportunities as they emerge. Such opportunities often are 'unplanned', responsive and spontaneous and can be both adult- or child-initiated. These spontaneous literacy opportunities occur during children's everyday play and so are usually focused on what children are interested in and when they are interested in it, and hence are highly relevant and meaningful for the child.

This approach fits well within a sociocultural model of literacy learning where literacy becomes part of the culture of the centre and literacy learning occurs through a process of social construction with adults, peers, places and things. In particular, through conversations with peers and adults children develop the narrative abilities that are so important for their comprehension of texts (reading comprehension) and writing. Such conversations provide the contexts that allow children to weave their own stories out of past and present, imagined and real events.

Peers develop children's narrative abilities during conversations that occur in child-initiated play. In this example, one child asks another what she is doing:

> I'm doing a treasure map.
> Actually it's a map to take you places.
> That's a dungeon.
> It looks a bit like a lemon cut in half, doesn't it?

On the other hand, adults also can support children's narrative abilities as the opportunities arise. Cullen (2002, p.74), for example, illustrates this storytelling process in an episode where a three-year-old (Linda) and her mother are choosing storybooks at the children's section in the local library. This conversation weaves past and present events together in a meaningful and coherent fashion and where the child's developing narrative abilities are evident.

> 'Tiger,' says Linda, 'red tiger.'
> 'Oh yes,' says Linda's Mum, 'it's like your red tiger. Do you want that one?'
> Linda: 'Tiger in ... car ... we went to shop.'
> Mum: 'Oh, yesterday, you mean. I hope Tiger didn't leap out.'
> Linda: 'Grrh.'

This chapter will consider the importance of child-initiated literacy play, including dramatic play based on stories and popular culture. Then, we provide a range of strategies and techniques that educators can use to capitalise on these informal literacy opportunities as they arise. It is in capitalising on these informal and spontaneous literacy opportunities where educators and children come to a 'meeting of minds'.

Supporting literacy through play

Play provides many informal opportunities for supporting children's literacy learning and narrative abilities. It provides children with a flexible forum through which they can engage with literacy at their own level and in ways that are meaningful to them. The open-ended nature of play allows children to explore, manipulate and practise many different concepts, processes, forms and functions of literacy and allows children with varying levels of literacy development to take part in literacy-related activities without risk of failure (Roskos & Christie, 2000).

As Davidson (1996) notes, play provides contexts where children can experiment with different types of language that fit the different roles that they take on in their play. The kinds of literacy talk that children engage in during play includes naming and negotiating the use of literacy tools and props, the meaning and use of print, as well as trying out and exploring the sounds of words. While this talk can be solo, it is often social (Neuman & Roskos, 1990, in Klenk, 2001). Child-initiated play is an essential part of children's literacy learning.

(i) Dramatic play

Children's narrative abilities, literacy skills and understandings are enhanced through dramatic play. Such literacy play can be entirely spontaneous and incidental; occurring within the context of children's general dramatic play; or play that is facilitated through a more structured and planned thematic play area. All of these forms of dramatic play are characterised by the need to do something in the real world through the replication or approximation of the way in which literacy is used in everyday situations. Thus dramatic play offers a valid, authentic and appropriate vehicle for children to engage in rich and purposeful literacy learning (Hall & Robinson, 2000).

Dramatic literacy play can occur spontaneously, as children 'try on for size' what it is like to be a competent literacy expert – such as being a book reader, or a letter writer. This allows children to engage in literacy experiences regardless of their actual level of literacy knowledge and skill, and assists children to develop their understandings of the functions and purposes of literacy and develop their understandings and skills in the use of a wide range of literacy tools and activities. Through this children can come to better understand what it means to be literate. A centre with a rich literacy environment and routines provides many opportunities for such play to occur.

Example of spontaneous literacy play

One-to-one book reading is a regular routine in an infant centre. Anu (15 months) is familiar with the routine of sitting on an adult's lap, reading favourite stories, discussing the plot, characters and illustrations. In his own play with a doll, he picks up a nearby book, sits on a comfy pillow and 'reads' the book to the doll, engaging in a quiet conversation about the book.

Dramatic literacy play can also occur within the context of children's general dramatic play. Children's dramatic play is often based on their own experiences and interests outside of the centre, as well as shared centre experiences such as centre trips into the community and visitors to the centre. By adding print-rich materials, and realistic literacy props and tools to these play contexts, children are able to explore different forms and functions of literacy, relevant to their everyday life. Providing children with a wide range of literacy related experiences will ensure that children have a rich resource of experiences from which to draw within their play. This also provides ample opportunities for children to develop their narrative skills as they co-construct their literacy play with their peers. As Davidson (1996) explains, because the language children use to negotiate what is happening in their dramatic play is similar to the language of books, 'dramatic play provides practice for constructive narrative' (p.102).

Example of literacy within children's general dramatic play

After a centre visit to a local fish and chip shop, Hannah and Emily are both engaged in play based around fast-food restaurants. They have used the equipment from the dramatic play area and collage table to set up a counter and food preparation area and make play money and items of food.

They decide they need to have a menu and spend a long time discussing whether this should be on individual cards or on the wall. They also discuss the kind of foods to put on their menu and whether or not pictures are needed. Other discussion takes place around the taking and filling of orders.

Finally, dramatic literacy play can be facilitated through a more structured and planned approach to thematic play. Hall and Robinson (2000) suggest that planning a structured play area should start with the identification of a theme that relates to children's social and cultural lives. They suggest that play is likely to be richer if children have some understanding of the theme (e.g., café, shop, hospital, garage, travel agent). Visiting the area is a powerful way of consolidating and extending children's knowledge of the area and identifying literacy practices associated with the area. This enables the children to be involved in discussing, building and resourcing the area. Having chosen a theme, the task now is to identify all the literacy activities that are associated with it, giving the children opportunities to explore and use a range of literacy activities that are appropriate and interesting. This is related to the range of roles that the structured play area involves and the literacy associated with these roles. Depending on your knowledge of the children in your context you may begin by encouraging the children to play independently, then subtly or more explicitly start to intervene in order to extend the play.

Example of facilitating structured literacy play

❖ Visit a café: Prepare questions before visit. Take photographs, talk about signs, menus, roles of workers, ordering, cooking, types of food, safety etc.

❖ Creating a café: Making decisions about where to build the café, what resources are needed and what to call the café. Providing literacy resources: menus; order pads; posters; signs; special offers; home delivery telephone numbers; name tags etc.

❖ Running the café: Identifying and applying for jobs. Recipes. Setting the tables. Opening and closing times. Numbers allowed in café. Notice board etc.

❖ Extending play: Introduce a problem – how can you accommodate babies in your café? Resources (high chairs), facilities (changing room, heating milk), food (special menu), room (prams) etc.

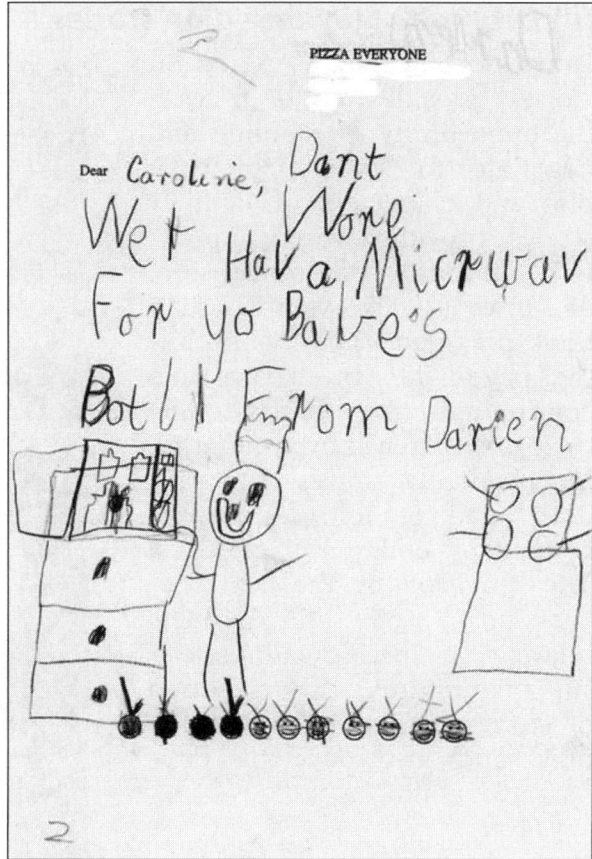

Solving a problem. Translation: Dear Caroline, don't worry. We have a microwave for your baby's bottles. From Darien.

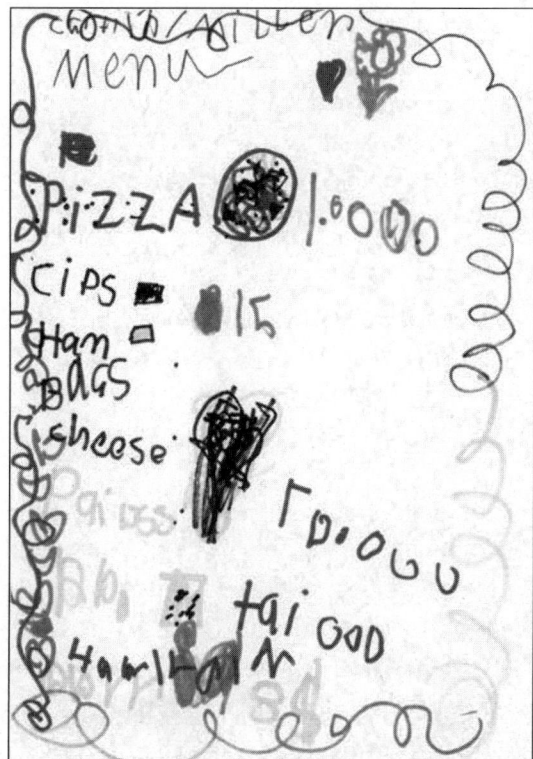

Writing menus for the café

(ii) Dramatic play based on stories

Dramatic play that is based on stories provides children with the opportunity to examine and negotiate in some depth the plot and characters of familiar stories, providing strong support for children's comprehension. As Rowe (2000) explains, such book play can bring 'books "off the page" into the space–time continuum of everyday life' (p.26). Children may dramatise, independently, stories they have been read or told, or stories created by children themselves. The provision by the centre of dress-ups, props and puppets relating to specific stories can support children's dramatisation of stories within their dramatic play, and also develops their narrative abilities.

Dramatic play allows children to really explore the characters of stories

The Three Billy Goats Gruff

A group of three-year-old children is playing the *Three Billy Goats Gruff*. They select suitable dress-ups for each character and decide what they can use as the bridge. Much of their play revolves around discussion and negotiation about who will play each role, the order in which the billy goats cross the bridge, what the troll and billy goats say, when the troll will jump out and what happens to the troll in the end.

Where the Wild Things Are

'I'm in the boat. Sailing in the boat. To the wild things in the jungle. Daniel, he's sailing with me. I'm being Max. Daniel is being Max and I am too.'

(iii) Dramatic play based on popular culture

Popular culture, including television programs, films, popular music, along with computer, electronic and arcade games, are playing an increasingly significant part in the lives of many children in Western societies today. There is a growing body of research (Arthur, 2001; Dyson, 1997; Marsh, 2000), which confirms what many early childhood educators already know, 'that popular culture is indeed popular' (McNaughton, 2002, p.195). The enthusiastic interest many children show in the stories, characters and behaviours associated with popular media culture is often demonstrated in children's informal play.

The benefits of such play are similar to that of dramatic play based on stories as children play out and explore the characters, roles and plots of favourite programs and games. As children play they can be encouraged to engage with a range of literacy tools and props as well as in narrative conversations with their peers and others, which supports their literacy learning. Where educators engage children in conversations about these scripts, they can also support children to analyse and critique popular media (particularly in relation to the behaviours and motivations of popular characters and storylines).

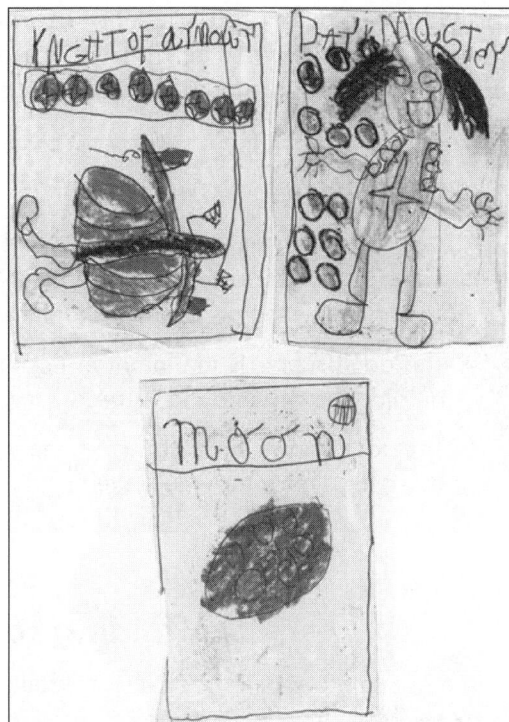

Literacy learning through popular culture

Strategies to support informal literacy learning

Educators can support informal literacy learning through fruitfully harvesting the myriad of opportunities provided by the centre routines, planned experiences and children's play. Educators who know each child well and who are observant are able to recognise learning opportunities and can tailor their support to meet individual children's strengths, interests and current literacy understandings. As Davidson (1996) explains, the adult's role is to observe 'children's current knowledge and help them to consolidate and extend this knowledge' (p.233). By observing what children are doing, adults are also able to sensitively encourage children to incorporate relevant literacy resources and behaviours into their play (Fields & Spangler, 2000).

There are a wide range of teaching techniques and strategies available for educators (and peers) to draw on in order to support and extend children's language and literacy learning and development. As there are no simple formulae for deciding which of these strategies is most appropriate to use at any one moment, educators need to engage in ongoing reflection about the teaching strategies and techniques they select and how they apply these in practice to best support the literacies of the children with whom they work.

Presented here is a range of broader teaching strategies that educators and peers might usefully draw on when supporting children's informal language and literacy learning and development; we have adapted these for literacy purposes from MacNaughton and Williams (1998). These broad teaching strategies are derived from a sociocultural perspective and they acknowledge children's own literacy experiences and understandings, the significance of language for early literacy, and emphasise the negotiation of shared meanings particularly through conversations. This is not intended to be a complete list but a sample of key strategies frequently used in early childhood settings to assist educators to build on informal literacy opportunities. Each strategy highlights the importance of social construction in children's literacy learning.

(i) Scaffolding

Scaffolding involves the educator working with a child within their 'zone of proximal development', which is the gap between what a child can do on their own, and what they can do in collaboration with another, more competent, person. In order to successfully scaffold, children's literacy learning educators need to have an ongoing and in-depth knowledge of each child's level of literacy abilities and development. The educator can then provide the child with temporary guidance and support, which they gradually reduce as the child's competence at the task increases until, eventually, the child is able to complete the task independently.

Scaffolding how books are read

❖ The adult selects a book and reads it to an infant, turning pages as she says 'Turn the page'. The infant sits passively throughout the process.

❖ The adult supports the infant in turning the pages of the book by separating each page and guiding the child's hand as necessary, saying 'Turn the page'.

❖ The adult allows the child to turn the pages independently, indicating when this should be done by saying 'Now turn the page'.

Scaffolding comprehension of the plot

The educator reads a book to the infant, pointing out significant elements in the illustrations and plot – 'Look, there's Mr Rabbit'.

As the infant's experience and understanding of the process and the story develops, the educator asks the child questions about the characters and plot, followed by the answers – 'Who's that? It's Mr Rabbit'.

On repeated readings, the adult waits for the child to identify key elements of the story:

Adult – 'Who's that?'
Child – 'Rabbit.'
Adult – 'Yes, that is Mr Rabbit.'

Later, the adult simply pauses as the child identifies aspects of the story on their own and then supports her efforts.

Child – 'Rabbit.'
Adult – 'Yes, that's Mr Rabbit.'

(ii) Co-construction

Co-construction is a term that describes the educator and child engaging in joint activity involving the negotiation of meanings, understandings and perspectives. Within co-construction the knowledge and experiences of *both* adult and child are valued, and therefore it involves a sharing of power and sense of partnership (Hedges, 2000). When considered in relation to literacy, educators engaging in co-construction respect and value children's voices, literacy knowledge, experiences and understandings and strive to understand these while also assisting the child with understanding other literacy perspectives. Co-construction can also occur between children.

For example

Educator and child are engaged in a discussion about the construction of a shop in the dramatic play area. Rather than simply describing or suggesting what a shop should include, the educator engages in discussion with the child about what they think is needed in a shop, what they think happens, what literacy materials might be needed, why they think this, and so on. Both educator and child share their experiences of shops as they exchange and explore ideas together.

(iii) Deconstruction

Deconstructing involves pulling apart and exploring literacy understandings and meanings to get a better understanding of where they come from, and of the assumptions on which they are based. This strategy is very useful when supporting children to challenge and critique the views and messages inherent within texts and identify the basis for them. Deconstructing can be valuable, for example, when children feel that they or others are not capable of aspects of literacy learning or participating in certain literacy endeavours.

> **Deconstructing texts**
>
> During the making of Mother's Day cards, the children compared their own mothers' lives to the portrayal of the women in the Mother's Day catalogues. They also looked at the gifts that were advertised in the catalogues and began to talk about the purpose of Mother's Day. Through this analysis the children were able to begin to challenge some of the assumptions about mothers, what mothers like and the commercialisation of Mother's Day.

> **Deconstructing literacy self-perceptions**
>
> When the educator suggests that James writes to a friend who has recently moved to another centre, James is adamant that he can't. The educator talks with James about why this is and discovers that James feels he can only 'write' once he starts school. The educator explores different ideas about learning, school and writing with James. The educator helps James write the letter.

(iv) Problematising

Problematising is similar to deconstructing in that it involves exploring children's assumptions and concepts, and challenges children to think more deeply about underlying issues and ideas. This strategy is particularly useful in relation to comprehension as it encourages children to explore the meanings and messages inherent in stories in more depth.

> **For example**
>
> After reading a story about a child and her cat who move from house to house before finally settling down, the educator asks the children how this child felt about moving house so often. The educator listens to and acknowledges the children's responses and then poses some more challenging questions about why she was unhappy moving house, how this child understood how her cat felt, how her mother might have felt, and why friendships, familiar things and the idea of having a home are important. The aim of this discussion is not about finding the 'correct' answers, but to encourage the children to think more deeply about friendships, familiar things and the concept of home.

(v) Modelling

Providing literacy-rich environments is not enough. Literacy elements and practices need to be highlighted for children so that children are not only aware of them but they see that they are useful. Educators can use modelling to strengthen and extend children's understanding of the range of forms, functions and ways of exploring and using different aspects of literacy (Einarsdottir, 2000). While modelling is important in itself, educators can then draw children into the literacy practices being modelled.

Ways educators can be literacy models within the centre

❖ modelling the use of centre resources purposefully such as writing reminder notes and putting them on the message board, using the writing centre to write notes and letters, entering the book corner and reading books, reading the signs around the centre out loud

❖ carrying out centre administrative tasks where children can see, rather than completing them in the office, for example, filling in the roll, ordering centre supplies, finding phone numbers, taking messages, writing shopping lists

❖ filling in centre forms such as sleep charts with infants, toddlers and young children. Also explain the purpose of writing things down (e.g., 'that was a long sleep. Let's write down what time it is so Dad will know how long you slept').

As children take notice of these types of modelling and become interested, they can then be appropriately drawn into the literacy activity.

(vi) Facilitating

Facilitating relates to the adaptation of the learning environment to enhance its effectiveness in supporting children's learning. Those aspects of a literacy-enriched environment discussed in Chapter 5, including the provision of literacy tools and props and environmental print, are examples of ways in which educators can facilitate literacy learning within the centre environment. Facilitation also relates to the organisation of time, including regular routines, planned events and activities and the daily planning of the centre, as discussed in Chapter 6.

Having books within easy reach

To facilitate effectively, it is important that educators first carefully observe what is happening and consider those aspects of the environment that are limiting a child's literacy learning as well as how the environment could be adapted to enhance their learning.

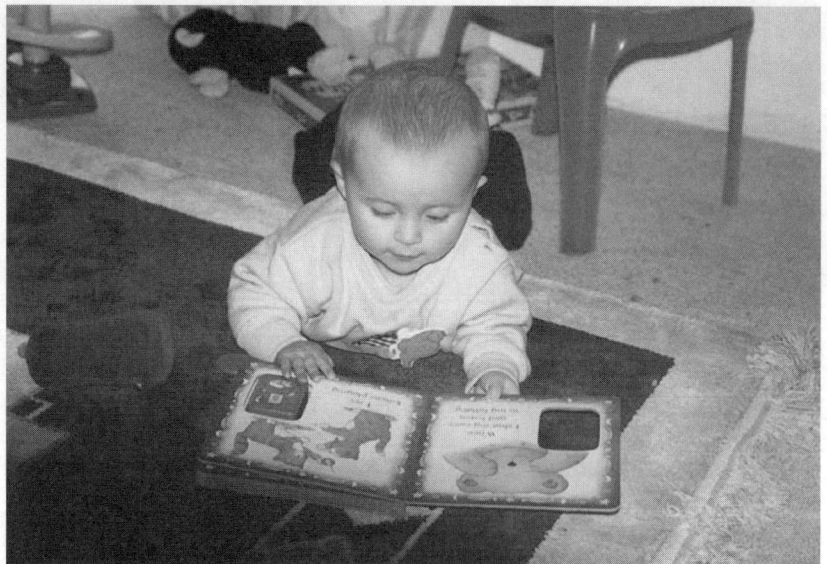

For example

An educator places an infant down on his front with a number of brightly coloured toys. However, shortly after, the educator notes that the infant has knocked all the toys away and is becoming frustrated. The educator decides that the infant may be finding the toys too stimulating so she moves the toys out of the way, goes to the bookshelf and finds a small sturdy cardboard book with clear, simple illustrations. She places this in front of the infant who lifts his head and looks at the pictures intently. The educator watches for signals from the infant before turning the page.

Techniques to support informal literacy learning

There is also a wide range of more specific teaching techniques that educators can utilise to build on and create informal literacy opportunities. Some particularly useful teaching techniques are discussed below and we have again adapted these from MacNaughton and Williams (1998) for the purposes of supporting children's growing language and literacy expertise. These can be used on their own or may be used as part of one of the broader teaching strategies discussed previously. Each technique highlights the importance of social construction in children's literacy learning.

(i) Demonstrating

At times, giving children the information they need to successfully engage with literacy tools and props is important. This allows them to practise and extend their literacy skills and processes. When deciding whether or not to use this technique the educator needs to consider whether the child is capable and ready to learn this skill or process, or whether demonstrating its 'correct' use may limit the child's ability to explore their own understandings about that literacy skill or process.

> ### For example
>
> Moana (15 months) approaches an educator carrying out an observation on another child. Moana touches the pen. 'Would you like to do some writing too?' Moana indicates 'yes', and the educator gives her some paper and a pen. Moana holds the pen and paper looking at the educator. The educator clicks her pen on and off so Moana can see, saying 'Push this button to make it work'. The educator then carries on writing. Moana pushes the top of her pen on and off a few times and then draws lines on her paper.

(ii) Suggesting

Suggesting involves offering children ideas and advice while leaving the final decision up to the child. This technique is particularly useful when the educator knows that the child has had a range of literacy experiences to draw on that can be highlighted for the child through suggestion ('Perhaps you could write a letter, maybe phone her?').

7

> ### For example
>
> A group of young children is involved in dramatic play. One child announces he is going shopping. An educator working with children at a table nearby suggests he may need a shopping list. The child decides he does and uses a pad and pencil already beside the play stove and writes letters in lines on the page, while asking the other children whether they need certain grocery items.

(iii) Describing

The technique of describing can be useful for highlighting aspects of objects, processes, events or emotions. Describing can be helpful in supporting children's comprehension, such as describing elements in a story and introducing descriptive vocabulary. Describing is also useful for highlighting literacy forms and functions both within the centre and during trips into the wider community.

For example

An educator joins a small group of toddlers playing with shells in the water trough. As the toddlers pick up and explore the shells, the educator uses a range of words to describe their various shapes, textures and colours.

(iv) Recalling

This technique assists children to draw links between past and present literacy experiences, reinforcing their ideas and knowledge, and assisting children in expressing and exploring their literacy understandings. Recalling past events helps children to develop their understanding of story narratives by reflecting on what is significant when describing an event, the sequence of events, key players and their roles. This technique is useful when recording children's stories and documenting their work. It is also a useful technique to use when reading storybooks to assist children to focus on key elements of the plot (Didn't she have a piece of cake before?).

For example

Omar wants to write a story about a recent centre trip but is not sure how to start. The educator talks with Omar, helping him to recall the events that had occurred throughout the trip, discussing the order in which they occurred and other significant aspects of the trip. After this discussion, Omar is able to identify elements of the trip he wants to include in his story and dictates these for the educator to record.

(v) Questioning

This is a very powerful strategy that educators can use to extend children's thinking and understanding about literacy forms and functions. Open-ended questions in particular are useful when exploring the possible direction and implications of a storyline ('I wonder what she's going to do now?' 'Why do you think he was so angry?'). They are also useful in assisting children with exploring their own literacy knowledge and understandings ('What do you think the sign should say?', 'Whose name begins with a /p/ sound?') and they help develop children's narrative abilities. There are different levels of questions that can be used according to the children's level of understanding and the literacy activity they are involved in. Moving from literal questions ('where was Little Red Riding Hood going?'), to inferential questions ('Why was she afraid of the wolf?') to evaluative ('Do you think it was a good idea to go through the forest alone?') helps children to develop higher-order thinking. This sort of challenge has been identified as one of the most critical factors in determining children's literacy achievements (Stahl *et al.*, 1996).

(vi) Using humour

Finally, humour is a useful technique that educators can draw on to encourage children to play with, notice, reflect on and enjoy aspects of literacy. Playing with words (silly, billy, willy, nilly) can be great fun while also developing phonemic awareness. Humour can also support comprehension in an enjoyable and non-threatening way by highlighting elements of stories and literacy play that do and don't fit ('He put on his banana? his house? his coat?').

For example

When reading a favourite book to two toddlers, an educator mistakenly calls the main character 'Scary Maclary'. The educator puts down the book, looks at the children and exclaims 'It's not *Scary* Maclary! Is it *Deary* Maclary?' The children smile and respond 'No!' loudly. The educator continues 'Is it *Weary* Maclary?' 'No!' 'Is it *Hairy* Maclary?' 'Yes!' The educator replies 'Oh yes, that sounds right' and continues with the story.

Sharing a sound story

Concluding comments

- Educators and children can capitalise on the informal literacy opportunities generated by a literacy-enriched early childhood environment.

- Dramatic play supports children's literacy learning by providing a flexible forum through which children can engage with literacy at their own level and in ways that are meaningful to them.

- Educators can draw on a broad range of teaching strategies that create and build on informal literacy opportunities and acknowledge children's literacy experiences and understandings.

- There is also a range of specific teaching techniques that educators can draw on to support and extend children's informal literacy learning and development, particularly through the negotiation of shared meanings.

Section Three

Special Topics in Literacy

Chapter 8

Highlighting Approaches to Book Reading

Book reading is a valuable and common literacy activity in early childhood centres which provides children with the opportunity not only to enjoy books but to develop their knowledge and understanding about books and reading. Book reading can involve adults reading to larger groups in a more structured and formal way, adults spontaneously reading to an individual child or a small group of children in a less formal way, or children freely choosing books and reading them to themselves and their friends. These forms of book reading can occur at any age, and the earlier the better.

It is important to recognise that children from different cultural backgrounds will have different understandings of the concept of 'story', the way books are read or shared, and the purposes for reading books (Jones Diaz & Harvey, 2002). For example, in some families there may be few books but a rich oral tradition of storytelling through dance and music, or through the practice of 'oral literature' and 'oral history', and these storytelling practices may be particularly important in some Indigenous families (Hanlen, 2002). The recognition of the multiplicity of literacy practices that children bring to the centre and the incorporation and extension of these practices is central to an effective approach to book reading.

Books are an excellent way of acknowledging and accessing the culture of the community. As Anstey and Bull (1996) suggest, 'Texts in children's literature need to be seen not only as sites where imagination and response come into play, but also as places where culture is produced or reproduced' (pp.201–2). In particular, culture is reproduced in books as either non-fiction or fiction. Non-fiction books offer children the opportunity to access information about the world, to find out how to make or do something, and to support literacy learning, such as alphabet books and number books. Fiction books, which include poetry books, rhyming books and picture books, invite 'readers to re-create and examine familiar and unfamiliar worlds and experiences and offer[s] readers the opportunity to know themselves, others and the world more fully' (Browne, 2001, p.64). This chapter examines the importance of book reading and the strategies and techniques by which educators can support co-constructed and interactive fiction and non-fiction book reading.

Learning about book conventions

The importance of book reading

The benefits of both more formal (large group) and informal (small group and individual) book reading are many and it is not surprising that book reading forms the backbone of most centre literacy practices. Book reading has been found to be important for the learning of book conventions, to help children learn more about aspects of book language, to assist in developing children's comprehension, to support prerequisite decoding skills, and for motivational and attitudinal reasons.

Research shows that book reading in the earliest years (Bus, Van Ijzendoorn & Pellegrini, 1995; Wells, 1985), in addition to rhymes and language play (Bryant & Bradley, 1985), has the potential to bring about improved language and literacy outcomes for children. In addition, research indicates that exposure to rich vocabulary and stimulating discussion in the years before formal school predicts literacy development in the first year of school and literacy achievement in fourth and seventh grade (Dickinson & Tabors, 2002). Further, while a rich vocabulary may be achieved through discussion of everyday experiences, exposure to the rich and complex language of books may promote the more complex language associated with school (Frijters, Baron & Brunello, 2000). Being able to use more grammatically complex sentences enables children to express a greater number of meanings and access specific types of language, such as the language of science and mathematics.

A range of extension activities can emerge out of book-reading events. Book reading provides an excellent opportunity to acknowledge and support children's home languages, inviting community elders/leaders, parents/carers and other family members (where possible) to share stories or read to children in home languages. Tapes, dual text books and children's own stories are also very important resources for supporting community languages. In addition, stories that are culturally appropriate, highly visual, repetitive, or have a chorus, enable children who are learning English as an additional language to make meaning from the story and to tune in to the sounds of English without any pressure to respond.

(i) Motivation and attitudes

Book reading with children plays an important role in the development of children's motivation and attitudes towards becoming readers. As Fields and Spangler (2000) explain, 'when we read stories to young children, we introduce them to the magic of books and awaken their desire to read for themselves' (p.82). Strengthening this desire through book reading is an important way of empowering children so that they can gain full benefit from the experiences of the centre and the literate community. In addition, learning to read is not always an easy process and with positive attitudes to literacy, children are better able, in formal schooling, to overcome any difficulties that may arise during the process of learning to read.

Informal book reading, in particular, with individuals or small groups of children, in English and home and community languages, provides rich opportunities for close interaction between adult and child. Where such reading experiences include familiarity and routine, children come to see reading as a warm, friendly, safe and pleasurable activity (Shuker, 2001). As Barton (1999) notes, it is through such book-reading opportunities that 'children can learn attitudes and values associated with reading' (p.147) and about literacy and literature in general.

In summary, educators who give attention to book reading and provide a range of regular and positive book-reading experiences send strong messages to children that reading is valued and is an important, worthwhile and enjoyable activity.

(ii) Book conventions

Book reading provides ideal opportunities for children to develop their understandings and concepts about how books work and the conventions of fiction and non-fiction books. As Fields and Spangler (2000) suggest, 'being read to regularly is the best way for children to become familiar with the conventions of written language' (p.81). However, just being read to does not always ensure that children learn the necessary book knowledge and conventions and adults also need to actively highlight and scaffold these aspects (as we discuss later in this chapter).

Book conventions include

❖ books have covers and pages

❖ books are read from left to right (in alphabetic scripts)

❖ there are authors, illustrators, pictures and words

❖ books are handled and looked after in particular ways

❖ books and print communicate meaning

❖ sharing books involves some specific shared routines

❖ there are different types of books – narrative, factual, rhyming, joke, etc.

(iii) Book language

The language of books has some interesting and unique characteristics that children need to learn about, such as more complex grammatical structures, specialised forms of narrative and text constancy. These specific aspects of book language can be learned through book reading.

Book language includes a wider range of *grammatical structures* and so is different to the language of everyday speech (Barton, 1999). As Adams and Jackson (2002) point out, book language includes a wide range and variety of syntax patterns and these more complex grammatical forms 'provide the child with mental models of language which they can then draw upon when they read texts for themselves' (p.192).

The language used in fictional books also uses a specialised form of *narrative*, and skilled narrative book reading can help children to 'deconstruct' these narratives. As Adams and Jackson (2002, p.193) explain:

> Narratives, according to Whitehead (1999), are the organising systems underpinning stories, the 'backbone' structure which forms a particular and carefully chosen selection of events and happenings (real or imaginary). Children's literature involves the core components of narrative – time (the sequencing of events, whether in the past, present or imaginary future) and values (the choice of what to include and exclude). Whitehead (1999) argues that an understanding of narrative is 'the most crucial and basic of all language activities'. (p.28)

When children retell stories these forms of book language and narrative structures are developed. In addition, the language of written text in books also doesn't change (*book constancy*). As Adams and Jackson (2002) point out, children can learn about this aspect of book language from hearing favourite texts being read and re-read. 'When the parent [or educator] misreads and the child says, "That's not how it goes," it is clear that the child has developed an expectation that print will hold the meaning constant from one reading to the next. These understandings can develop in a pre-reading stage, before the child has any knowledge of the alphabet letters and how they code meaning' (p.191). Interestingly, Nicholson (2000) notes that when asked to retell a familiar story by referring to the illustrations, a child with an understanding of book constancy will attempt to repeat the actual part of the story that relates to the illustrations, whereas a child who does not have this understanding is likely to simply describe what she sees. Reading a non-fiction text involves different skills and understanding about how the information is presented (captions, photographs, diagrams, lists etc), organised (non-narrative, non-linear) and accessed (contents, index); in addition some recent non-fiction texts have supporting CD ROMs and links to Web pages.

(iv) Decoding skills

Book reading provides many opportunities for educators to assist children in developing a range of prerequisite language areas important for decoding text, such as phonemic awareness and letter–sound knowledge. While these aspects are discussed in considerable depth in the next chapter, Adams and Jackson (2002) suggest that skilled book reading can help children 'gain familiarity with the shapes of the alphabet letters; learn about letters and their names; they can learn that there is a phonemic relationship between letters and particular sounds; they can develop various print-related concepts such as "letters", "words", punctuation marks, and directionality' (p.192).

(v) Comprehension

Book reading also provides a range of opportunities to develop aspects that support the development of children's comprehension (understanding), such as discussion and questioning techniques, contextualising or decontextualising the book language and extending vocabulary understandings.

Book reading provides educators with ample opportunities to *discuss* with children such areas of a book as storylines, characters and illustrations to help children understand more deeply the nature of a book's content, and through conversations to help children develop a sense of story. Non-fiction books give educators the opportunity to discover children's interests and knowledge and help children become familiar with new vocabulary, ideas and information. Information can be cross-checked and extended using other texts and the information can be used for a variety of purposes. A range of strategies and techniques have been covered in depth in the previous chapter to help educators build on these informal literacy opportunities, and these apply equally well to formal and informal book reading. Children can be supported to develop their own strategies and techniques for examining books, including developing their questioning skills in order to make meaning from books and work out the meanings of words. Additionally, children can be encouraged to retell stories that develop their narrative abilities and comprehension.

8

Book reading also provides opportunities to help children to either contextualise or decontextualise the language of books. Both areas have been found to be important for developing children's comprehension and both areas are commonly required in formal schooling. *Contextualised* language is where language is related to a specific context. For example, Adams and Jackson (2002) argue that 'book reading is one of the first contexts where it is explicitly demonstrated to children that language can be used as a tool to transmit, explain, use and exploit knowledge regarding specific contexts in real life' (p.193). In other words, educators can help children to make explicit links between aspects that occur in a book and similar aspects in the real world. This process develops children's comprehension through building on children's contextual knowledge which is of relevance to their day-to-day lives.

Conversely, a range of book reading experiences can encourage children to do the opposite, to *decontextualise* language (Wells, 1986). That is, as Adams and Jackson (2002) explain, where children 'create these scenes, characters and events in their imagination, a cognitive achievement, as they make meaning from the words they hear. The places, people or objects have no context beyond the written or spoken words' (p.192). Decontextualised language is commonly used in formal schooling settings and

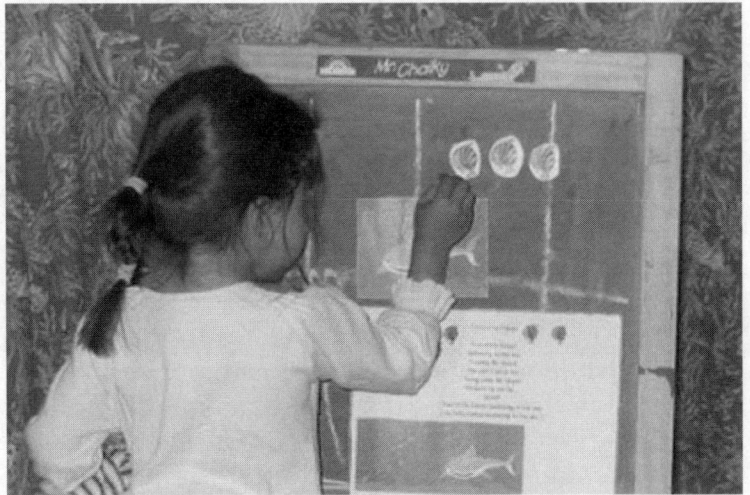

Re-creating a story

children are often asked to take broad ideas, concepts and understandings and apply these to alternative contexts and situations, which is a fundamental higher-level thinking skill.

The language of books also tends to be richer and more diverse than that used in everyday speech. In particular, the breadth of *vocabulary* in books read to children helps to increase children's vocabulary and their ability to understand and use these new words appropriately in context. However, as Adams and Jackson (2002) note, depending on the nature of the book-reading experiences, there are differences in the rate of children's vocabulary development. These authors write that 'both Senechal (1995), and Dickinson and Smith (1994) in research on four-year-olds found that children who were *actively* involved in responding to the story made greater gains in vocabulary knowledge' (p.192).

Strategies to support co-constructed and interactive book reading

We have argued that book reading should be an important part of the centre program. However, the literature in the area is now making a clear distinction between just engaging in book reading and providing sound and effective book-reading experiences for children. As Tizard (1993) notes, 'reading aloud *on its own*, especially to groups, does not ensure that children will make a connection between meaning and print, or have any understanding of written language' (p.82; emphasis added).

So what are the implications of this for educators? In order for book reading to be more meaningful, useful and effective for children's language and literacy learning the literature suggests that book reading should become a co-constructed, regular and interactive part of centre life. Frequent book-reading experiences, then, provide opportunities for the 'co-construction' of aspects relating to literacy learning. The broader area of co-construction, and its theoretical underpinnings, is covered earlier in this book. In short, instead of just reading to children, educators can ensure that meanings, learning directions and approaches are negotiated and mediated between the adult and the children. As Barton

(1999) puts it in relation to storybook reading, 'this is not purely a story being told by one person to another; rather, we have a story around a story, a narrative which is being *co-constructed* by the participants' (p.144). These narratives have their precursors in the early pre-verbal and verbal conversations adults have with infants and toddlers.

As Nicholson (2000) concludes, reading to children is important but on its own is not sufficient to help children learn about reading. Instead, adults need to *actively* work with children to construct meaning – meaning about the story, and meaning about other aspects of literacy, such as alphabet knowledge and book conventions. Inherent in this co-construction process is ensuring that book reading is *interactive*. Without interaction and discussion, shared meanings cannot be constructed.

A large number of strategies for developing co-constructed and interactive book reading have been suggested in the literature (e.g., see Barton, 1999; Dunn, Beach & Kontos, 2000; McGee & Richgels, 1996; Nicholson, 2000; Reynolds, 1998; Whitehead, 1999). Here we will consider six key strategies that apply to informal book-reading opportunities (as well as other formal and informal interactions). These strategies are designed to complement, and should be read in conjunction with, the broader strategies to support the informal literacy learning considered in the previous chapter.

(i) Start with what the child knows

This means starting with children's current literacy understandings, theories, meanings, experiences and practices and building on these; and adjusting the reading style to match the child's ability to participate.

> **For example**
>
> The educator is aware that Ethan is very interested in dinosaurs but finds it difficult to sit still for long. She selects a book about dinosaurs that provides a lot of opportunity for Ethan to join in with dinosaur noises and movements as she reads.
>
> To encourage Ethan to focus on elements of the story the educator asks him questions about the kind of noises and movements each dinosaur would make, based on the different characteristics of the dinosaurs in the book.

(ii) Actively encourage discussion

This can be done by asking children to elaborate on and clarify their responses; providing positive feedback to children's comments and questions; asking children to engage in some higher-order thinking such as analysing and predicting; and putting the children's questions and queries above the need to finish the book.

> **For example**
>
> During the reading of a story about a child who is frightened by sounds at night, the educator asks the children if they are sometimes frightened by night-time noises. One child replies that he is frightened by scary noises. The educator encourages the child to elaborate by asking what kinds of noises are scary, why they are scary, what makes these scary noises and why they are more scary at night.

(iii) Make links to the child's own life experiences

Relating the events, characters and places of the story to children's own lives where possible is a powerful way of engaging children with the story, and bringing the child into the narrative.

> ## For example
>
> During the reading of a story about a child and her pet cat, the educator stops to ask the children if they have pets, what kind of pets they have, their names and so on. The educator then pauses regularly while reading to ask children to reflect on similar experiences with their pets.

(iv) Challenge assumptions within texts

Helping children to identify and question the way the world is represented in texts is an important aspect of early literacy learning. Often referred to as critical literacy, this is not about being 'politically correct' or taking away the joy of reading. First, it is about giving children the opportunity to ask how they, their family and their culture are being represented in text (e.g., what are the girls/boys doing?). Second, questions about the way texts are constructed and how texts represent different groups of people give children the opportunity to explore and contest different views of the world (e.g., do all children live with a mum and a dad?). O'Brien and Comber (2000, p.156) suggest the following questions as a means of helping even young children to begin to look at texts critically:

    a)   Questions about texts

        What kind of a text(s) is this?

        How can we describe it?

        Where else have you seen texts like this?

        What do these kinds of texts usually do?

        Who would produce (write/draw) a text like this?

        Who do they produce (write/draw) it for?

        For what kind(s) of readers (viewers/listeners) is this text intended?

    b)   Questions about how texts represent groups of people

        How does the text portray gender, age, culture etc? What words are used?

        What are the girls like in these texts? What are the boys like?

        What do the texts show boys and girls doing and saying?

        What do the texts show old people/young people doing and saying?

        What does the writer think about these people?

        Why might the writer have written about these people in this way?

        How else could it have been written?

        What else could the writer have the people say?

> ## For example
>
> When reading a story in which a family's holiday has to be cancelled because the car breaks down, the teacher (who is aware that the children she is reading to are from affluent backgrounds) talks with the children about why this family couldn't just get the car fixed or use another car. This leads to a discussion with the children about differing levels of family income and how this can impact on their own and others' lives.

(v) Monitor and modify interactions

Educators need to constantly monitor and modify their book reading to take into account children's interests and understandings, such as:

❖ changing the pace of reading such as speeding up to maintain interest or slowing down to emphasise an important aspect of the plot

❖ explaining new vocabulary and concepts (non-fiction)

❖ relating the captions, texts to the illustrations/diagrams (non-fiction)

❖ providing more elaboration to help flesh out the children's understanding

❖ moving the discussion on so the plot is not lost

❖ stopping the story to move straight to an extension activity.

An example using *Trug and Leaf*

Marie Clay (1998, pp.178–9) highlights the importance of adapting storybook reading to meet the needs of individual children. In this transcript she annotates how the educator takes particular care with the introduction to the story *Trug and Leaf* (by Phillis Flowerdew), as it was thought too difficult for the child to understand unscaffolded.

Setting the topic, title and characters

Teacher: I've got another book about Trug for you. It's about Trug and Leaf this time, and poor Leaf is ill.

Probing to find out what the child knows

Teacher: Do you know what it means when you are ill?
Child: (No response.)
Teacher: It means you are sick, and Trug's going to try to look after her. Look, she's in bed.

Asking the child to work with new knowledge

Teacher: Trug's going to get some water for her. What do you think water might start with?
Child: W.
Teacher: I bet you can show what word says *water*.

Accepting partially correct responses

Teacher: That word does start with w. It says *will*.

Tightening the criteria of acceptability

Teacher: Can you find another?
Child: (Locates 'water')
Teacher: That's got w, hasn't it? Right, he's going to get some water.

Prompting constructive activity (to understand the plot)

Teacher: He's trying to carry it in his hands. Is that working? It drips on the mud, doesn't it? That's not much good. Look, it's still dripping! Has he got any water left? I wonder how he is going to get the water. What does he see? What can he use?
Child: The egg.
Teacher: Where has the baby bird come from?
Child: The egg.
Teacher: He's come out of the egg, hasn't he? What's Trug going to do with the egg?
Child: Put water in it?

Providing a model (of reflecting on the story)

Teacher: He had a good idea, didn't he? And he can take the water to Leaf. She might get better now she's got a drink of water, mightn't she? Do you think so? Because she's ill, isn't she?

8

(vi) Model reading strategy use

Educators often need to explicitly model or voice aloud reflective strategies which the children may need for reading. Such skills and strategies give the children the cognitive tools they can use themselves at a later point.

For example

❖ 'Where do we start?'

❖ 'What do you think is going to happen next?'

❖ 'Why are they doing that?'

❖ 'Turn the pages one at a time.'

(vii) Use the 'hand-over' principle

Wherever possible, it is helpful to use the 'hand-over' principle. This involves encouraging children to take an increasingly more active part in the book reading during the session and over time. This might involve such aspects as letting the children find the books, turn the pages, identify key characters, read the story themselves, asking children to discuss the illustrations, and generally letting children take over wherever possible. This 'hand-over' principle is a form of scaffolding discussed in the previous chapter.

An example of the hand-over principle in action

Educator reads the book to Anna. Anna doesn't make any verbal or non-verbal communication during the story. At the end of the book:

Anna says: 'I will read to you ta'.

Anna holds the book and turns the first page. 'See, egg on leaf and moon'.

Educator: 'What's on the next page?'

Anna turns the page. 'Very hungry caterpillar – he eats lots', turning the pages quickly.

Anna: 'Leaf, strawberry …' naming all the foods and pointing to each item.

Anna: 'Caterpillar is fat, makes a shell'. She slowly turns the page: 'Ah, turns into a beautiful butterfly'.

The educator congratulates Anna and thanks her for a lovely story. Anna smiles and returns the book to the shelf.

Techniques to support co-constructed and interactive book reading

There is also a range of techniques that specifically support and extend co-constructed and interactive book reading and help children to make the most of these literacy opportunities. Effective book reading needs to be well managed and organised by the educator, and the children should be meaningfully engaged in the book reading. However, in order for book reading to be both co-constructed and interactive it is valuable for children to be aware of some important book-related foundations, such as book conventions, aspects of book language and some prerequisites of decoding.

This creates an interactive spiralling learning process in the broader sense around the book-reading experiences. When educators integrate important book-related foundations into their book reading, children learn a number of basic literacy 'tools' which educators can further capitalise on. In effect, the more children know about these book-related foundations, the easier it is for the educator to build on this information and support children's literacy learning with the range of broader strategies mentioned previously. In addition, as children's literacy knowledge increases, the more they will regularly want, and be able to engage in informed co-constructed and interactive literacy experiences – whether with the educator in formal and informal settings, or on their own or in peer groups. Through this process educators increasingly empower children to self-direct and self-motivate their own, and others', literacy learning. These techniques are designed to complement, and should be read in conjunction with, the broader techniques to support informal literacy learning considered in the previous chapter.

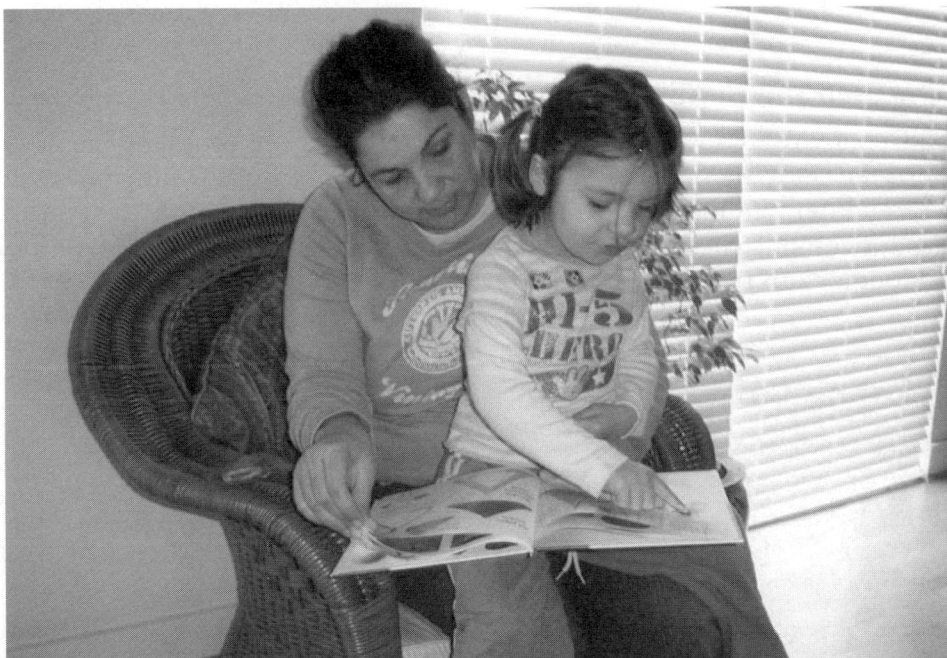

Asking questions about the story

8

(i) Managing book reading

Both formal and informal book reading need to be well managed. This does not mean that the educator dictates or dominates the experience, but rather, that the educator is organised and flexible in their approach to the reading process. The children, also, should understand the sorts of boundaries and social rules that apply for all children involved in the book reading. As McGee and Richgels (1996) highlight, sharing books also involves some specific shared routines for successful book reading to occur.

Techniques for managing book reading

❖ Give clear instructions to the children about how you would like them to act during the book reading, including how discussion and questioning should occur (more important for larger groups).

❖ Encourage and be enthusiastic when approached to read to children or when children wish to read.

❖ Ensure that the book is at an appropriate level for the children involved.

❖ Ensure that all the children are comfortable.

❖ Hold the book steadily and so all children can see it.

❖ Use eye contact to include all children in the group and regularly scan the children to see that they are still interested.

❖ Speak clearly and confidently.

❖ Vary the tempo (speed up, slow down, pause) to reflect the action in the story.

❖ Keep the listening period within the children's attention span.

❖ Model the ways in which books should be handled and book reading carried out.

❖ Don't worry about stopping the book reading at any time or changing your approach if the children are not interested.

❖ Adjust your managing strategies in response to the children's feedback.

(ii) Engaging children in book reading

Keeping children involved during book reading is not usually a problem, particularly if the children chose the book themselves. However, it is useful to use a range of techniques to help the children interact more meaningfully with the educator and the text and to support opportunities for co-construction. These sorts of conversations are important because they help infants, toddlers and young children develop a sense of story.

Techniques for engaging children in book reading

❖ Ask frequent questions – questions that encourage children to participate generally need to be open-ended questions (e.g., What's happening now? What is a dump truck used for?) rather than closed (e.g., What's that? Can you see the dog?). Questioning can encourage young children's involvement as long as the adult knows the child well enough to ask questions that the child is capable of answering.

❖ Invite predictions and inferences – encouraging children to discuss photographs/illustrations in non-fiction texts or predict events or infer motives, actions and relationships in fictional texts can be a useful source of discussion.

❖ Respond warmly to children's ideas and comments.

❖ Build on the children's ideas and answers to extend their learning.

❖ Respect the viewpoints and knowledge of the children.

❖ Personalise the story or information – relate events and ideas to the child's experiences.

❖ Read dramatically – using facial expressions and gestures can help with children's involvement in the story, and also can provide additional clues as to the story's meaning.

❖ Recap – discuss aspects of books after they have been read and during the reading.

❖ Encourage extension opportunities based on the book reading.

(iii) Teaching book conventions

There is an important range of book conventions that educators can help children to learn. Although these are more technical in nature than other aspects of books and literacy they provide children with the expert 'jargon' or terminology that is central to any co-construction of book reading. It is difficult for an educator to provide an interactive book-reading experience without the children having some knowledge of the key terms relating to books themselves. Give time to reading and discussing these as important information, for example, by looking to find other books by the same author/illustrator, talking about how long ago the book was written, or what 'copyright' means.

Examples of important book conventions

The following terms and basic understandings should be frequently used and seamlessly integrated during book readings:

❖ Books have covers, titles, authors, illustrators and publishers.

❖ Books comprise blocks of text, words, letters and page numbers.

❖ Words on a page are read from left to right, and top to bottom (alphabetic scripts).

❖ The story starts at the front of the book and ends at the back.

❖ Information in non-fiction texts is not necessarily linear.

❖ The illustrations are designed to enhance the meaning of the story or information.

❖ Stories/information have punctuation marks (e.g., exclamation marks, full stops, commas, question marks, speech marks etc).

❖ There is a wide range of specialist language associated with reading and talking about books (e.g., 'word', 'letter', 'page', 'contents', 'index', 'author' etc).

(Adapted from: Adams & Jackson, 2002, p.187)

(iv) Highlighting book language

It is important for children to learn about book language in order to engage more meaningfully in co-constructed and interactive book reading. For example, educators can develop strong and interesting lines of discussion and questioning around such areas as plots, characters, vocabulary and so on, but these conversations will be more effective if children are first more fully aware of the nature of this book language. Children can learn about book language when educators build these sorts of discussions into their book-reading experiences. This is particularly important in relation to non-fiction texts, in order to access information children need to be able to ask questions about where to find the information, which part of the text relates to their investigation, what the information means and how they can use it.

8

Techniques for highlighting book language

In fiction texts:

❖ Pay attention to narrative elements, such as 'characters, actions, relationships between events and character motivation' (McGee & Richgels, 1996, p.54).

❖ Focus attention on structural elements – to help children gain a sense of story structure they need to know about beginnings and endings, storylines and plot organisation.

❖ Reflect on interesting or difficult words – these can be discussion pointers and aid the learning of vocabulary.

- ❖ Provide labels for objects and characters in the stories.
- ❖ Highlight that the story comes from the text and the illustrations also provide support.
- ❖ Point out that the text and illustrations of the book remain constant from one reading to the next.

In non-fiction texts:
- ❖ Highlight the way in which the book is structured to help find information such as contents page, index, page numbers, headings, captions.
- ❖ Point to the relationship between page title, text, illustrations, diagrams.
- ❖ Read short segments of information and discuss.
- ❖ Explain new vocabulary and concepts.
- ❖ Where possible create experiences that relate to the information such as growing vegetables, looking after pets.

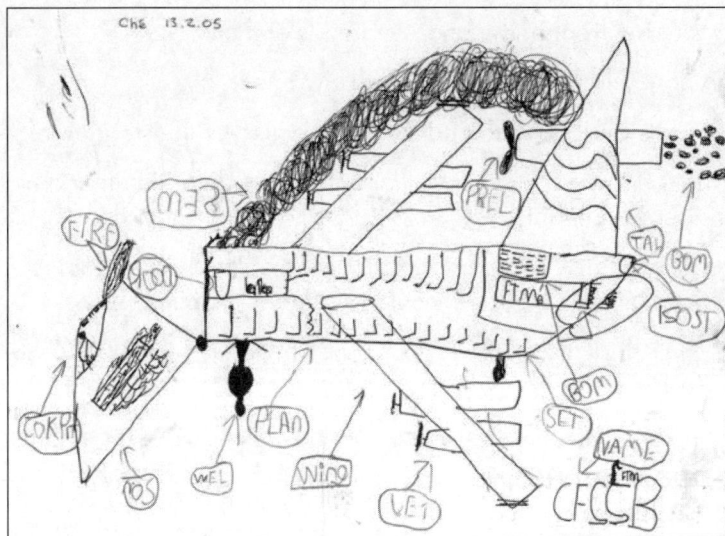

Knowledge of non-fiction texts transfers to drawing and writing

(v) Facilitating the prerequisites of decoding

Book reading provides a range of opportunities to help children learn the prerequisites of decoding text in appropriate ways and in authentic situations. The area of phonemic awareness, letter–sound relationships and decoding in general is covered in depth in the next chapter. However, informal and more formal book reading contexts allow the educator to use a range of techniques to introduce aspects related to decoding in co-constructed and interactive ways.

Techniques for facilitating important decoding prerequisites

- ❖ Increasing alphabet knowledge – using the names of letters frequently during reading.
- ❖ Raising phonemic awareness – pointing out and playing with syllables, rhymes and rhyming, onset/initial sounds and rimes.
- ❖ Highlighting and discussing print – using the appropriate print labels ('word', 'letter'), pointing out one-to-one relationships and demonstrating the directionality of print (left to right).

❖ Combining alphabet letters and their sounds – naming letters, highlighting their shapes and modelling the sounds of the letters.

❖ Pointing to differences between written scripts with which children are familiar (e.g., logographic scripts and alphabetic scripts).

(vi) Selecting styles of reading aloud

McNaughton (2002) and Phillips, McNaughton and MacDonald (2001) identify three storybook-reading techniques – the 'item-learning' style, the 'performance' style and the 'narrative' style. Educators can draw upon each style to best meet the needs of their children, the particular context, the purposes of the activity, the narrative style of the book and the age of the child. Each style has its relative strengths and as McNaughton (2002) points out 'These styles are not necessarily used exclusively – even during one session with the same book, families [educators] can switch with "textual dexterity" between styles to meet different purposes' (p.169).

The *item-learning* style involves focusing on specific items in the book such as colours, letters or things and this interaction style tends to take a question-and-answer format.

Example of the item-learning style

Teacher: What's on there?
Child: It's a fish.

(Phillips, McNaughton & MacDonald, 2001, p.58)

This style is useful as a way of developing vocabulary, engaging children early on in the storybook-reading session, showing how illustrations support the text; it often suits infant picture books. It is a style that tends to involve closed questions and consequently needs to be used thoughtfully, taking children's response to the style into account. This style forms part of the storybook reader's pedagogical repertoire but exclusively using this technique risks limiting children's interactions with the text and the educator.

The *performance* style involves 'modelling and imitation, through which the child is enabled to recite parts or even all of the text' (McNaughton, 2002, p.169). This interaction style tends to involve the reader leaving out parts of the text that children are able to fill in themselves (often from memory of previous reading or because of the repetitive style of the text).

Example of the performance style

Teacher: Likes to hide in …
Child: Boxes.
Teacher: The cat from France likes to sing and …
Child: Dance.
Teacher: But my cat …
Child: Hides in boxes.

(Phillips, McNaughton & MacDonald, 2001, p.59)

This style is used as a way of actively engaging children by participating in the book reading. It emphasises the repetitive, predictable and generative features of the text and helps children develop phonological awareness particularly through the emphasis on rhyming. It is a style that is fun and is particularly suited to those story and poetry books

8

that have repeated phrases and clear rhymes. Educators can support children to get the idea that they can add the missing words and 'read' for success and can be used as part of the 'hand-over' technique discussed earlier in this chapter. The performance style can quickly provide opportunities for children to demonstrate their expertise at identifying and playing with rhyming words and phrases.

The third technique is the *narrative* style, which involves focusing on the text meaning. 'The interactions are like conversations during which the reader provides scaffolding that guides the child into understanding and even debating text meanings' (McNaughton, 2002, p.169). This interaction style tends to involve the reader and the child engaging in conversations where the meanings and structures of the text are co-constructed.

Example of the narrative style

Teacher: Oh what has happened there (referring to the illustration)?
Child: They snapped the …
Teacher: Snapped the what?
Child: Stick, the stick.
Teacher: Oh, so what happens when it snaps the stick?
Child: Um.
Teacher: Has he got no stick left?
Child: Yep.
Teacher: Oh, that's good.

(Phillips, McNaughton & MacDonald, 2001, p.59)

This style is used as a way of engaging children in exploring what is happening in the story. It provides opportunities for highlighting and developing reciprocal conversations around a range of aspects relating to narrative structures, such as plots, characters, events, and their relationship to the child's life. This technique can be used with children of all ages, with the educator adapting their level of input based on the child's language. However, regardless of age, this style provides the opportunity for educators to actively listen and respond to the child's voice. It is an empowering approach.

Concluding comments

* Book reading is a valuable and common literacy activity in early childhood centres that provides children with the opportunity to not only enjoy books but to develop their knowledge and understanding about books and reading.

* Book reading has been found to be important for motivational and attitudinal reasons, for the learning of book conventions, to help children learn more about aspects of book language, to support prerequisite decoding skills and to assist in developing children's comprehension.

* Educators can draw on a broad range of teaching strategies to support co-constructed, regular and interactive book reading experiences and develop children's knowledge and understanding about books.

* There is a range of specific techniques that support and extend co-constructed and interactive book reading and help children to become aware of some important book-related foundations, such as book conventions, aspects of book language and some prerequisites of decoding.

Chapter 9

Highlighting Phonemic Awareness and Letter–Sound Relationships

Phonemic awareness and letter–sound knowledge are key areas that underpin beginning reading (also see the learning debate in Chapter 4). As Rohl (2000) argues, the most accurate predictor of achievement in reading is an *explicit* awareness of the sound structure of language. Consequently it is worth highlighting these areas separately in order to emphasise their importance for children's early literacy and language development. (Both these areas also continue to develop as children learn to formally read and write at school.)

The development of phonemic awareness in children begins with infants being immersed in the sounds of their own language. As children develop in an environment full of rhythms and rhymes they will increasingly develop an intrinsic awareness of the sounds of language and of sounds within words. This awareness gradually moves from the implicit and unconscious to the explicit and conscious (Ericson & Julicbo, 1998; Layton, Deeny & Upton, 1997). Educators can support children to develop an awareness of language sounds by helping them to become *conscious* of the sounds of words and the sounds within words. This is done largely through playing with, openly talking about and exploring word sounds and rhymes (Burns, Snow & Griffin, 1999).

Children's explicit knowledge of phonemic awareness develops through a gradual process of refining their understandings about language; starting from the most basic distinctions between the broad range of general sounds in their lives, and moving towards distinguishing the ever finer gradations between the more discrete sounds of spoken language – syllables, rhyming, onset/initial sounds, alphabet letter–sounds and phonemes. This phonological sensitivity underpins children's ability to decode print (Tunmer & Chapman, 2003).

While these areas are discussed here in relation to the degree of refined segmentation of spoken words, they can all be introduced and used in a range of ways from infants to young children but given different emphases and depth depending on the interest and awareness demonstrated by each child. Although a toddler might not be able to write letters as well as a five-year-old, that doesn't mean toddlers should not be encouraged to engage in writing activities. This section will provide a brief sample of the possibilities for developing each of the important areas that provide a sound foundation of prerequisite reading skills.

It is important to note that this chapter focuses only on the development of children's awareness of the sounds of spoken language specifically relevant to literacy learning. Once children have these essential skills and knowledge in place, this gives them a firm foundation for learning to actually read (decode) written letters on a page (which often

9

occurs simultaneously during children's writing – see Chapter 10). While many older children in a centre will be able to read one or more letters, it is useful for these prerequisite language skills to also be well established.

Table 9.1: Developing phonemic awareness			
General sounds	environmental sounds (e.g., scissors cutting, body sounds) language sounds ('sssss' 'mmmmmm')		
Syllables	bis/cuit	tel/e/phone	pic/nic
Rhymes	the cat in the hat fuzzy wuzzy buzzy scary wary hairy		
Onset-rimes	onset – rime c – at h – at s – at	onset – rime d – og fr – og l – og	
Alphabet letter–sounds	letter name b s t	letter sound 'b' 's' 't'	
Phonemes	c–a–p	s–o–k	b–r–u–sh

(Adapted from Rohl, 2000, p.69)

General sounds

Focused listening activities support children's abilities to hear, focus on and detect the sounds in words. As discussed in the learning debate (see Chapter 4), phonemic awareness involves focusing on the sound rather than the meaning of words. Encouraging children to listen to what they *actually* hear and not what they *expect* to hear encourages active, attentive and analytical listening (Adams *et al.*, 1998). In addition, as Layton, Deeny and Upton (1997) explain, when children enjoy discovering sounds and similarities in sounds they will want to continue doing so, thus 'reinforcing the tendency to reflect on the intrinsic value of speech sounds themselves, aside from their role in conveying sense and meaning' (pp.1–2).

There are a number of different aspects of 'careful' or 'focused' listening that adults can incorporate into their interactions with children of all ages. Children gain benefit from focused listening to a wide range of general sounds as well as the sounds of spoken words. Three sets of examples of sound games that educators can easily engage in and co-construct are listed below.

Focus on, listen to, discover, explore and make a variety of different sounds, including

❖ environmental sounds such as listening to the rain on the roof, the sounds of cars, scissors cutting, identifying sounds on a tape

❖ body sounds such as walking feet, clapping hands, tapping fingers, clicking tongues

❖ vocalisations such as repeating an infant's vocalisations, making fun noises or nonsense words

❖ sounds created using a range of props such as running a stick along a fence, using musical instruments, the sound of pouring water

❖ generally 'developing children's sensitivity to the sounds of language – the same, the similar, the near-echoes and all sorts of variations ...' (Whitehead, 1999, p.65).

Focus on and listen to the different qualities of sounds, including

❖ loud and soft, long and short both in relation to general sounds and spoken words and phrases. For example, different kinds of claps, saying words in different ways (fast, slow, high, low, using a funny voice etc), and varying volume, tempo and pitch when reading or reciting stories and rhymes

❖ sounds and words that are the same, different and similar such as emphasising rhyming words, asking 'what sounds like this?'

❖ comparing names and repeating and highlighting words such as 'Tom and Tim', 'going, going, going, gone'

❖ reading or reciting poems, songs, nursery rhymes and rhyming stories using gestures, regular beats and pauses to emphasise rhyming words and the rhythm of the language

❖ emphasising and discussing long words and short words such as 'hippopotamus' and 'cat'.

(Adams, Foorman, Lundberg & Terri, 1998; Early Childhood Literacy Project, 1999; Layton, Deeny & Upton, 1997)

Provide experiences that highlight 'moving to' and 'feeling' sounds such as

❖ environmental sounds – moving like the wind, banging like a hammer

❖ music – moving in response to a range of musical styles and 'moods'

❖ the rhythms of language – gently bouncing an infant to the rhythm of a nursery rhyme, marching or clapping to a chant or poem

❖ touching and moving infants to the words of an infants rhyme – 'Two little hands go clap, clap, clap …'

❖ moving to the sounds and meanings of words such as marching, stomping, tip-toes, swooping.

Developing children's sensitivity to the nature and qualities of general sounds, as considered above, supports a broad range of learning areas within the early childhood curriculum, such as music, drama and movement. It is also a useful precursor and 'primer' for the sorts of phonological sensitivity that are relevant for developing children's phonemic awareness.

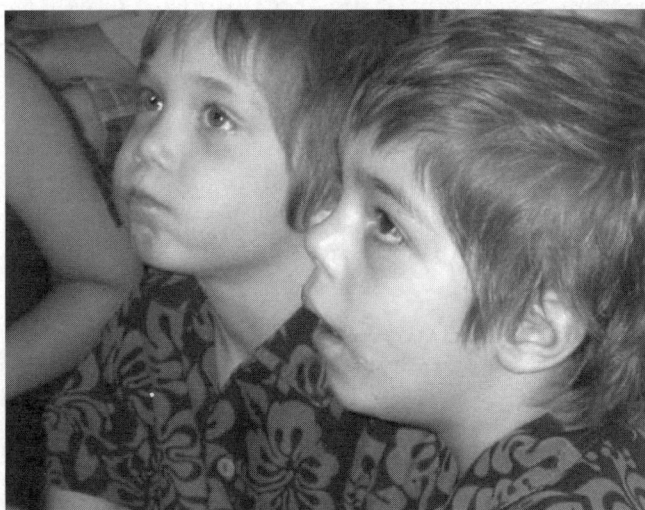

Listening to a sound story

9

Syllables

Developing an ability to detect syllables in spoken words provides children with a strong basis from which to develop finer levels of phonemic awareness. When children have developed a sensitivity to general sounds the scene is set for them to begin to 'recognise the beats or syllables in words' (Early Childhood Literacy Project, 1999, p.44), for example, bis/cuit, tel/e/phone and pic/nic. As Nicholson (1999) explains, syllables are generally emphasised through normal speech and so are often easy for children to identify. Highlighting and 'playing' with syllables can easily become a part of everyday centre life and can involve infants, toddlers and young children.

Syllables can be highlighted for children in a range of ways, including

❖ through movement – moving to the rhythm of the language of songs, poems and rhymes might involve gently rocking or bouncing an infant or stepping, jumping or stamping with toddlers and young children

❖ clapping and touching helps children to physically feel the rhythm in words (e.g., clapping names – Sam/, A/shad, A/nu/sha)

❖ adding percussive sounds to mark the 'beats' or syllables in words, using a range of resources such as hands, feet, voices, percussion instruments

❖ rhythmic chanting to and with children, encouraging them to hear and participate in emphasising the syllables in speech such as 'What did you eat for break/fast?'; 'Co/co/pops /and /yog/hurt, toast /and /jam', or fun chants such as 'Bippity, boppity, bumble bee, tell me what your name should be'

❖ once children are able to identify syllables, they can explore words by comparing and 'measuring' them based on the number of syllables, for example, 'Does Tim's name have one, two or three claps?'

(Adams et al., 1998; Early Childhood Literacy Project, 1999; Layton, Deeny & Upton, 1997)

Rhymes

Listening to and playing around with rhymes and rhyming words helps children to become aware of similar sounds within words. In particular, rhymes assist children to hear and become conscious of the end-sounds of words that are similar or the same, which is a vital precursor to their ability to divide words into onsets and rimes (discussed in the following section). As Layton, Deeny and Upton (1997) explain, 'children's knowledge of nursery rhymes when they are three and a half years old is a good predictor of their ability to make judgments on the onsets and rhymes of words before they start school' (p.11).

Fortunately there is a rich source of rhymes available to early childhood educators in the form of nursery rhymes, finger plays, poetry, songs and rhyming stories. These rhymes can be used with all ages and in any situation.

The 'rhyming' part of rhymes can be emphasised in a wide range of ways, including

❖ using vocal variations, music and percussion that coincide with the rhyming words

❖ using movement and touch, similar to the ways discussed above for highlighting the qualities of sound and the beats of syllables

❖ pausing before saying rhyming words to give emphasis to the rhyme and to provide children with an opportunity to fill in the rhyming word themselves.

Invented and nonsense rhymes encourage children to play with and explore rhyming words and sounds

❖ Many books, songs and poems provide examples of nonsense rhyming such as 'Wibbily wobbily woo, an elephant sat on you …', and 'Fuzzy wuzzy was a bear …'

❖ Adults can model playing with and inventing silly rhymes just for the fun of it. Rhymes can be made up about an everyday event, for example, 'Splish, splash, splosh. Have a nice wash', as well as a number of familiar rhymes like 'See ya later alligator', or 'Pass the cheese please Louise'.

Reading, singing, reciting, making up and talking about silly rhyming shows children that playing with and making up rhyming words is fun and is something that very young children can do as well (Early Childhood Literacy Project, 1999; Layton, Deeny & Upton, 1997).

For example

Ashleigh (four years old) is reading on her own in the book corner. She stops, looks closely at the picture, then says 'Scary wary hairy from Donaldson dairy' and laughs.

Rhymes can also be focused on in more depth with children who show a clear awareness of rhyme. Here, a focus on having fun with words is important and, in this way, can occur in everyday contexts whenever the opportunity presents itself.

Examples of more focused rhyming exploration include

❖ developing and adding to rhyming patterns such as 'Dutter, mutter, gutter, rutter. Shall we have some bread and butter?'

❖ identifying the odd one out such as 'bat, cat, hat' but not 'ham'

❖ rhyming riddles such as 'I am thinking of an animal that is green and jumps and rhymes with log'

❖ rhyming games such as 'I hear with my little ear something [a word] that rhymes with …'

❖ changing the rhyming words of well-known nursery rhymes to make nonsense to see if children notice the 'mistake' e.g., 'Twinkle, twinkle little car'; 'Humpty dumpty wall on a sat', 'One, two, shuckle my boo'

❖ creating new rhymes from traditional ones, e.g., 'Humpty Dumpty went for a walk, he met Razwana who wanted to talk'.

Rhyming games can become progressively more challenging, moving from rhyme judgement – 'does this rhyme?', to rhyme detection – 'which word rhymes?', and on to rhyme production – 'tell me a word that rhymes with …'.

(Adams *et al.*, 1998; Early Childhood Literacy Project, 1999; Layton, Deeny & Upton, 1997)

9

Onset/initial sounds and rime

A finer gradation in the development of phonemic awareness is the ability to detect onsets and rimes. Developing this level of phonemic awareness requires a child to break a heard syllable into its onset (the beginning consonant(s)) and rime (referring to the remainder of the syllable which includes the vowel and remaining consonants); for example, c/at, c/an, d/og, fr/og (Nicholson, 1999). The detection of rimes, or the end-sounds of words, supports later reading as they help children to quickly learn a group of words. For example, knowing the rime /-at/ assists children to easily read a list of words (or word family) that end with '-at', such as bat, cat, fat, hat, mat, pat, sat and so on. Supporting a general awareness of rhymes will strongly support rime detection, and has been covered in the section discussed above.

Developing an ability to detect onset means being able to detect the first *sound* of words. It is important to note that the focus here is on the beginning sounds (e.g., the fr in fr/og) as opposed to the first letter of words (e.g., 'f'). Children's ability to detect onset sounds provides strong support for letter and letter–sound learning. Here are some ideas for supporting children's ability to detect onset phonemes by highlighting, emphasising and isolating the initial sounds of words.

Educators can

❖ emphasise alliteration or onset sounds in songs, stories, rhymes, finger plays and poems such as 'Ssslippery, ssslimy sssnake', 'Peter Piper picked a peck of pickled peppers'

❖ highlight and play with alliteration that occurs in everyday speech by adapting familiar songs to emphasise onset phonemes such as 'Old Macdonald had some (chickens, cheese, chocolate) … with a /ch/ /ch/ here a /ch/ /ch/ there …' (Smith, 2000).

Children can

❖ judge onsets, such as 'all the children whose name starts with /mmm/ can wash their hands' or 'is there a /t/ in Tama?'

❖ detect onsets, such as 'guess whose name I am going to say, /p/ /p/ /p/ /p/ … Paul'; 'I hear with my little ear, something that starts with /mmmm/'; 'which one doesn't fit /p/ /p/ pig, /p/ /p/ pan, /p/ /p/ pot, /g/ /g/ goat'

❖ produce onsets, such as 'what sound does 'Riaz' begin with?'

(Layton, Deeny & Upton, 1997)

Alphabet letter–sounds

Learning the names of alphabet letters *and* their sounds is a complex process for children as it involves linking the individual sound of each letter to the name of that letter – this is often termed learning the 'alphabetic principle'. To assist in this process it is suggested that a letter name should generally not be given to children without its sound to ensure that children understand that alphabet letters have specific speech sounds attached (Adams *et al.*, 1998; Nicholson, 1999).

Being able to detect and identify onset sounds provides children with a strong foundation for developing their knowledge of alphabet letter–sounds. For example, once children are familiar with a range of onset phonemes, they can be introduced to the letter names that relate to those phonemes. And once children are aware of letter names and their sounds, recognising and decoding that written letter is only a very small step away.

Using Alphabet letter–sounds in the centre

❖ It is generally easier for children to learn the letters that have names similar to the way they sound (such as 'm', 's', 't', 'p'), making it sensible to introduce these first.

❖ Children's interest in their own name usually makes the initial letter of their own name (and other significant names) a useful starting place (Arrow, 2002).

❖ There is a wide range of alphabet-related resources available in most early childhood centres, including alphabet songs, rhymes and tapes.

❖ The development of letter–sound knowledge can be supported using similar ideas as discussed for the development of onset detection, by simply adding the letter, both by name (and in written form – lower case), alongside its sound ('whose name starts with /t/ /t/ 't'?).

❖ The traditional alphabet song gives children the names of each letter but does not give the letter sounds and so is a precursor to developing phonemic awareness. The 'Singing Alphabet' song (Love & Reilly, 1994 cited in Early Childhood Literacy Project, 1999) uses the letter sounds and names (e.g., 'Ugly Uncles, uuu'). Songs like this can be easily adapted to include children's names; for example, 'Shelley is shaking, sh, sh, sh', 'Tina is talking, t, t, t'.

It is a logical extension from here for children to be able to, and want to, start reading some of these letter names. As we discuss in the Conclusion, there is no reason to hold children back from this as long as such experiences are enjoyable and relevant for them.

For example

❖ Children might wish to read the letters in their own name, especially during name writing.

❖ There is an endless resource of letters contained in the environmental print of the early childhood centre.

❖ In the wider community, educators can highlight letters in print in everyday contexts, supporting children in 'discovering' letters in a range of words (e.g., /mmm/ like a McDonald's 'm'; /ssss/ for 's' in stop).

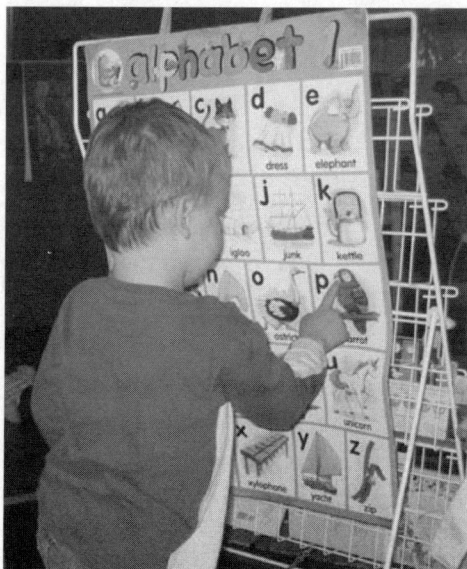

Matching the sound to the picture

9

Phonemes

A more detailed and difficult level of phonemic awareness is the ability to detect and to break words down into their individual phonemes (e.g., /c/ /a/ /p/, /s/ /o/ /k/, /b/ /r/ /u/ /sh/) – the smallest sounds of spoken language. When children have this level of phonemic awareness, they have a very strong foundation for learning to read. However, as Layton, Deeny and Upton (1997) explain, breaking words down into individual phonemes is very hard to do because it results in distortion. As most non-readers cannot divide words into single phonemes, this level of detection may well not be achieved during the early childhood years. However, it is useful for early childhood educators to be aware of this next step to highlight how the preceding steps of awareness, as discussed above, lay the foundation for this higher level of phonemic awareness, and to provide some direction to support children whose awareness has developed this far.

'Sounding-out' phonemes while writing for a real purpose

Che: I'm writing to Grandma. Thank – you – for – the – potato – race. I – loved – it. Can – we – have – another – one – at – my – next – birthday?

Mum: Great!

Che: Now tell me how to write the rest of 'potato – race'.

Cymi: Why you trying to write that? Cat race!

Che: I've scrubbed that out [potato race]. I'm going to write 'cat – race'. What does it start with? ... /c/ ... /c/ ... cat.

Mum: Yes the sound /c/.

Che: There. [points to the alphabet chart] My name starts with that.

Mum: The letter 'c' makes the sound /c/. /c/ for cat.

Che: Cat ... /t/ ... /t/ ... like that [writes 't']. But what's in the middle?

Mum: /c/ ... /a/ ... /t/. It's the sound /a/.

Che: /a/ ... /a/ ... 'a'... these! [points to 'a' on alphabet chart]

Mum: Yes, 'a'. That's right – well done!

Where children are interested in the individual phonemes of words

❖ Educators can support them to break simple words down into their component phonemes (d/o/g) and then putting them back together again ('dog').

❖ Gough (in Nicholson, 1999) suggests the idea of using a very slow-talking turtle puppet whose slow talk accentuates the different phonemes of words and, as children talk slowly back, supports them in blending phonemes.

❖ Children who are experimenting with writing letters and words can be encouraged to sound out the individual phonemes and letters and then blend these back into the whole word.

Concluding comments

- The development of phonemic awareness is an important foundation for the development of text decoding skills.

- There is a range of aspects and levels of phonemic awareness such as a general sensitivity to the sounds of language, the detection of syllables, rhymes, onset-rimes and phonemes.

- The development of phonemic awareness begins from birth and is developed and refined when educators and parents/carers engage children in highlighting, playing with and exploring the sounds of language and spoken words.

- Learning the names of alphabet letters *and* their sounds is a fundamental prerequisite of learning to read those letters (and words) and educators are encouraged to provide regular literacy opportunities where children can engage with a variety of alphabet letter–sounds.

- Learning to break words down into their individual phonemes and putting these phonemes back together into words is an advanced language skill that not all early childhood children will master. However, it is an important fundamental skill and helpful for early reading.

- Learning to read written letters and words is much easier for those children who have some understanding of phonemic awareness as well as knowledge of letter–sound relationships.

9

Chapter 10

Highlighting Children's Writing

Expert writing is not an easy, quickly learned or 'natural' activity. Turning their spoken language into written symbols is one of the hardest tasks a society asks of children. Aside from children 'having something to say', they also need to exhibit expert fine motor skills, to have a solid knowledge of written letter–sound relationships and the conventions of print and spelling, and to understand the broad range of functions, forms and purposes of print. All this as well as being able to read what they have written. We also assume that children have already acquired some fairly advanced semantic, syntactic and phonological understandings from their language acquisition.

It is for these reasons that formal schooling devotes considerable time to writing, both in its more technical and broader sense, and why families and early childhood education nurture the early development of children's understandings and skills in this area. This chapter seeks to highlight some key issues relating to writing in early childhood education, including the importance of children's writing, their writing and spelling expertise and the weaving of writing throughout the centre. We finish the chapter with a discussion of shared, modelled, guided and independent writing approaches.

The importance of children's writing

The benefits of supporting and fostering children's writing in early childhood centres are many. Children's writing, in whatever forms it takes, is empowering, motivating and strengthens children's feelings of self-worth. There are also strong links between writing and reading, which are reciprocally interactive. Children have the opportunity to learn about a range of book and print conventions during their writing, and critical phonemic awareness and letter–sound knowledge are also learned. Encouraging children to write at their own pace in early childhood education centres has many benefits for children's self-esteem, their ability to tell their stories, their literacy learning, and their active involvement with our literate society.

(i) Empowerment, motivation and self-identity

> Children want to write. They want to write the first day they attend school. This is no accident. Before they went to school they marked up walls, pavements, newspapers with crayons, chalk, pens or pencils … anything that makes a mark. The child's mark says, 'I am'.
>
> (Donald Graves cited in Morrow, 2001, p.279)

A child's writing reflects their own world, their narratives and voices, provides a means for self-expression, and is an integral part of their self-identity. Dyson (1989), for example, has written extensively on this aspect. She argues that writing becomes an integral part of the child's world and that print becomes a part of the 'scripts of children's everyday lives'. Their everyday lives, she suggests, involve a process of discovering how to negotiate among multiple worlds – 'the symbolic or imagined worlds brought to life through various media, the social world, and the wider experienced world' (p.25). This conception of writing reflects the sociocultural views we have considered in this book concerning the nature of 'the literate child'. In other words, 'the imaginative worlds children construct are *embedded* in their social and experienced worlds' (Dyson, 1989, p.10) and writing forms an intrinsic part of this process.

Cymion creates his own board game after playing this at home

10

In addition, children's writing can be viewed as a two-way interaction. Children are not only 'literacy apprentices' as they increasingly learn about the complexities of literacy, but their ability to write becomes a tool with which they can become active participants in a literate society. Children want their voices to be heard and writing becomes a crucial part of their imaginary worlds and narratives. Children become motivated to write because they can influence their world, and also because writing provides them with the cognitive tools to express their own views. Writing, fundamentally, is a potent social tool that empowers children, links them into their communities, and helps them develop strong reciprocal and responsive relationships with people, places and things.

It is important, then, that children retain a feeling of 'ownership, power and control over their own writing, and, eventually, their own lives' (Whitehead, 1997, p.139). Accepting writing based on the children's oral language is an important part of recognising and building on children's linguistic and cultural experiences, particularly in relation to languages other than English where initial 'marks on paper' may represent non-alphabetic scripts and Aboriginal English, in which the linguistic features (grammar, vocabulary, pronunciation) differ from Standard Australian English (DEET, no date). It is these feelings of control over their own voice that provide children with writing self-efficacy, and without this, they lose the creative urge to write for self-expression and can feel less confident in participating in a literate society. If writing is viewed as a chore, a boring activity, or something one has to do, then this will inevitably affect children's motivation and achievement in this area. McNaughton, Parr and Smith (1996) noted in their New Zealand study of young children's writing over the transition to school that the good writers 'offered words to the effect that writing was a means of personal expression and exploration and a way of communicating thoughts and feelings to others' (p.88).

On the other hand, the statements of poor writers indicated that 'they believed that writing was done primarily as school "work". Writing provided them with opportunities to show the teacher and others what they had learned. They reported engaging in writing for the purposes of doing their work, getting it right and making a finished product which could be assessed by the teacher' (pp. 88–9). What is worrying about this is that these young children on just starting school had strong *extrinsically* motivated beliefs about writing, while another group of children had much more powerful intrinsic beliefs about the purposes and functions of writing. Interestingly, Wylie's (2002) Competent Children project also found similar patterns for children at ages 8 and 10. As Wylie (2002) pointed out, 'a sign that a child needs more support with their reading is that they read *only* the books given to them for homework, or restrict their writing activity to copying' (pp.219–20).

Some forms of writing experiences can discourage children from writing and dent their writing self-efficacy. On the other hand, when educators provide learning environments where any writing approximations are valued, where writing is encouraged as a self-expressive activity, and where writing is supported as an important way for children to build their self-identity and narrative voice, children come to view themselves as active, expert participants in their literate world.

(ii) The links between writing and reading

Children's writing is important for literacy because there are strong links between writing and reading. This is reflected in the Quality Area 4.3 of QIAS as well as in state curriculum documents. Research suggests that as children develop an awareness of the relationship between the sounds of spoken language and the symbols (letters) of written language, they are simultaneously developing knowledge of how to encode (write) and decode (read) print – thus reading and writing are inextricably interconnected. Clay (1991) notes, 'It is important to foster the child's desire to explore writing at the same time as he is learning to read ... what is learned in writing becomes a resource in reading and vice versa' (p.96). She points out that 'what the child writes gives a rough idea of what he is noticing about printed language' (p.97). This highlights the value of writing in providing clues to educators about children's literacy learning in general and that there is a reciprocal and valuable relationship between the two areas.

In *By Different Paths to Common Outcomes* (1998) Marie Clay argues that writing contributes to the 'building of almost every kind of inner control of literacy learning that is needed by the successful reader' (p.130). She also analyses that when children write they engage in a range of the following fundamental reading-related competencies:

❖ 'They attend closely to some features of letters.

❖ They learn about letters, distinguishing one from another.

❖ They access this letter knowledge in several different ways.

❖ They work with letter clusters, as sequences or chunks.

❖ They work with words, constructing them from letters, letter clusters, or patterns.

❖ They work with syntactic knowledge of what is likely to occur in the language and what does not happen.

❖ They use their knowledge of the world to compose the message and anticipate upcoming content.

❖ They direct attention to page placement of text, directional rules, serial order, and spaces.

❖ They work with some sense of the sequence rules and probability status of any part of the print.

❖ They break down the task to its smallest segments while at the same time synthesising them into words and sentences' (pp.130–1).

Sharing a group made book based on a language experience

In *Change Over Time* (2001) Clay again asserts that despite 'proposals, critiques and publications which have raised or lowered the interest in early writing none has made significant changes to how we understand the *reciprocity* of learning to read and write. A better understanding about reciprocity could lead to more effective teaching interactions in both activities' (p.11). In particular, she recommends that children be involved in authentic writing and reading experiences and that it is important that educators understand 'what is going on before their eyes, as reading and writing come together and influence each other' (p.12). She warns against treating reading and writing activities as separate, and against educators (and parents) focusing on either one before the other. In other words, reading experiences support writing and vice versa.

Writing and reading also share three common elements. First, writing, like reading, has a similar *function*, purpose and use in society and this impacts on children's motivation to

10

write and read. Wanting to become a part of a literate society is a powerful motivator for children. Second, writing shares a range of common *forms* like reading, such as books, labels, recipes, poems, magazines, lyrics and signs. Finally, writing shares a number of common *conventions* (as we discuss in more detail next), such as comprised of letters, words, goes left to right and top to bottom, punctuation, spacings and so on. In sum, children's writing is an important opportunity for children to learn about a range of fundamental language and literacy areas, each having valuable spin-offs for their reading as well.

(iii) Book and print conventions

Children's writing provides many opportunities for learning about the broader conventions of books and print. In this book, and many other texts, the specific conventions of books and the conventions of print are often combined and used interchangeably. However, it is useful here to separate out the conventions that specifically relate to print, when one is solely focusing on children's writing, from those conventions that specifically relate to books, which can be focused on when encouraging children perhaps to make their own 'books'.

a) **The conventions of books.** Book conventions can be incorporated into children's writing in a number of ways. A common approach is where children are encouraged to make their own shorter books comprising illustrations and shorter captions, or they may also be able (with the educator's support) to create even longer books with lengthier more descriptive texts.

Examples of the conventions of books

Children can be encouraged to learn the following book conventions when making their own books:

❖ books have covers, titles, authors, contents pages, indexes and illustrators

❖ text conveys the main meaning, and illustrations clearly support the storyline

❖ stories start at the front of the book and end at the back, have sequentially numbered pages, and the left page is read before the right

❖ books have a clear overall structure – an opening, a setting, a plot, a style, characters, organisation, timeline, and an ending

❖ books come in a range of forms (e.g., picture books, pop-up books, large books)

❖ books have a range of functions (e.g., for poetry, for reference, to scare, to delight)

❖ books need to be cared for and stored in specific ways.

(Based on Adams & Jackson, 2002; Browne, 2001)

b) **The conventions of print.** When educators support children's writing there are ample opportunities to discuss the conventions of print. This more technical knowledge provides children with the standard terms and understandings necessary to further their literacy learning. As Clay (2001) points out, writing is important because it also provides opportunities for children's attention to be drawn to aspects of print, such as the features and differences between letter forms.

Examples of the conventions of print

Children can be encouraged to learn the following print conventions when writing:

❖ 'Letters' are written together to form words and each letter has its own unique upper case and lower case shape. There are 26 letters in the alphabet. The same letter can look slightly different depending on whether it is word-processed or handwritten.

❖ 'Words' are clusters of individual letters ordered in a special way, separated by spaces, which are read from left to right, and top to bottom. Each individual word means something and maps one to one with written text. Grouped together, words make sentences and paragraphs.

❖ Writing comprises blocks of text which progress one line after the other from the top to the bottom of the page, in sequences of paragraphs.

❖ Writing also involves punctuation marks (e.g., exclamation marks, full stops, commas, question marks, speech marks etc). Each punctuation mark means something and contributes significantly to the comprehension or meaning of what is being written.

(Based on Adams & Jackson, 2002, p.187)

(iv) Phonemic awareness and letter–sound knowledge

Writing is an extremely valuable opportunity for helping children learn phonemic awareness and written letter–sound knowledge. In authentic situations in centres children grapple with the nature of letters, their sounds and how these fit together to help them tell their stories. Such informal opportunities allow the educator to introduce aspects related to word decoding in co-constructed and interactive ways. Clay (2001), for example, notes that 'Young readers and writers have to become aware of phonemes ... whether children can break up what they say into parts' and, 'When children are writing they need to separate the sounds within the words they are trying to write in order to be able to find some letter forms to represent these sounds' (p.21).

Raising phonemic awareness during writing experiences

❖ pointing out and playing with syllables (e.g., Chris/to/pher; Ma/nu)

❖ highlighting rhymes and rhyming as they arise

❖ demonstrating written onset (initial) sounds and rimes (e.g., c/an, p/an, r/an). Common simple 'word families' include -ad, -ag, -al, -am, -an, -ap, -at, -aw, -ay, -eg, -en, -et, -id, -in, -ip, -ir, -it, -og, -op, -ot, -ow, -ug, -um, and –up

❖ blending written letter sounds into words (e.g., s-a-t = sat).

Increasing alphabet knowledge during writing experiences

❖ highlighting and naming individual written letter names

❖ highlighting and modelling individual written letter sounds

❖ highlighting and modelling letter shapes

❖ discussing the upper and lower case forms of letters

❖ discussing the beginning and end sounds of words

❖ highlighting interesting clusters of letters within words (including rimes)

❖ pointing out the words within words (e.g., particularly relevant if they link to the children's names such as the 'and' in Andy).

10

In order for children to be able to write so that they can be understood by others, they need to break down their oral language into spoken letters, put these letters into a written form, group those letters back into their own words, and then understand their own writing – a complex linguistic feat. This is the reason why this book continually highlights phonemic awareness and letter–sound relationships as an essential support for reading, writing and literacy development in general.

Children's writing and spelling expertise

While formal writing and spelling instruction in both its more technical and broader senses begins when children start school, children begin to learn about and engage with these aspects of literacy from a very early age. This section looks at how 'writing' and 'spelling' are conceptualised, the importance of pre-writing areas (drawing and scribbling), the emergence of beginning and semi-phonetic writing and spelling expertise, and briefly discusses the principles of flexibility and generativity along with 'invented' spelling.

(i) Conceptualising writing and spelling expertise

The way we conceptualise how children learn about writing and spelling in the early years affects the way we view children's writing and spelling, what sort of literacy resources and experiences we provide for children, and the ways in which educators support children's practices. The area of writing and spelling is full of complex, varying, and at times conflicting, viewpoints and issues. There are a wide range of taxonomies, developmental stages, systems, continuums, phases and so on in the literature, each seeking to explain how children develop writing and spelling expertise in the early years.

Many of these theories are fairly rigid and prescribed, and more recent literature has criticised elements of these approaches as not fully describing the complexity of children's growing writing and spelling expertise. Instead, recent literature (e.g., Clay, 1998, 2001; McNaughton, Parr & Smith, 1996; Morrow, 2001; Smith & Elley, 1997) suggests that children should acquire an increasing repertoire of writing- and spelling-related expertise that they can use in a variety of creative and original ways.

We agree. In this chapter we argue that there are overlapping broad bands of children's writing and spelling expertise that are *not* 'developmental', necessarily age-linked, or strictly sequential, but which become part of a *broader* and *expanding* repertoire of strategies that children can utilise as they require. This helps explain why even young children can still incorporate into their writing aspects of drawing, writing and spelling that they used at a considerably younger age.

In this section we will focus on some important pre-writing areas, and then the two overlapping broad bands of children's writing and spelling expertise found in early childhood centres – the beginning band and the semi-phonetic band. While each 'band' is broad, debatable and has 'fuzzy' boundaries, we suggest that these categories are useful for early childhood educators because they indicate and represent significant and observable shifts in children's thinking about the nature of writing and spelling. The main distinction between children's writing and spelling in each of these two categories is that in the beginning band children do *not* make use of letter–sound relationships and hence are writing in a non-phonetic way, while in the semi-phonetic band, children write making partial use of letter–sound relationships. It is this understanding and use by children of written letter–sound relationships, we would argue, that marks a significant change in children's writing and spelling expertise. We have based the following detailed information mainly on the literacy projects undertaken by the Education Department of Western Australia (EDWA, 2004) and Learning Media (1992).

(ii) Before writing

As soon as a child is able to pick up a crayon, make marks in sand or in other materials, they are able to scribble and draw. Scribbling and drawing are valuable symbolic experiences for children and should be encouraged at every opportunity. Children also learn a range of basic tools from this scribbling and learning which their future writing expertise can draw on. However, children's early scribbling, drawing, painting and the like are important activities in their own right and educators should first be aware of the purposes of children's drawing/painting/scribbling. Indeed, children's drawings are not always 'about' something. Children may be exploring shapes, textures, sensations, colours or the use of different writing and painting tools.

We need to be careful that we do not undervalue the role of early scribbling, drawing and painting in its own right in children's *overall* learning. As Whitehead (1997) points out, the increasing interest in children's early writing 'has also had the effect of diminishing attention, support and resources for drawing in the early years curriculum. Young children's pictures and experiments with markers are now scanned by teachers for letters, numerals and letter-like forms but their intrinsic value as drawings is in danger of being ignored' (p.135).

When children later come to engage in what we term 'beginning writing', their ability to scribble, draw and paint becomes a strength in the child's overall toolkit for expressing themselves. Meier (2000), for example, highlights that drawing, painting, scribbling, and writing and reading fit equally well together in early childhood education to comprise a more holistic and balanced understanding of children's representations of the world. And, as Morrow (2001) points out, children's representational work is often an intriguing creation where drawings and writing are often mixed; messages are invented; letters, symbols and words are used as decoration; and multi-media is used for a range of purposes.

Each of these sorts of activities, Whitehead (1997) suggests, are dynamic, exploratory problem-solving experiences, which 'are produced together and, like so much play and pretending, they may be doing many things: communicating messages or standing for experiences, ideas and sensations' (p.134). Importantly, young children often use these various forms of drawings and invented forms of writing even after they begin to master more conventional forms of print. Isolating any one area of the ways in which children engage symbolically with the world reduces the broad palette children have to express themselves.

(iii) Beginning writing and spelling

The point when these sorts of 'before writing' activities become 'writing' is usually viewed as being when children are aware that their print carries a message and some known letters are used. Writing, then, is when print and language come together. As Clay (1991) explains, 'The child invents a sentence which could describe a picture. Or, he writes a simple word like "is" and proudly names it something else like "run". Print and language are equated' (p.78). While we use the simpler term 'beginning writing', a range of relatively equivalent terms is used in the literature, particularly in relation to spelling, such as 'preliminary' and 'precommunicative'.

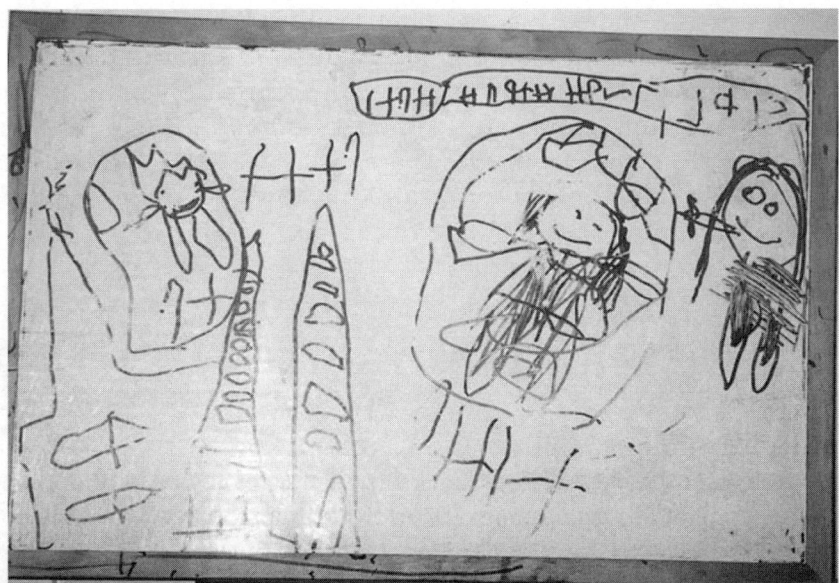

This is a story being told by a four-year-old girl of a princess in a castle who got stuck in a spider web. She made up the story then drew the pictures when she re-told it.

10

This beginning category of writing and spelling expertise involves children writing letter-like shapes, symbols and scribbles that are broadly intended to represent letters and words but which are difficult to recognise as such because the child hasn't yet become aware of, or isn't using, a full range of alphabet letters or written letter–sound relationships. While it may be difficult to identify precisely when 'writing' starts, the following list details the sorts of expertise that might include children in this beginning writing category.

Children's growing repertoire of beginning writing and spelling expertise

The beginning writer:
- ❖ is aware that print carries a message
- ❖ is not aware of letter–sound relationships
- ❖ uses a variety of writing-like symbols
- ❖ uses some known letters or approximations of letters
- ❖ assigns a message to own symbols
- ❖ knows that writing and drawing are different
- ❖ mixes upper and lower case letters
- ❖ writes the first one or two letters of own name or word correctly and may finish with a random string of letters (often repeating the same letter several times)
- ❖ writes own name correctly by rote
- ❖ names or labels own 'writing' and pictures (using a variety of symbols)
- ❖ notices environmental print
- ❖ is willing to try writing speech
- ❖ likes sharing writing discoveries with others.

(Education Department of Western Australia, 1994; Learning Media, 1992)

(iv) Semi-phonetic writing and spelling

The semi-phonetic category of writing and spelling expertise involves children writing symbols, which may be hard to read but do actually in parts represent an understanding of written letter–sound relationships and take the approximated form of alphabet letters. Words are often represented by a short cluster of letters that are now based on the sounds of the words (often termed invented spelling). Mapping when children precisely move from the beginning to the semi-phonetic category is not necessarily an easy, useful or desirable task. Young children tend to make the transition mainly to semi-phonetic writing over a period of time from within their *overlapping* beginning and semi-phonetic bands of expertise. To some extent these categories are artificial, but they do capture the significant conceptual shift in children's thinking towards understanding the link between written letters and sounds.

Children's growing repertoire of semi-phonetic writing and spelling expertise

The semi-phonetic writer:
- ❖ uses the most obvious sounds to spell whole words. This may be the initial sound (D-down), initial and final sounds (DN-down), or initial, middle and final sounds (DON-down)

- uses letter names to represent each syllable, e.g., AT (eighty), U (you), R (are)
- uses an initial letter to represent most words in a sentence, e.g., s o i s g to c a s (Someone is going to climb a slide)
- writes one or two letters for sounds, then adds random letters to complete the word, e.g., greim (grass), rdms (radio)
- correctly uses a small bank of known sight words
- starts using left to right and top to bottom directionality
- knows the names of the letters of the alphabet
- recognises some simple written words
- recognises and copies words from environmental print
- leaves spaces between word-like letter clusters, e.g., I h bn sik (I have been sick).

(Education Department of Western Australia, 2004; Learning Media, 1992)

The ingenuity and creativity of children's semi-phonetic writing never fails to amaze us. Here are some more examples from Kress (1997, pp.80–1).

Lunch list	
A request by Michael for lunch next Saturday	
Matad chese and tmatew and bacn ol on a biscat into the coca tem ac a piser. And da tric of cold tholt.	Melted cheese and tomato and bacon all on a biscuit in the cooker to make a pizza. And a drink of cold chocolate.

The bee and the rhinoceros	
A six-page illustrated storybook	
The bii and the rinocrs.	title page
Oaes a pan tim their was a bii and a rnacrs.	Drawing of bee and rhinoceros on p.2 and text on p.3.
Wan day the rinosrs met a bii.	again, drawing of bee and rhinoceros on p.4 and text on p.5.
And the bii sdg hem saw the rinosrs pact the bii. And that's The End.	p.6

(v) The flexibility and generative principles

In their learning about writing and spelling, children come to understand two key principles – the flexibility and the generative principles.

The *flexibility principle*, as Clay (1998) describes it, is where children experiment with the shapes of letter forms. In effect, they are seeking to push the limits and boundaries of what is and what is not a 'letter' and in turn learn more about the identity and nature of letter symbols. Educators play a critical role both in guiding and facilitating this process.

As Clay (1998, p.142) puts it, children explore such questions as:

- When is a sign not a language sign?

- When is a sign a new sign?

- Can you turn this letter around, or begin on the right-hand side of the page or at the bottom?

The *generative principle* is where children come to understand, as Clay (1998) describes, the process of 'generating new from known' (p.143). In the case of writing, Clay argues that children come to understand that from their knowledge of the alphabet, the alphabet letter–sounds relationship and the shapes of written letters, they can generate

10

in writing any word they may wish to write, at least phonetically. And, from their existing grammatical knowledge they can generate written sentences that make sense to people other than themselves. This is not to say that, particularly for children in early childhood settings, their spelling or grammar will be technically 'correct', but that at least what children may be communicating in writing is able to be understood with some careful deciphering.

This diagram from Kress (1997, p.67) gives an interesting insight into the flexibility and generative principles through name writing and outlines one child's practice and experimentation over a period of one year from the age of four years to five years, one month. The power of names, both to the children themselves and to sustaining such an ongoing self-reflective task, is obvious here. As Kress (1997) puts it 'it is clear to me that this is *creative* activity, transformation, and not, decidedly not, copying. There is no question of lack, error, of "not yet good enough"' (p.66). Out of Emily's self-reflection, and the pushing of the limits and boundaries of her literacy knowledge, has come some major progress in her writing achievement.

(1) November

(2) November

(3) November

(4) December

(5) March

(6) March

(7) May

(8) May

(9) July

(10) October

(11) November

(12) December

(13) December

(14) December

There are many areas of interest to consider in Emily's name writing and Kress (1997) suggests that Emily is going through a reflective ongoing process of asking herself many questions about name writing, such as: how many bars in an 'E'; which way should the letters be written; when should I use upper and lower cases; what distinguishes an 'i' from an 'l'; how many letters are in my name; how should the letters be sized, spaced and ordered; do the letters have to be in a horizontal straight line; how does my name go with other words; and so on. It looks as if Emily in November (1, 2, 3) and December (4) could probably be placed in the *overlapping* categories of advanced beginning writing and early semi-phonetic writing. Her grasp of letter–sound relationships and conventional alphabet letter forms between December (4) and March (5) seems to have strengthened markedly, which probably demonstrates a significant shift in her thinking from beginning writing to semi-phonetic writing.

Critically, it is important to note that the changes each month were not linear improvements, but an ongoing grappling with the large number of conventions of print that conventional writing requires. This individualised process has important implications for how we view the writing of each child in a centre. Ultimately, Emily has come to understand the principles of flexibility and generativity through engaging with this serious problem-solving process of how to write her name.

(vi) 'Invented' spelling

This term, as Smith and Elley (1997) explain, relates to any attempts by children to write words which are not spelled in the accepted conventional way. Schools, of course, aim to teach children how to spell words correctly in a variety of ways. However, encouraging children to use invented spelling has sometimes been viewed as a negative approach to supporting children's writing and it is sometimes assumed that invented spelling is encouraged without any emphasis on conventional spelling. On the contrary, as Smith and Elley (1997) point out, invented spelling is a learning process associated with writing 'that children pass through on their path to becoming proficient spellers' (p.104).

If in early childhood settings one corrected children's spelling all the time, they would probably stop any attempts to write at all (and this applies to most other areas of children's activities and experiences in early childhood as well). As we have discussed in this chapter, it is the act of children learning to communicate freely in writing that needs to be supported and encouraged, and conventional spelling or writing develops gradually throughout this process under the careful guidance of educators as children learn more about literacy. However, it is important to remember that for some children 'taking risks' and writing words that are incorrectly spelt may be seen as culturally inappropriate. Discussion with parents/carers and children about the way in which 'invented spelling' supports early writing attempts and leads to more conventional spelling is crucial to helping children and parents/carers feel comfortable and confident in this approach.

Weaving writing throughout the centre

In Chapters 5, 6 and 7 we discussed the creation of literacy-enriched early childhood centres. We covered a range of aspects relating to weaving writing resources into the centre environment, incorporating writing into centre routines and activities, and building on informal writing opportunities. We suggest at this point that the reader review these chapters, specifically noting the information related to writing. This section aims to extend the information provided there, and consider some new areas as well. We consider next a broader range of writing implements, tools and props; detailed information on creating writing centres; look at the types of print models writers might need; examine book writing by children; and provide some ideas for building on informal writing opportunities in the centre.

10

(i) Writing implements, materials and equipment

There are a wide range of writing tools and props that a centre may find useful, and we have grouped these into implements, materials and equipment. These can be stationed in a range of dramatic play environments so that they are to hand for children and educators. Such writing tools and props can also be made into portable writing kits that children can take away and use as required. These, perhaps, could be individualised and specially labelled for each child.

Writing tools and props in action

(ii) Writing centres

Besides weaving writing resources throughout the centre, specialised *writing centres* can provide children with writing resource areas as well as spaces in which they can engage in a range of literacy tasks (Shuker, 2001). When children are using the writing centre, educators can engage children in trying out and refining their literacy skills and understandings. Owocki (1998) notes that, while following the child's lead, adults can simply support and encourage the child by listening, making suggestions or helping children to organise or extend their literacy ideas. For example, educators can discuss with a child the shape of letters they want to form, or explain the different literacy forms being used such as birthday or 'thank you' card messages.

Equipment, materials and implements for writing centres

Writing centre equipment should include suitable seating and desk space sufficient for a group of children to work together, for example, desks with drawers, or a table with boxes or a shelf unit for storing writing materials and implements.

Writing centres can be well stocked with a range of:

❖ writing materials such as plain white paper, note pads, envelopes, bank slips

❖ writing implements, including pens, pencils, felt pens, coloured pencils

❖ associated writing tools such as rulers, erasers, sharpeners, staplers, cellotape and scissors.

Print models for writing centres

Writing centres can also display print models such as: copies of the alphabet in standard print in both lower case and upper case (e.g., alphabet friezes, laminated sheets etc). See the section on print models below for further information.

(iii) Print models

Print models provide children with a range of letters and words in their environment which they can immediately call upon as required. Some examples of letter and word models that can be used in writing centres, or generally around the centre, are outlined below. Children can also be encouraged to look at other print resources around the centre such as books,

books that children have written, or other forms of print in the centre or community. Additionally, educators can develop their own print models and shapes out of whatever is to hand – buttons, stones, blocks, dough or collage materials.

Letter models

❖ copies on paper of the alphabet in standard print in both lower case and upper case (e.g., on laminated sheets)

❖ a variety of physical letters such as magnetic, plastic or wooden

❖ alphabet friezes

❖ sets of alphabet letters individually written on lino squares for hardier uses such as letter/word games and play etc

❖ published alphabet books (the more interesting the better)

❖ original alphabet books which the children can make and illustrate for themselves.

Word models

❖ cards with each child's name written on them

❖ individualised cards or booklets for children with letters and words added as the child requests them, such as names of the child's family members and their own full names

❖ words chart comprising frequently requested, high-interest and high-frequency words (e.g., words could be velcroed on the wall under each alphabet letter for easy removal and use by children).

(iv) Book writing

Encouraging children of all ages to write and 'publish' books is an exciting outcome of a rich literacy environment. Of course, the definition of what a 'book' is varies on whether the child is an infant, toddler or young child, and we would expect the complexity and detail to increase accordingly. However, book publishing is an important way of showing the child and the centre community that you value children's writing, irrespective of the child's age and writing experience.

Educators are able to get the child's voice heard in a variety of ways. This might involve such

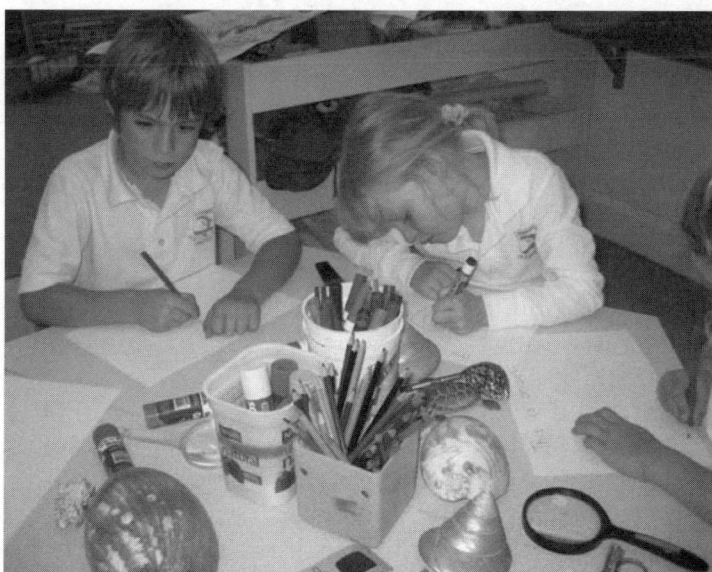

Making a class book about the sea shore

10

techniques as transcribing the child's story, writing captions underneath the child's writing, or encouraging children to copy transcribed writing. Educators can also build book writing into their planned activities such as group books about trips, visitors, themes, incorporating illustrations, photos and mixed media. Books can be displayed in frieze form on the centre walls, or be put into more traditional small or large booklet formats. Children's books don't have to be long, just personalised and interesting. Computers can be useful here in a range of ways both for the child and educator. Groups of children can create co-authored books as well. Such books can then be shared and celebrated by the educator with the children and the centre community.

Types of books children could write

Big books, books made at home, books with audio tapes/CDs, books written for younger children, centre diaries and large calendars, cartoons and comics, dual language stories, flap books, imaginative stories, information and reference books, joke books, life stories (e.g., the child, a friend, family member), magazines and newspapers for the centre community, personal stories, poetry books, recipe books, retelling of favourite stories, stories based around photos, stories based on 'super heroes'.

(Adapted from Browne, 2001, p.114)

Children's stories can be short and to the point. Here is an example of a story by a four-and-a-half-year-old child which provides a lot of action in a concise format. This example is taken from an illustrated collection of stories, transcribed by an adult, called *The Monster That Came To Tea, And Other Short Stories.*

The Man That Hopped to the Top of the Hill!

Once upon a time, there was a man.

He hopped to the top of the hill, but he did not know how to get down.

He tried to run but he rolly-pollied head-bottom, head-bottom, head-bottom, all the way home to the end of this story.

THE END

(v) Building on informal writing opportunities

When literacy resources are woven throughout the centre and integrated into the planned routines and experiences of the centre informal writing opportunities should arise frequently. Children will be involved in independent writing and drawing on a regular basis, and a range of valuable literacy learning opportunities can be capitalised on by the centre staff.

Informal writing opportunities, as Browne (2001) suggests, might involve encouraging children to write labels, captions and stories for drawings, diagrams, models, photos, displays; draw and write a variety of signs useful for dramatic play and other activities; posters for centre visits and events; cards, invitations and letters that require a response from others (inside or outside of the centre); faxes and emails that also require responses; and instructions and leaflets for equipment, games etc.

Educators can help children's writing by supporting children to:

❖ believe in themselves as writers

❖ become active participants in their own writing development

❖ be free to express their voice

❖ take lots of chances, experiment, and take risks without censure

❖ gain independence

❖ enjoy themselves and have fun

❖ communicate.

(Adapted from Browne, 2001)

During informal writing opportunities educators can aim to:

❖ make writing/communication easier for the child (such as through ensuring writing resources are close to hand, or supporting the child in such ways as transcribing or writing captions)

❖ work from an understanding of where the children are at as opposed to imposing a specific 'writing regime' on them

❖ provide plentiful writing-associated resources, routines, experiences, and informal learning opportunities for all children in the centre

❖ encourage positive attitudes to their writing

❖ not be overly concerned with correct spelling, neatness, letter shapes (but keep tactfully discussing with children ways to gradually improve these)

❖ provide plenty of opportunities for different forms and functions of writing.

(Adapted from Browne, 2001)

In sum, weaving a range of writing resources throughout the centre in the form of writing implements, materials and equipment is an effective way of placing literacy tools easily within reach of children and educators. If writing equipment is nearby, children will be more inclined to use them and educators can more easily incorporate writing tools into children's activities. In addition, writing centres can provide more formal places for specialised writing equipment and experiences. Children require a range of writing models, particularly in the form of letter and word models that are close to hand. Book writing is an activity that all centre children can engage in and enjoy, the only challenge for educators is to look at the levels of support that are required for different groups of children. Finally, with all these writing areas in place, many informal writing opportunities will arise, which educators can use to support children's learning.

Shared, modelled, guided and independent writing

A common approach in the literacy literature for structuring writing and reading programs involves 'modelled', 'shared', 'guided' and 'independent' writing and reading. This approach clearly defines the relationship between the educator, the child and writing and reading programs and interactions. This approach is used in many early childhood settings across Australia, however, in adapting this approach for early childhood education it is important to note that each approach should be tailored sensitively for enhancing the writing of infants, toddlers or young children.

10

Clay (2001), in particular, points out that educators are critical in this complex process of helping children to learn to write. She notes that 'there are some cultural processes which help children to learn the links between what they say and how they might create a record of it. To notice a preschool child's changing responses to print is valuable but to believe that writing is going to emerge without the influence of tutors or models is to deny the child access to the arbitrary rules of writing systems' (pp.34–5). It is these interactions, modelled, shared and guided, which are critical for the growth of children's writing expertise.

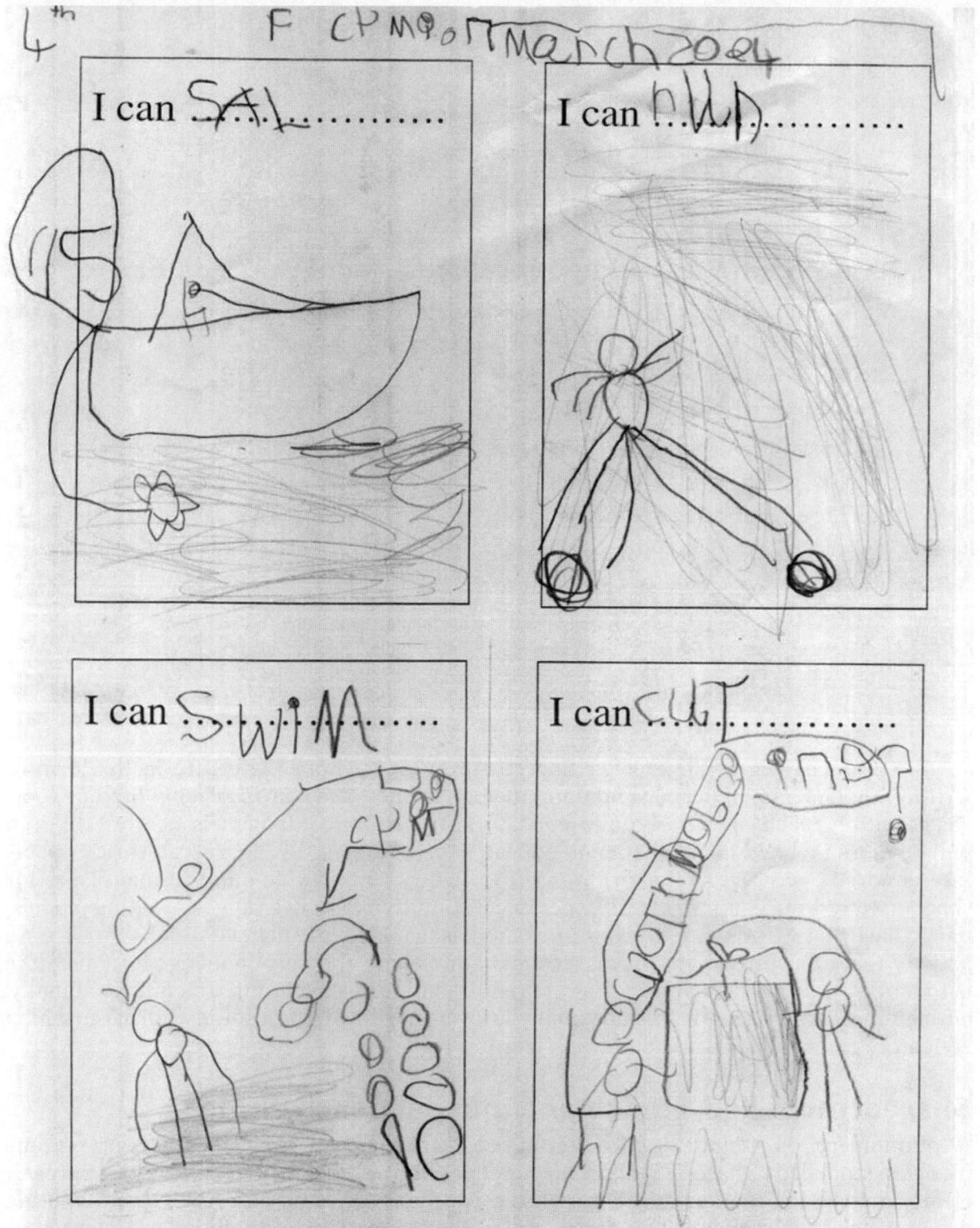

Scaffolding writing

(i) Shared writing

Shared writing is an approach to working with early childhood children where the *educator* facilitates children's writing by doing most of the work. As the physical and cognitive acts of writing can be arduous for young children, adults can help children put their words down on paper more easily as the circumstances arise. Clay (1991), for example, suggests that educators can dictate or transcribe children's stories. In the centre context this might mean asking children for captions to their drawings and paintings, writing down stories for children if they wish, writing words on signs and posters for children and so on.

There is also ample opportunity during shared writing to discuss all sorts of areas related to writing, including print conventions, letter–sound relationships, and clarifying and refining what the child means. Clay (2001), for example, notes how in the early intervention program called Reading Recovery (used in the Junior School) the use of writing can be used to teach children to 'hear the sound sequences in words and to construct words in writing from the sounds or sound patterns they hear … Teachers give children credit for their attempts, and prompt them to articulate the word slowly to hear the sounds, but teacher and child share the writing of the hard or new parts' (p.16). Such shared approaches would be equally as useful in early childhood centres when used appropriately.

Many centres engage in shared writing on a daily basis with their children. Centre children usually generate a lot of ideas and stories during their time in the centre and dictating or transcribing helps the child's voice to be recorded and valued. The short story quoted earlier, 'The Man That Hopped to the Top of the Hill' is an example of the way in which the transcriber (the adult) provided the child with structure that validated the experience of storytelling. Additionally, other literacy areas can be usefully integrated into these shared writing experiences.

(ii) Modelled writing

Modelled writing is used by the educator to demonstrate particular aspects of writing while composing a particular type of text. This is an especially useful strategy for children who have begun to master some of the early skills of writing and are interested in creating more complex texts. The educator 'thinks aloud' while making decisions about what to write, where to start, how to organise the information and revising and editing the text. The focus will vary according to the aspects of writing that are being modelled. The process is owned by the educator and gives children the opportunity to observe how a text is constructed as they develop a growing understanding of the processes, forms and conventions of writing. For example the children may be planning to celebrate a festival by doing some baking, and this gives the educator the opportunity to model by writing a recipe with the children, explaining the list of ingredients and the importance of a sequence of instructions.

(iii) Guided writing

Guided writing is an approach to working with early childhood children where the *child* actively does most of the work and the educator guides and scaffolds the writer. Clay (1991), for example, suggests that educators can support children's writing through guiding their writing, copying and retelling. In the centre context this might mean encouraging children to write for themselves when the occasions arise. For example, children can be encouraged to write their own captions or stories for their drawing. Depending on the age or literacy experiences of the child this could produce nothing, scribbles, some letters, or even words and short sentences. Whatever is produced should be supported, praised, enjoyed, and used as starting points for further literacy discussion.

Children can also be encouraged to copy written text. We don't mean sitting children at desks for endless hours of copying alphabet letters and worksheets. Instead, children usually enjoy being encouraged to scribble, trace over the educator's words, or copy underneath your words. This becomes more meaningful when the words they copy are of their own creation. The overall aim is to keep developing children's writing expertise instead of just focusing on getting some aspect of their writing 'correct'. In other words,

10

copying experiences provide rich opportunities for guiding children's understandings about the functions of writing and the conventions of print.

Retelling is another powerful method for guiding children's writing in the broader sense. The educator may have dictated or transcribed some form of text for the child (be it a story, caption, sign etc), and encouraging the child to 'read' the text is a learning opportunity too valuable to miss. In centres, we would expect the child's 'reading' or retelling to generally be an approximation and will most likely more closely reflect the meaning as opposed to the actual written words. However, what is important at this point is that such experiences provide many opportunities for talking about meanings, print, print conventions and letter–sound relationships. For primary educators, Clay (1991) also suggests that they can ask children to point to their text when they retell their 'story' by asking them to 'read it with your finger'. This is an advanced reading skill not expected of most centre children, but it does provide the educator with information about the children's levels of understanding of directionality and the one-to-one correspondence of the spoken and written word.

Clay (1991) points out that each of these areas alone – of transcribing for children, writing, copying and retelling – are powerful literacy learning opportunities. However, when any of these are combined in various ways using children's own voices and stories the benefits are increased. It is very empowering for children to be able to both 'read' and 'write' their own ideas. Every literacy demonstration by a child should be viewed as an achievement, whether it is a scribble, or wobbly written letters, or even written words.

The overall goal in early childhood education of guided writing is not to teach children to write, copy or retell 'correctly' although many children will gain a broad range of valuable writing experience through their experiences in the centre. Instead, the goal should be to provide more regular and increasingly sustained guided and scaffolded experiences that provide rich opportunities for educators to engage in meaningful literacy-related talk with children about the things that matter to them – their writing; their ideas; their captions, letters or stories (however long or short); and their ongoing ability to express themselves more effectively.

(iv) Independent writing

Independent, or personal, writing is where the child is the writer and the educator is an observer. Centre children can be supported to become independent writers where they are encouraged and facilitated to write for a variety of their own purposes; where they have access to a wide range of writing implements, materials and equipment across the

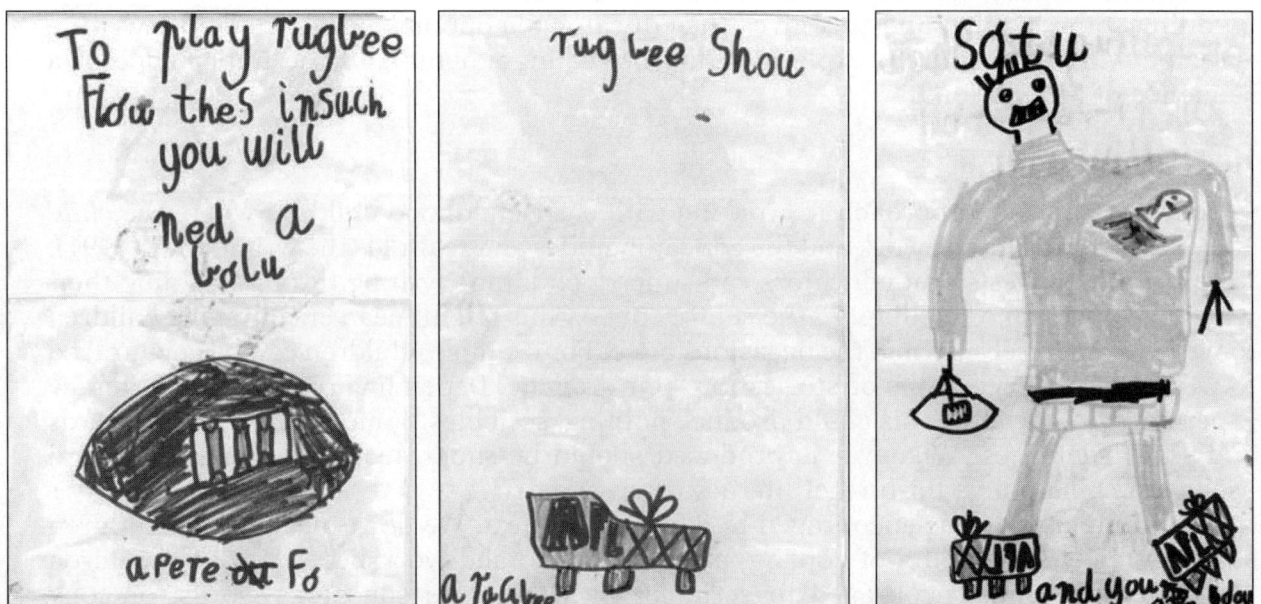

Making a book about rugby. Translation: To play rugby follow the instructions. You will need a ball, a pair of rugby shoes, suit and you are done

centre; where children have ample time and space to undertake a variety of meaningful writing activities; and where children are provided with many opportunities to initiate writing experiences for themselves. It is here that the educator, as an informed literacy professional, exercises their judgement when deciding whether to let the child continue to work independently or whether to assist the child in the activity they are engaging in.

Concluding comments

- Writing, in whatever form it takes, is an important way for children's voices and narratives to be recorded and shared.

- Infants, toddlers and young children can be encouraged to be involved in writing activities, no matter what form they take.

- Writing and reading share a range of important areas and each provides special opportunities for learning about the other.

- Children's experiences before writing, such as drawing, scribbling and painting, are valuable tools which later writing can draw on.

- Children's beginning writing and semi-phonetic writing are distinguished by significant and observable shifts in children's thinking in relation to written letter–sound awareness and the use of conventional alphabet letters.

- Writing can be woven throughout centres in the form of tools and props where children might need them, in specialist writing centres, and through the provision of print models and undertaking book writing.

- Educators can support children's writing on a continuum between undertaking most of the writing work for the child through to facilitating independent writing in all its forms.

10

Conclusion

Creating literacy-enriched early childhood environments is, in many respects, little different from integrating any other aspect into centre life. However, it is important that sound and informed literacy policy is developed and Section One of this book covered these areas in detail. When integrating literacy policy in practice, educators can concentrate on three core areas that we covered in Section Two. Weaving literacy resources throughout the early childhood centre gives children access to a range of literacy resources and opportunities to engage with literacy in meaningful ways. Planning for literacy experiences in the everyday routines, activities and events of the centre also provides regular, ongoing literacy experiences for children. When educators create and build on informal literacy opportunities in their everyday interactions with children, powerful literacy learning is also reinforced. For educators, these sorts of interactions are made considerably easier when the first two core approaches are in place.

In Section Three, we highlighted three main themes in this book: the importance of book reading, phonemic awareness and letter–sound knowledge, and children's writing. Book reading is the foundation of literacy practices in many centres and because of this we have focused on its importance and on a range of strategies and techniques to improve its effectiveness in centres. Both phonemic awareness and letter–sound knowledge have been found to be key prerequisites in helping children to decode text, in other words, the technical act of actually reading letters and words. This area is relatively easy for educators to strengthen in their centres because many early childhood practices already revolve around nursery rhymes, songs and various alphabet practices. Children's writing, like book reading, is a fundamental part of the literacy practices of many centres, and children expand their writing and spelling expertise well before starting school. Again, while this area is embedded in the three core approaches discussed, it has been highlighted to signal the importance of the area and to provide more detailed practical ideas to help educators implement this aspect of literacy in their centre.

In summary, these four chapters on policy debates, the three chapters on literacy practice, and the last three chapters on special topics should come together to help educators and the centre community to develop a literacy-enriched early childhood program. Figure 1 outlines this process and highlights that the literacy policy debate should continually influence literacy practices in the centre. When these two aspects of literacy policy and practice come together, sound and informed literacy approaches will become an integral, appropriate and meaningful part of the overall centre program.

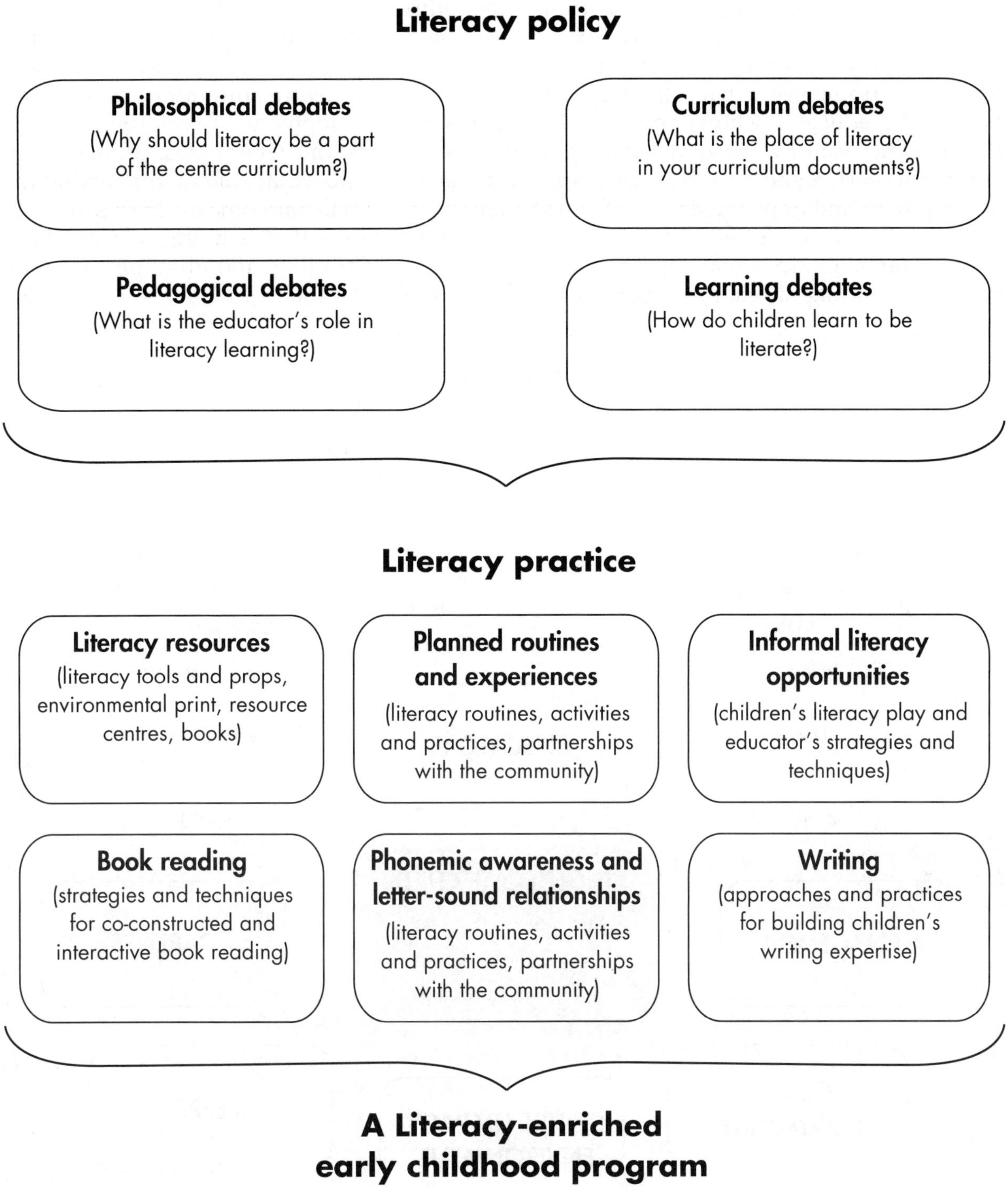

Literacy policy

Philosophical debates
(Why should literacy be a part
of the centre curriculum?)

Curriculum debates
(What is the place of literacy
in your curriculum documents?)

Pedagogical debates
(What is the educator's role in
literacy learning?)

Learning debates
(How do children learn to be
literate?)

Literacy practice

Literacy resources
(literacy tools and props,
environmental print, resource
centres, books)

**Planned routines
and experiences**
(literacy routines, activities
and practices, partnerships
with the community)

**Informal literacy
opportunities**
(children's literacy play and
educator's strategies and
techniques)

Book reading
(strategies and techniques
for co-constructed and
interactive book reading)

**Phonemic awareness and
letter-sound relationships**
(literacy routines, activities
and practices, partnerships
with the community)

Writing
(approaches and practices
for building children's
writing expertise)

A Literacy-enriched
early childhood program

Figure 1: Developing a literacy-enriched early childhood program

Informed literacy professionals, who help create such literacy-enriched programs, are not only able to justify their contribution to children's literacy development, but are able to ensure that early childhood literacy practices are appropriate and meaningful for this age group. All too often educators are encouraged to use external literacy models, packages and approaches that may be inappropriate and can turn children off wanting to learn to read and enjoy literature. This book is designed to empower educators with the theory, knowledge and ideas that will assist them to confidently and competently develop sound and appropriate literacy-enriched early childhood programs.

Early childhood educators, along with the other members of the centre community (including parents), create a literate community which in turn nurtures the development of literate children. Figure 2 weaves together the key components of a literate centre community, each of which plays an important role. Hence, the centre provides a rich literacy environment that comprises a variety of quality literacy resources, routines and opportunities. Within this environment children engage in reciprocal and responsive relationships with a range of others, including peers, parents/carers and members of the centre community. Significant here is the educator who supports and enhances the development of children's literacy through the use of a range of effective literacy strategies and techniques. Management and kindergarten and preschool principals also have an important role in supporting the development and implementation of sound literacy policy. The outcome of these processes is that over time children learn to enjoy the diverse richness that is literacy, learn about a broad range of areas that support literacy learning and reading, and ultimately develop an understanding of what it is to be a literate person and an active member of a literate society.

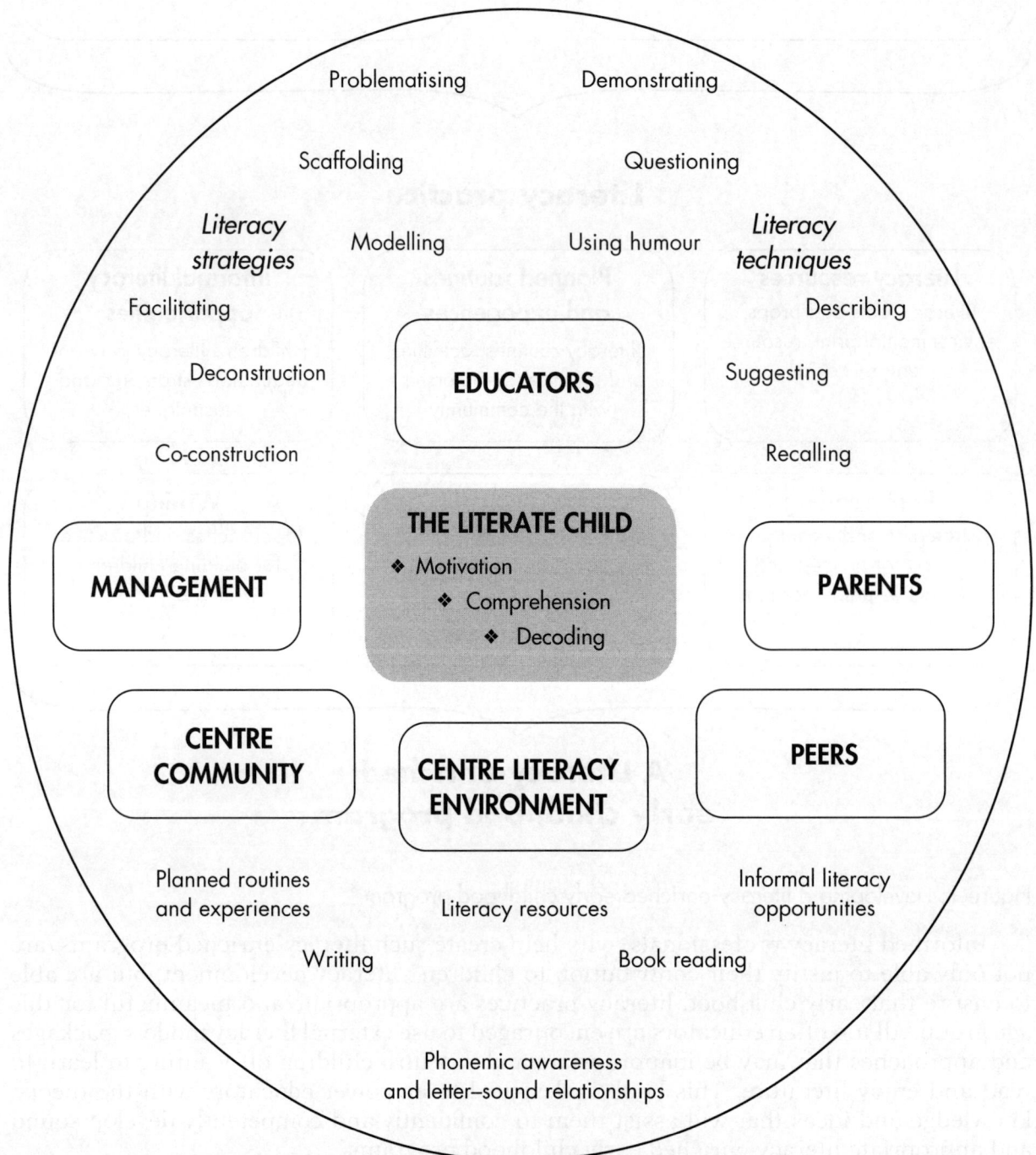

Figure 2: Supporting the literate child in the early childhood centre

In conclusion, we hope that you will find this book a useful source of information and ideas. We would appreciate suggestions or feedback from you and we would love to hear of any literacy policy or practice ideas that you have found to be valuable in your own centre and practice. You can contact us by email on c.barratt_pugh@ecu.edu.au.

References

Adams, M. J. (1990). *Beginning to read: Thinking and learning about print*. Cambridge, MA: MIT Press.

Adams, M. J., Foorman, B. R., Lundberg, I. & Terri, B. (1998). *Phonemic awareness in young children: A classroom curriculum*. Baltimore: Paul H. Brookes Publishing.

Adams, P. & Jackson, W. (2002). Literacy in home contexts: Creating effective home literacy environments. In P. Adams and H. Ryan. (Eds) *Learning to read in Aotearoa New Zealand: A collaboration between early childhood educators, families and schools*. Palmerston North: Dunmore Press.

Anstey, M. & Bull, G. *The literacy labyrinth*. Sydney: Prentice Hall Australia.

Arrows, A. (2002). *I know my name is BEN. What reading and spelling skills do preschoolers have*. Paper presented at the NZARE Conference, 5–8 December, 2002 Palmerston North, NZ.

Arthur, L. (2001). Popular culture and early literacy learning. *Contemporary Issues in Early Childhood* (2) 3, 295–308.

Arthur, L. & Makin, L. (2001). *Australian Journal of Early Childhood, 26.* 14–19.

Australian Bureau of Statistics (1996). *Census of the Commonwealth of Australia: Australia Now*. Canberra: Australian Bureau of Statistics.

Australian Bureau of Statistics (2005). *Census of child care*. Canberra: Australian Bureau of Statistics.

Australian Early Childhood Association. (1991). *Code of ethics*. Watson, ACT: AECA.

Australian Early Childhood Association (1995). *The policy handbook*. Australian Capital Territory: Australian Early Childhood Association.

Barbour, A. C. (1998/99). Home literacy bags: Promoting family involvement. *Childhood Education, Winter*, 71–5.

Barratt-Pugh, C. (1997). 'Why d'you speak funny?': supporting all children learning to talk and talking to learn. In Abbott, L. and Moylett, H. (Eds), *Working with under threes: Responding to young children's needs*. Milton Keynes: Open University Press.

Barratt-Pugh, C. (2000). The sociocultural context of literacy learning. In C. Barratt-Pugh and M. Rohl (Eds), *Literacy learning in the early years*. NSW: Allen & Unwin.

Barratt-Pugh, C. (2002). The socio-cultural context of literacy learning. In C. Barratt-Pugh and M. Rohl (Eds) (2000). *Literacy learning in the early years*. NSW: Allen and Unwin.

Barratt-Pugh, C., Breen, M., Kinder, J., Rohl, M., & House, H. (1996). *Learning in two languages: Models of bilingual education*. Canberra: NLLIA project.

Barton, D. (1999). *Literacy: An introduction to the ecology of written language*. Oxford: Blackwell Publishers.

Bergen, D. & Mauer, D. (2000). Symbolic play, phonological awareness, and literacy skills at three age levels. In K. A. Roskos and J. F. Christie (Eds), *Play and literacy in early childhood: Research from multiple perspectives*. Mahwah, New Jersey: Lawrence Erlbaum.

Bertanees, C. & Thornley, C. (2001). *Critical literacy in teacher education*. Paper presented at the NZARE Annual Conference, Christchurch, New Zealand, December 6–9.

Bloodgood, J. W. (1999). What's in a name? Children's name writing and literacy acquisition. *Reading Research Quarterly, 34, 3*, 342–67.

Breen, M., Louden, W., Barratt-Pugh, C., Rivalland, J., Rohl, M., & Rhydwen, M. (1994). *Literacy in its place. Literacy practices in urban and rural communities*. Vols 1 & 2. Canberra: DEET.

Bronfenbrenner, U. (1979). *Ecology of human development*. Cambridge, MA: Harvard University Press.

Browne, A. (2001). *Developing language and literacy 3–8*. (2nd Edn). London: Chapman.

Bryant, P. E. & Bradley, L. (1985). *Rhyme and reason in reading and spelling*. Ann Arbor: University of Michigan Press.

Burns, M. S., Griffin, P. & Snow, C. E. (1999). *Starting out right: A guide to promoting children's reading success*. Washington, DC: National Research Council.

Bus, A. G., Van Ijzendoorn, M. H. & Pellegrini, A. D. (1995). Joint book reading makes for success in learning to read: A meta-analysis on intergenerational transmission of literacy. *Review of Educational Research, 65*, 1–21.

Cairney, T. (2002*)*. Bridging home and school literacy: In search of transformative approaches to curriculum. *Early Childhood Development and Care*. 172, 2, 153–72.

Cairney, T. & Ruge, J. (1998). *Developing partnerships: The home, school and community interface: Towards effective support for students*. Canberra: DETYA.

Cairney, T., Ruge, J., Buchanan, J., Lowe, K. & Munsie, L. (1995). *Community literacy practices and schooling*. Canberra: DEET.

Carle, E. (2003). *The very hungry caterpillar*. London: Puffin Books.

Carr, M. (1998). *Assessing children's experiences in early childhood*. Wellington: Ministry of Education.

Carr, M. (1999). Some thoughts about effective assessment. *Early Education, 21*, Spring/Summer.

Chapman, J. & Tunmer, W. (2002). Reading self-perceptions: What beginning readers think about themselves as readers and why some become negative. In P. Adams and H. Ryan (Eds), *Learning to read in Aotearoa New Zealand: A collaboration between early childhood teachers, families, and schools*. Palmerston North: Dunmore Press.

Clay, M. (1991). *Becoming literate: The construction of inner control*. Auckland: Heinemann.

Clay, M. (1998). *By different paths to common outcomes*. Maine: Stenhouse.

Clay, M. (2001). *Change over time in children's literacy development*. Auckland: Heinemann.

Crooks, T. (2000a). *Planning, assessment and reporting*. Wellington: NZEI (www.nzei.org.nz).

Crooks, T. (2000b). *Assessment – challenges for early years education*. Paper presented to TRCC course, Dunedin, 9–13 April, 2000.

Cullen, J. (2001). An introduction to understanding learning. In V. Carpenter, H. Dixon, E. Rata and C. Rawlinson (Eds), *Theory in practice for educators*. Palmerston North: Dunmore Press.

Cullen, J. (2002). The social and cultural contexts of early literacy: Making the links between homes, centres and schools. In P. Adams and H. Ryan (Eds), *Learning to read in Aotearoa New Zealand: A collaboration between early childhood educators, families and schools*. Palmerston North: Dunmore Press.

Cummins, J. (1993). Bilingualism and second language learning. *Annual Review of Applied Linguistics*. 13, 51–70.

Curriculum Council (1998). *Curriculum framework*. WA: Curriculum Council. http://www.curriculum.wa.edu.au.

Davidson, J. (1996). *Emergent literacy and dramatic play in early education*. New York: Delmar.

Department of Education (2002). *Essential learnings framework*. Tasmania: DE.

Department of Education (2005). *Curriculum framework*. Northern Territory: DE.

Department of Education and the Arts (2004). *Early years curriculum guidelines*. Queensland: DEA.

Department of Education and Community Services (2001). *Curriculum for ACT*. ACT: DECS.

Department of Education, Employment and Training (no date). *Langwij comes to school: Promoting literacy among speakers of Aboriginal English and Australian Creoles*. Canberra: DEET.

Department of Education, Employment and Training & Youth Affairs (1998). *Literacy for all: The challenge for Australian schools*. Canberra: DEETYA.

Department of Education, Science and Training. (2005). *National Indigenous English literacy and numeracy strategy*. Canberra: DEST.

Department of Education & Training (2002a). *Curriculum and standards framework*. Victoria: DET Services.

Department of Education & Training (2002b). *Curriculum framework for children's services*. New South Wales: DET.

Department of Education, Training & Employment (2004). *Curriculum, standards and accountability framework* (SACSA). South Australia: DETE.

Dickinson, D. & Tabors, P. (2002). Fostering language and literacy in classrooms and homes. *Young Children*, 57 (2), 10–18.

Dunn, L., Beach, S. A. & Kontos, S. (2000). Supporting literacy in early childhood programs: A challenge for the future. In K. A. Roskos and F. J. Christie (Eds), *Play and literacy in early childhood. Research from multiple perspectives*. New Jersey: Lawrence Erlbaum.

Dyson A. (1997). *Writing superheroes: Contemporary childhood, popular culture, and classroom literacy*. New York: Teacher's College Press.

Dyson, A. (1989). *Multiple worlds of child writers: Friends learning to write*. NY: Teacher's College Press.

Early Childhood Literacy Project (1999). *Issues and practices in literacy development. Linking: sessional preschool, child care settings, family involvement*. Canberra: Australian Early Childhood Association.

Education Department of Western Australia (1994). *Spelling: Developmental continuum*. Sydney: Longman.

Education Department of Western Australia (2004a). *First steps reading map of development addressing current literacy challenges* (2nd Edn). Melbourne: Rigby Heinemann.

Education Department of Western Australia (2004b). *First steps reading resource book addressing current literacy challenges* (2nd Edn). Melbourne: Rigby Heinemann.

Edwards, V. (1997). *The other languages: A guide to multilingual classrooms*. Newtown, NSW: Primary English Teaching Association.

Einarsdottir, J. (2000). Incorporating literacy resources into the play curriculum of two Icelandic preschools. In K. A. Roskos and J. F. Christie (Eds), *Play and literacy in early childhood: Research from multiple perspectives*. New Jersey: Lawrence Erlbaum.

Ericson, L. & Juliebo, M. F. (1998). *The phonological awareness handbook for kindergarten and primary teachers*. Newark, Delaware: International Reading Association.

Ferguson, C. J. (1999). Building literacy with child-constructed sociodramatic play centres. *Dimensions of Early Childhood, 27, 3*, 23–9.

Fields, M. & Spangler, K. (2000). *Let's begin reading right: A developmental approach to emergent literacy* (4th Edn). New Jersey: Prentice Hall.

Fleet, A. & Lockwood, V. (2002). Authentic literacy assessment. In L. Makin and C. Diaz (Eds), *Literacies in early childhood: Changing views, challenging practice*. Sydney: MacLennan & Petty.

Freebody, P. (1992). A sociocultural approach: resourcing four roles as a literacy learner. In A. Watson and A. Badenhop (Eds), *Prevention of reading failure*. Sydney: Ashton Scholastic.

Frijters, J. C., Baron, R. W. & Brunello, M. (2000). Direct and mediated influences of home literacy and literacy interest on prereaders' oral vocabulary and early written language skill. *Journal of Educational Psychology, 92*, 466–77.

Gee, J. (2002). A sociocultural perspective on early literacy development. In S. Neuman and D. Dickinson (Eds), *Handbook of early literacy research*. NY: Guilford.

Gough, P. B. & Tunmer W. E. (1986). Decoding, reading and reading disability. *Remedial and Special Education, 7*, 6–10.

Gregory, E. (1996). *Making sense of a new world: Learning to read in a second language*. London: Paul Chapman Publishing Ltd.

Hall, N. (1998). Young children as story tellers. In R. Campbell (Ed.), *Facilitating preschool literacy*. Delaware, USA: International Reading Association.

Hall, N. & Robinson, A. (2000). Play and literacy learning. In C. Barratt-Pugh and M. Rohl (Eds), *Literacy learning in the early years*. Sydney: Allen & Unwin.

Hamer, C. (1999). *Observation, a tool for learning*. Wellington: The Open Polytechnic of New Zealand.

Hamer, J. & Adams, P. (2002). Literacy policy in early childhood settings: Becoming informed literacy professionals. In P. Adams and H. Ryan (Eds), *Learning to read in Aotearoa New Zealand: A collaboration between early childhood educators, families and schools*. Palmerston North: Dunmore Press.

Hanlen, W. (2002). Indigenous literacies: Moving from social construction towards social justice. In L. Makin and C. Jones Diaz (Eds), *Literacies in early childhood: Changing views, challenging practice*. NSW: MacLennan & Petty.

Harris, S. (1990). *Two way Aboriginal schooling: Education and cultural survival.* Canberra: Aboriginal Studies Press.

Hedges, H. (2000). Teaching in early childhood: Time to merge constructivist views so learning through play equals teaching through play. *Australian Journal of Early Childhood,* 25 (4), 16–21.

Hill, S., Comber, B., Louden, W., Rivalland, J. & Reid, J. (1998). *100 Children go to school: Connections and disconnections in literacy development in the year prior to school and the first year of school.* Canberra: DEET.

Hill, S., Comber, B., Louden, W., Rivalland, J. & Reid, J. (2002). *A hundred children turn 10: A longitudinal study of literacy development from the year prior to school to the first four years of school.* Canberra: DEET.

Hood, H. (2000). *Left to write too: Developing effective written language programmes for young children.* Palmerston North: Dunmore Press.

Hoover, W. & Tunmer, W. (1999). The components of reading. In G. Thompson, W. Tunmer and T. Nicholson (Eds), *Reading acquisition processes.* Clevedon: Multilingual matters.

Jackson, W. & Adams, P. (2002). Parents as literacy partners: Strengthening the links between homes, centres and schools. In P. Adams and H. Ryan (Eds), *Learning to read in Aotearoa New Zealand: A collaboration between early childhood educators, families and schools.* Palmerston North: Dunmore Press.

Johnston, P. & Rogers, R. (2002). Early literacy development: The case for 'informed assessment'. In S. Neuman and D. Dickinson (Eds), *Handbook of early literacy research.* NY: Guilford.

Jones Diaz, C. (Ed.) (1999). Bilingualism, biliteracy and beyond. In *Bilingualism: Building blocks for biliteracy.* Conferences proceedings of the Bilingual Children's Interest Group and the Language Acquisition Research Centre. Sydney: University of Western Sydney.

Jones Diaz, C., Beecher, B. & Arthur, L. (2002). Children's worlds and critical literacy. In L. Makin and C. Jones Diaz (Eds), *Literacies in early childhood: Changing views, challenging practice.* NSW: MacLennan & Petty.

Jones Diaz, C., Beecher, B., Arthur, L., Ashton, J., Hayden, J., Makin, L., McNought, M. & Clugston, L. (2001). *Literacies, communities and under 5's. The early literacy and social justice project.* NSW: NSW DET.

Jones Diaz, C. & Harvey, N. (2002). Other words, other worlds: Bilingual identities and literacy. In L. Makin and C. Jones Diaz (Eds), *Literacies in early childhood: Changing views, challenging practice.* NSW: MacLennan & Petty.

Klenk, L. (2001). Playing with literacy in preschool classrooms. *Childhood Education,* 77, 3, 150–7.

Knobel, M. & Healey, A. (1998). Critical literacies: An introduction. In M. Knobel and A. Healey (Eds), *Critical literacies in the primary classroom.* Newton, NSW: Primary English Teaching Association.

Kress, G. (1997). *Before writing: Rethinking the paths to literacy.* London: Routledge.

Laster, B. & Conte, B. (1998–99). Emerging literacy: Message boards in preschool. *Reading Teacher,* 52, 4, 417–20.

Layton, L., Deeny, K. & Upton, G. (1997). *Sound practice: Phonological awareness in the classroom.* London: David Fulton Publishers.

Learning Media (1992). *Dancing with the pen: The learner as a writer.* Wellington: Learning Media.

Lee, C. & Smagorinsky. P. (Eds) (2000). *Vygotskian perspectives on literacy research: Constructing meaning through collaborative inquiry.* Cambridge: Cambridge University Press.

Lee, W. & Carr, M. (2002). Documentation of learning stories: A powerful assessment tool for early childhood. Paper presented at the Dialogue and Documentation: Sharing our Understanding of Children's Learning and Developing a Rich Early Years Provision. Corby, United Kingdom. 9 March 2002.

Louden, W., Rohl, M., Barratt-Pugh, C., Brown, C., Cairney, T., Elderfield, J., House, H., Meiers, M., Rivalland, J. & Rowe, K. (2005). *In teachers' hands: Effective literacy teaching practices in the early years of schooling.* Canberra: DEET.

Luke, A. & Freebody, P. (1997). Shaping the social practices of reading. In S. Muspratt, A. Luke, and P. Freebody (Eds), *Constructing critical literacies: Teaching and learning textual practice.* NSW: Allen & Unwin.

MacNaughton, G. & Williams, G. (1998). *Techniques for teaching young children: Choices in theory and practice.* New South Wales: Longman.

Makin, L. & Diaz. C. (2002). *Literacies in early childhood: Changing views, challenging practice.* Sydney: MacLennan and Petty.

Makin, M. & Groom, S. (2002). Literacy transitions. In L. Makin and C. Jones Diaz (Eds), *Literacies in early childhood: Changing views, challenging practice*. NSW: MacLennan & Petty.

Marsh, J. (2000). Teletubby tales: Popular culture in the early years language and literacy curriculum. *Contemporary Issues in Early Childhood* (1), 2, pp. 119–33.

Martello, J. (2002). Many roads through many modes: Becoming literate in early childhood. In L. Makin and C. Jones Diaz (Eds), *Literacies in early childhood: Changing views, challenging practice*. NSW: MacLennan & Petty.

McCulloch, G. (Ed.) (1992). *The school curriculum in New Zealand*. Palmerston North: Dunmore Press.

McGee, L. M. & Richgels, D. J. (1996). *Literacy's beginnings. Supporting young readers and writers*. (2nd Edn). Boston: Allyn & Bacon.

McLaughlan-Smith, C. & Shuker, M. J. (2002). The foundations of literacy: Promoting literacy development in the early years. In P. Adams and H. Ryan (Eds), *Learning to read in Aotearoa New Zealand: A collaboration between early childhood educators, families and schools*. Palmerston North: Dunmore Press.

McLaughlan-Smith, C. & St. George, A. M. (1999). Parental beliefs and literacy practices with kindergarten aged children. *Early childhood folio 4: A collection of recent research*, 1999 (37–40). Wellington: NZCER.

McNaughton, S. (1995). *Patterns of emergent literacy: Process of development and transition*. Auckland: Oxford University Press.

McNaughton, S. (2002). *Meeting of minds*. Wellington: Learning Media.

Meier, D. (2000). *Scribble, scrabble: Learning to read and write*. NY: Teachers' College Press.

Miller, L. (1999). Literacy interactions through environmental print. In R. Campbell (Ed.), *Facilitating preschool literacy*. Delaware, USA: International Reading Association.

Milne, R. & Clarke, P. (1993). *Bilingual early childhood education in child care and preschool centres*. Victoria: FKA Multicultural Resource Centre.

Morrow, L. (2001). *Literacy development in the early years*. MA: Allyn and Bacon.

Mullen, S. (2000). A whole school approach incorporating home literacies into teaching and learning programs. *Practically Primary, 5(3)*, 14–18.

National Childcare Accreditation Council (2001). *Putting children first*. Sydney: NCAC.

National Childcare Accreditation Council (2005). *National standards for family day care*. NSW: NCAC.

National Childcare Accreditation Council (2005). *Quality improvement and accreditation system*. NSW: NCAC.

Nel, E. M. (2000). Academics, literacy, and young children. *Childhood education*. 76 3, 136–41.

Nelson, C. J. (1999). I can write my name! How implementing a sign-in routine in your head start classroom fosters emergent literacy. *Children and Families, 8, 1*, 36–8.

Neuman, S. (1998). How can we enable all children to achieve? In S. B. Neuman and K. A. Roskos (Eds), *Children achieving: Best practices in early literacy*. Delaware: International Reading Association.

Neuman, S., Copple, C. & Bredekamp, S. (2000). *Learning to read and write: Developmental appropriate practices for young children*. Washington: NAEYC.

Nicholson, T. (1999). *At the cutting edge: Learning to read and spell for success*. (2nd Edn). Wellington: NZCER.

Nicholson, T. (2000). *Reading the writing on the wall. Debates, challenges and opportunities in the teaching of reading*. Palmerston North: Dunmore Press.

Nutbrown, C. (1997). *Recognising early literacy development: Assessing children's achievements*. London: Paul Chapman Publishing.

O'Brien, J. & Comber, B. (2000). Negotiating critical literacies with young children. In C. Barratt-Pugh and M. Rohl (Eds), *Literacy learning in the early years*. Sydney: Allen & Unwin.

OECD (2000). *Thematic review of early childhood education and care policy Australian background report*. Canberra: DETYA.

Owocki, G. (1998). Facilitating literacy through play-centered experiences. In R. Campbell (Ed.), *Facilitating preschool literacy*. Delaware USA: International Reading Association.

Pellegrini, A. (2002). Some theoretical programmes: The intersection of curriculum, readers and educators. In P. Adams and H. Ryan (Eds), *Learning to read in Aotearoa New Zealand: A collaboration between early childhood educators, families, and schools*. Palmerston North: Dunmore Press.

Raban, B., Griffin, P. & Coates, H. (2000). *Preschool profile*. Canberra: DETYA (Indigenous Education Branch).

Reynolds, B. (1997). *Literacy in preschool: the roles of teachers and parents*. Oakhill: Trentham Books.

Reynolds, B. (1998). To teach or not to teach reading in the preschool...that is the question. In R. Campbell (Ed.), *Facilitating preschool literacy*. Delaware, USA: International Reading Association.

Rivalland, J. (2000). Linking literacy learning across different contexts. In C. Barratt-Pugh and M. Rohl (Eds), *Literacy learning in the early years*. NSW: Allen & Unwin.

Roberts, B. (1998). 'I No EvrethENe': What skills are essential in early literacy? In S. B. Neuman and K. A. Roskos (Eds), *Children achieving: Best practices in early literacy*. Delaware: International Reading Association.

Rohl, M. (2000). Learning about words, sounds and letters. In C. Barratt Pugh and M. Rohl (Eds), *Literacy learning in the early years*. NSW: Allen & Unwin.

Roller, C. (1998). *Understanding the complexity of reading*. Newark, Delaware: International Reading Association.

Roskos, K. & Christie, J. (2000). *Play and literacy in early childhood: Research from multiple perspectives*. New Jersey: LEA.

Rowe, D. (2000). Bringing books to life: In K. Roskos and J. Christie (Eds), *Play and literacy in early childhood: Research from multiple perspectives*. New Jersey: LEA.

Salinger, T. (2002). Assessing the literacy of young children: The case for multiple forms of evidence. In S. Neuman and D. Dickinson (Eds), *Handbook of early literacy research*. NY: Guilford.

Shuker, M. J. (2001). Fostering literacy in early childhood – why should we bother? *Early Education, 25*, 21–6.

Siraj-Blatchford, I. & Clarke, P. (2000). *Supporting identity, diversity and language in the Early Years*. Buckingham: Open University Press.

Smith, J. (2000). Teaching reading: Singing and songwriting support early literacy instruction. *The Reading Teacher, 53*, 8, 646–9.

Smith, J. & Elley, W. (1997). *How children learn to write*. Auckland: Longman.

Snow, C. E., Burns, M. S. & Griffin, P. (Eds) (1998). *Preventing reading difficulties in young children*. Washington, DC: National Academy Press.

Stanovich, K. E. (1986). Matthew effects in reading: Some consequences of individual differences in the acquisition of literacy. *Reading Research Quarterly, 21*, 360–407.

Tayler, C. (2000). Monitoring young children's literacy learning. In C. Barratt-Pugh and M. Rohl (Eds), *Literacy learning in the early years*. NSW: Allen & Unwin.

Tizard, B. (1993). Early influences on literacy. In R. Beard (Ed.), *Teaching literacy: Balancing perspectives*. London: Hodder and Stoughton.

Tunmer, W. & Chapman, J. (2003). The relation of metalinguistic abilities, phonological recoding skill and the use of sentence context to beginning reading development: A longitudinal study. In R. M. Joshi and P. G. Aaron (Eds), *Handbook of orthography and literacy*. Mahwah, NJ: Erlbaum.

Wells, G. (1985). *The meaning makers*. Portsmouth, NH: Heinemann.

Wells, G. (1986). *The meaning makers: Children learning language and using language to learn*. London: Hodder & Stoughton.

Wells, G. (1999). *Dialogic inquiry: Towards a sociocultural practice and theory of education*. Cambridge: Cambridge University Press.

Whitehead, M. (1997). *Language and literacy in the early years*. (2nd Edn). London: Paul Chapman.

Whitehead, M. (1999). *Supporting language and literacy development in the early years*. Buckingham: Open University Press.

Whitehurst, G. & Lonigan, C. (2002). Emergent literacy: Development from prereaders to readers. In S. Neuman and D. Dickinson (Eds), *Handbook of early literacy research*. NY: Guilford.

Wink, J. & Putney, L. (2002). *A vision of Vygotsky*. Boston: Allyn & Bacon.

Wylie, C. (2002). Children's competency and reading: What children need to bring with them to school. In P. Adams and H. Ryan (Eds), *Learning to read in Aotearoa New Zealand: A collaboration between early childhood educators, families and schools*. Palmerston North: Dunmore Press.

Index